SOMATIC THERAPY FOR TRAUMA & SOUND HEALING FOR BEGINNERS

(2 books in 1) The home crash course to reawaken wholeness & vitality with vibrational power & somatic secrets anyone can do

ASCENDING VIBRATIONS

CONTENTS

Claim Your bonuses below   ix

PART I

SOMATIC TRAUMA HEALING

THE AT-HOME DIY CRASH COURSE IN
EXPERIENCING TRUE BODY AWARENESS
THROUGH SOMATIC SECRETS ANYONE
CAN DO & INSIDER TECHNIQUES YOUR
THERAPIST DOESN'T WANT YOU TO KNOW
ABOUT

Introduction   3

1. IF YOU UNDERSTAND SOMATIC THERAPY,
THEN YOU UNDERSTAND HOW TO ALTER YOUR
EXISTENCE FOREVER   7
Somatic Psychology and Psychotherapy   8
Key Somatic Therapy Concepts   10
Are There Limitations to Somatic Psychotherapy?   12
Different Types of Trauma Therapy   12

2. SOMATIC MINDFULNESS AND EXPERIENCING   15
Somatic Mindfulness   15
Somatic Experiencing   19

3. THE HEALING POWER OF BREATH—SOMATIC
BREATHWORK   24

4. EMPOWER YOURSELF BY UNDERSTANDING
PTSD AND ATTACHMENT TRAUMA   30
The Fight, Flight, Freeze, or Fawn Response   35
Grounding Exercise   39
Attachment Trauma   39
Attachment Trauma Exercise   41

5. TOWERING ABOVE PHYSICAL PAIN AND
ILLNESS   43
Sensory Motor Amnesia   44
Somatic Pandiculation   46

6. A TREASURE TROVE OF SOMATIC PRACTICES 52
Polyvagal Theory and the Vagus Nerve 52
Exercise #1 54
Exercise #2 55
Exercise #3 55
Exercise #4 56
Breathing Exercise #1 57
Breathing Exercise #2 58
Guided Meditation 58
Pendulation 59
Pendulation Exercise 60
Somatic Titration 61
Cognitive Behavioral Therapy 61
CBT Exercise #1 63
CBT Exercise #2 63
Energy Psychology 63
Energy Psychology Exercise #1 65
Energy Psychology Exercise #2 65
Energy Psychology Exercise #3 66
Sensorimotor Psychotherapy 67
Gestalt Therapy 69
Gestalt Therapy Exercise #1 71
Focusing Therapy 72
Psychodrama Therapy 75
Eye Movement Desensitization and Reprocessing
(EMDR) 79
EMDR Exercise #1 81

7. SHAME TRAUMA: HEALING THE INNER CHILD
AND CREATING BOUNDARIES 82
Healing the Inner Child Through Somatic Therapy 82
Shame 91
Setting Healthy Boundaries With Somatic Skills 96
Boundary Exercise #1 98

8. ANXIETY, SELF-LOVE, SELF-COMPASSION, AND
CRUSHING DEPRESSION 100
Depression and Somatic Therapy 107
Anxiety, Triggers, Stress Reduction, and Somatic
Therapy 109
Somatic Anger Release 112

9. DISCOVER NEW ROADS TO RECOVERY
(FURTHER TECHNIQUES TO HEAL TRAUMA)   114
Qigong and Shaking Practices   114
Somatic Yoga   116
Movement-Based Techniques   119
Trauma Clearing Shaking   120
Somatic Art Therapy   121

10. DO THESE PERSONALITIES SOUND FAMILIAR?   124
Narcissistic Personality Disorder   124
Borderline Personality Disorder   129
Abusive Partners in Relationships   130

11. WHERE TO GO FROM HERE—HOW TO KNOW
YOU'RE HEALING   132
How to Know When You Are Healing   132
What to Look For in a Somatic Therapist   134
Finding Meaning After Trauma   135
The Somatic Daily Ritual for Empowered Healing   136

Afterword   141

PART II

SOUND HEALING FOR BEGINNERS

SONIC MEDICINE FOR THE BODY, CHAKRA
RITUALS, AND WHAT THEY DIDN'T TELL
YOU ABOUT VIBRATIONAL ENERGY

Introduction   147

12. UNDERSTANDING SOUND CAN ALTER YOUR
EXISTENCE PROFOUNDLY   151
How Do We Hear?   154
Types of Sound Therapy and the Instruments Used   158
Solfeggio Frequencies   163
Meditation   164

13. THE FORGOTTEN SUPERPOWER: LISTENING   167
Deep Listening   168
What Is Mindfulness?   170
More Exercises in Mindfulness   173
Primordial Sound   176
Sound Healing for Tinnitus   177

14. CREATING MAGIC WITH VOCAL TONING   179
    How Does Vocal Toning Work?   179
    Exercise 1: Humming   182
    Exercise 2: Focused Humming   183
    Exercise 3: Open Voice   183
    The Power of Laughter   184
    Exercise 4: Laughing   184
    Toning Sounds for Different Parts of the Body   186
    Healing and Clearing the Chakras   186
    Exercise 5: The Role of Sound   188
    Shaman Sound Healing With Instruments   191
    Exercise 6: Using Your Voice as a Drum   191

15. FROM POLLUTION TO PANACEA   193
    Noise Pollution   193
    Healthy Sound Levels   194
    Use Sonic Transmutation   200
    Crystals   201
    Cleansing and Recharging Your Crystals With Sound   203
    Cleansing Smaller Crystals With a Singing Bowl   204
    Cleansing Larger Stones With a Singing Bowl   204
    Recharging and Retuning Your Crystals With Tuning Forks   204
    Recharging Crystals With Tingshas   206
    Retuning Your Crystals With Vocal Toning   206
    The Power of Music and the Voice   207
    A Reprogramming Visualization for Crystals   207
    A Cleansing Meditation for Crystals   208
    Choosing the Right Crystals   209

16. UNLOCKING YOUR MERIDIANS WITH SOUND   212
    Key Concepts in TCM   212
    The Meridians   213
    Opening the Flow of Qi With Sound   216
    The Five Elements   218
    An Exercise to Strengthen the Wood Element   218
    An Exercise to Strengthen the Fire Element   219
    An Exercise to Strengthen the Earth Element   219
    An Exercise to Strengthen the Metal Element   219
    An Exercise to Strengthen the Water Element   220
    Using the Associated Elemental Sounds   221

17. EMOTIONAL SOUND HEALING SECRETS 223
  The Relationship Between Sound Healing and Intuition 224
  What Is Intuition? 224
  Intuition and Music 224
  The Role of Intention 225
  Brain Wave States 226
  A Meditation to Slow Down 227
  Our Own Music 228
  The Heartbeat 228
  Breathing and Sighing 230
  A Meditation to Unify the Heart and the Breath 232
  Earth's Own Music 233
  Music Therapy 233
  Anxiety and Depression 234
  A Healing Meditation for Depression 235
  Binaural Beats 237
  ASMR 240
  Isochronic Tones 242
  Subliminal Message-Infused Passive Healing 242
  How to Make Your Own Subliminal Messages 243

18. TUNE YOUR BODY, MIND, AND SOUL INTO AN
  UPGRADED PARADIGM 245
  Recovery and Total Wellness Through Sound 245
  Vibrational Movement 246
  Energy Medicine 247
  Sound Balancing With Tuning Forks 252
  How to Use Tuning Forks to Relieve Pain 260
  Sound Healing With Singing Bowls and Crystal Bowls 264
  Singing Bowl Frequencies 265
  Adding a Water Dimension 267
  Using Singing Bowls in Your Yoga Practice 267
  How to Use Your Singing Bowl For a Sound Bath
  Meditation 269
  The Power of Harmonic Healing 272
  Harmonics in Meditation 276
  Harmonics in Healing 278
  Chakra Balancing 279
  The Ratios of Harmonic Intervals 281
  Learning to Practice Overtone Singing Yourself 282
  Toning the Vowels 283

19. MANTRA MAGIC   290
    The Anatomy of a Mantra   290

20. SOUND-POWERED GUIDED MEDITATIONS   297
    Turning Noise Into Healing Sounds   301
    Relieving Physical Pain   303
    Letting Go of Anxiety   305
    Anxiety in the Stomach   309
    Anxiety manifesting in Fidgeting Hands   310
    Anxiety manifesting in Jaw-clenching   312
    Loving and Forgiving Yourself   313
    Releasing Trauma   317
    A Humming Meditation   320

    Conclusion   323
    References   325
    Your Feedback is Valued   351
    Claim your Bonus audiobook   353

CLAIM YOUR BONUSES BELOW

To help you on your spiritual journey, we've created some free bonuses to help you clear energetic baggage that no longer serves you and manifest a life that suits you better. Bonuses include a companion video course with over 4.5 hours of empowering content, energy-tapping videos, powerful guided meditations, journals, and more.

You can get immediate access by going to the link below or scanning the QR code with your cell phone.

https://bonus.ascendingvibrations.net

Free Bonus #1: The 3-Step Chakra Tune-Up Course

Want to know a unique way to target the chakras? Elevate Your Existence by Targeting the Subconscious, the Physical, & the Spiritual

- Discover a unique 3-step chakra targeting method that so many people aren't taking advantage of!
- Hack your brain, elevate body, mind, and spirit, and release blocks holding you back from greatness
- Awaken amazing energy to tailor a reality that suits you better
- Stop wasting precious time on ineffective methods

Free Bonus #2: The Manifesting Secret Formula Toolkit
Are you done with settling in life, wasting precious time, and ready to
attract your highest potential to you?

Free Bonus #3: The Spiritual Cleansing Toolkit
Are you ready to drop all of the negative energy that no longer
serves you?

- Release energetic blocks that could be causing imbalances
- Awaken amazing energy to supercharge your aura
- Create a beautifully cleansed, energetic environment

**Free Bonus #4: A Powerful 10-Minute Energy Healing Guided
Meditation**

All of these amazing bonuses are 100% free. You don't need to enter
any details except for your email address.
To get instant access to your bonuses, go to

https://bonus.ascendingvibrations.net

❦ I ❦
SOMATIC TRAUMA HEALING

THE AT-HOME DIY CRASH COURSE IN EXPERIENCING TRUE BODY AWARENESS THROUGH SOMATIC SECRETS ANYONE CAN DO & INSIDER TECHNIQUES YOUR THERAPIST DOESN'T WANT YOU TO KNOW ABOUT

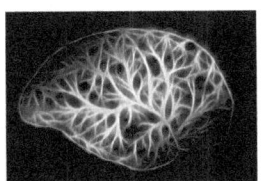

INTRODUCTION

It is a given that many of the books on Somatic Healing Therapy aim to help the reader with their myriad issues directly. However, the complex scientific terminology & hard-to-follow exercises common-place in such titles can often result in a perplexed reader left scratching their head. This book is different. This book is self-help in the truest sense of the word. Nothing in here is going to be complicated or bewildering. Everything I write is going to be easy for you to understand and easy to follow. If there are more challenging concepts contained within the chapters, then I will break them down to the point where anyone new to somatic healing will be able to understand. You won't need a doctor or a wall of scientific degrees to work out what the author is trying to convey. This book is for anybody and everybody.

The exercises contained in this book are not going to be so difficult that you need to go and get help from your neighbors or consult a professional Somatic Therapist to help you. No, these will be simple exercises that anybody, no matter how young or old, can easily follow and carry out in the safety of their home.

I appreciate that if you are interested in this book, it may well mean that you have been through some very stressful or traumatic experiences and are searching for healing. Please remember I am here to support you and encourage you through this journey. I will avoid using particular language and mentioning specific situations that could trigger a recurrence of that trauma in you. This book is a safe haven for you. You should always be able to find that peace and comfort whenever you are dipping into this book. It should be your guide when you need to practice exercises to help with your healing journey. These are not exercises to use just once and never bother with again. They are exercises that you can use daily to encourage the healing within you. Don't worry: You don't need to prescribe to some mystical religion or follow a shamanic leader to take part in recovery. Everything here is pragmatic and for your enjoyment, knowledge, and enlightenment. It does not require you to change your whole belief system to benefit from it.

I will also be discussing trauma and how it impacts and affects all our lives. No matter your age or gender, if you are a survivor of a traumatic experience, this book is here to help you in a way that won't burden you or bring you down. I will remind you what a unique and resilient person you are and how, if you embrace this healing journey, you can be the best possible version of yourself.

WE ARE NOT JUST OUR MINDS: HOW TRAUMA IMPACTS OUR BODY AND HEALTH

Trauma is an experience all humans have in common and something we all can relate to. Sometimes this can be obvious: We are in a car accident, or we lose a loved one unexpectedly—this can be a traumatic experience for us, but sometimes, the trauma is not so obvious. Maybe we have encountered conflict with a colleague at work; perhaps someone has insulted or belittled us. It may not sound like much, but these small things can also be traumatic experiences. The risk of trauma is something we live through every day. Our reaction to trauma varies from person to person because it is dependent on how each person's brain reacts to those situations—both at the time of the event and in the future.

The problem is that if trauma is not addressed, then it isn't just our brain that is impacted but our whole bodies. The effects of trauma can severely impact our well-being and health. It can affect everything from your digestion to your heart rate. It is important to remember that trauma is not something that only affects our mind: It can affect our whole body and any area of our health. Of course, it is essential that we clear the trauma from our bodies and learn to heal. Otherwise, it can lead to chronic illness. Trauma has led to illnesses such as type 2 diabetes, rheumatoid arthritis, and heart disease (Richmond, 2018). My dad was diagnosed with rheumatoid arthritis late in his life. Knowing what I know about trauma now, I wonder whether that was linked to his wife (my mother) dying. They had been together for a very long time. To say it was a shock to his system when she died would be an understatement. If only I had known about somatic healing therapy at the time, maybe I could have been more helpful to my dad in helping him navigate that traumatic experience. We all have different reactions, though, so I do want to reassure you that just because you have suffered a traumatic experience, it does not immediately mean you will suffer illness. But it does have the potential to do that if not addressed.

Something like trauma, often seen as a mental aspect, manifests itself in physical reactions such as headaches, muscle tension, fatigue, and stomach trouble (Richmond, 2018). It's the kind of constant physical pain that none of us want to endure unless we have to. It also plays out in our emotions and feelings. Some of us may feel bewildered; some may feel completely isolated; some feel trapped; some feel hopeless and as if they have no control over themselves; or some may stop feeling and stop caring about themselves and others altogether. Trauma may start in the brain, but it can affect our whole being if we don't learn to heal from it. That's the information I am going to attempt to provide to you. By following the advice and exercises provided in this book, you can begin your healing journey and learn to transform your life so that the past no longer dominates it. It's time for you to stop remembering the past and concentrate on shaping your future instead.

🦢 I 🦢

IF YOU UNDERSTAND SOMATIC THERAPY, THEN YOU UNDERSTAND HOW TO ALTER YOUR EXISTENCE FOREVER

T he word "somatic" originally comes from the Greek word *soma* which means "living body" (Erdelyi, 2019). This look at the word's origin gives you a good idea of what somatic therapy is. It is about listening to your body as well as your mind and making the connection between the two. By listening to the body and learning to heal the body, you will, in turn, heal your mind. The thinking behind somatic therapy is that much of what we suffer from now is due to past trauma. Much of this trauma is thought to have become trapped within our nervous systems. The symptoms and effects of trauma we display physically result from the instability of our nervous systems caused by those past experiences.

Some may dismiss this belief as hocus-pocus. Science is backing up this theory that the body and mind are connected. Morrisey once sang in The Smith's song "Still Ill": "Does the body rule the mind or does the mind rule the body? I don't know" (Morrisey & Marr, 1984). However, the more scientific and medical research executed in this area, the more we realize that the mind and the body are interconnected, and pain can work both ways. For example, a study carried out in 2005 concluded that chronic back pain often resulted in things like anxiety and extreme emotional responses (Von Korff et al., 2005). A study in 2020 focused on how social pain, i.e., isolating yourself or negative experiences of interaction, can result in physical pain (Zhang et al., 2020). Therefore, somatic healing is used as a therapy because it addresses both the mind and the body. It also addresses our emotions and feelings. It doesn't just assume physical pain can only be healed by physical therapy or that mental health can only be addressed via psychological therapy.

SOMATIC PSYCHOLOGY AND PSYCHOTHERAPY

Now it's time to introduce somatic psychology and psychotherapy. Somatic psychology encompasses therapeutic and holistic methods regarding the body, of which somatic psychotherapy is the largest branch.

Somatic psychotherapy also embraces the therapeutic and holistic approach of somatic psychology. It looks to address issues with the body, mind, and emotions within the process of healing. The belief is that a person's thoughts, outlook, principles, and emotions can impact their physical well-being, and physical things like posture, exercise, and diet can impact a person mentally. Anyone who saw Morgan Spurlock's 2004 documentary *Super Size Me* will know that Morgan had many wide-ranging physical issues caused by dining at a well-known fast-food chain and also suffered extreme mood swings. His mental health and not just his physical health, deteriorated due to the experiment.

Somatic psychotherapy is a method rooted in the connection between the body and the mind. Believers in somatic psychotherapy see the mind and body all as one, and any therapy should address both of these factors. They believe that the mind and the body can move toward healing when given the right approach, environment, social interactions, encouragement, and respect. If so, then the mind and the body can regulate themselves to cope with the stresses and strains of life. Otherwise, the trauma is stored in the body and can impact things like posture, facial expressions, and body language. Traditional therapies like talk therapy can help with trauma, but also adding a holistic approach such as somatic therapeutic techniques can work wonders. The same is true of body therapies: These may address physical issues and even some psychological issues, but they do not resolve deep-seated mental health problems.

Often, William Reich gets credited with forming the ideas behind somatic healing. However, he benefited from being a student of Sigmund Freud, who himself developed early thoughts about what we now think of as somatic healing. Pierre Janet is also an early contributor to these kinds of thoughts and ideas. However, Reich developed these views into much more of a progressive concept. He believed that human instincts were naturally good. From that belief, he formed a theory that incorporated the body. Reich's 1933 book *Character Analysis* suggested that the body was affected by buried emotions and even a person's personality. This could result in tension in the muscles, posture, and the way a person moves. He referred to this idea as "body armor." Therefore, he concluded that to release emotions trapped deep inside the body, some kind of physical force had to be applied to the body (Bell, 2017). Although some of Reich's later ideas were rejected by the psychology profession, he had laid the cornerstones for somatic therapy. It is widely accepted now that the mind and the body are much more aligned and not separate entities as previously believed. Many professionals dealing in mental health now support a more holistic approach when dealing with those affected by trauma.

Somatic psychotherapy works by paying attention to the body's signals—not only what our mind tells us. It may be tension in the muscles—usually around the head, neck, and shoulders—or it can manifest as digestion issues, hormonal problems, or sexual dysfunction. Somatic psychotherapists will help a person listen to their body and become aware of these signals. They will then assign the therapeutic technique they believe will best help to alleviate the problems. It could be such exercises as breathing techniques or something very physical like dance movement. The person may also discuss their behavioral habits and to note, in the future, the impact those habits have on any new thoughts and feelings that may crop up during somatic therapy.

Essentially, somatic therapy can help people with awareness of their bodies and minds and in assisting them with opening up and thinking more about their emotions and physical issues. As we will see in some later chapters, somatic therapy is very much becoming the norm for assisting those who have suffered post-traumatic stress disorder (PTSD). Understanding somatic therapy and including it into your routine can help address any number of issues such as dealing with stress, anxiety, and depression, assisting with relationship and interaction issues, or helping boost self-confidence and belief in oneself.

KEY SOMATIC THERAPY CONCEPTS

I will be discussing the key concepts contained in each chapter in much more detail as we go along. However, in this first chapter, I wanted to provide you with a brief outline of these essential concepts so that you will already have a basic understanding when we delve deeper into these ideas later.

Grounding

Grounding is a technique used on the body that enables one to feel themselves in the present moment. It uses the person's ability to sense their physical body, using their senses and feeling their feet on the ground. In essence, grounding is about managing the nervous system and learning to feel calm.

Boundary Development

Boundary development is all about the person concentrating on the here and now, giving them the tools to respond positively to their changing requirements, and setting clear boundaries. It enables a person to react to changing situations confidently and to establish a guard against becoming overwhelmed.

Self-Regulation

I think some people feel I could do with self-regulation when it comes to cakes or alcohol! Yet this concept is more to do with self-regulating your body, not necessarily your diet or your drinking habits (though self-regulating both is never a bad idea). It is the idea that the person stays aware and feels part of their body during deep emotions or sensations. The person learns to self-regulate any major physical sensibilities and can self-regulate them or respond appropriately at times of severe emotional impact.

Movement and Process

As I have outlined, somatic therapy is all about listening to one's body. This means that a person's posture, sense of space, and body language, such as gestures, can give an accurate understanding of the types of life experiences that a person may have been through. Movement can be something for a person to engage with to help with the issues they have.

Sequencing

Sequencing is all about how the tension built up by traumatic experiences may move around the body. For example, the tension may begin in the stomach. It may then move up the chest, which may tighten, and then move further up to the throat where, again, tightening may occur—making it difficult to breathe. Maybe the tension results in crying freely and tears coming out of the eyes, therefore bringing some release to the person and allowing them to breathe easier.

Titration

Titration is the procedure of encountering minor amounts of anguish while healing the person overall. A person will very slowly delve back into their past traumatic experiences, and as they do, the somatic therapist will check the responses and sensations in the body. They won't just keep an eye on the physical aspect: They will continue to talk to the person, but they will be watching out for things like difficulty in breathing, clenched fists, gnashing or grinding of teeth, or a difference in the sound of the voice.

Resourcing

Resourcing relates to the resources you can give a person to feel they have safe choices to make and do not become overwhelmed and anxious. The person will learn to identify places, people, and things to make them feel safe and calm. They will use these whenever they are feeling distressed. They will find out how to feel at peace with the world and what their body is feeling.

ARE THERE LIMITATIONS TO SOMATIC PSYCHOTHERAPY?

Although somatic psychotherapy is becoming more common as a therapy option for dealing with trauma, some concerns and limitations have been raised by those who oppose it. One such concern is touch therapy, which can sometimes be used as part of somatic therapy. Touch therapy is something many therapy professionals believe has ethical implications. Although it is recognized that some touch therapy can have a healing effect in reducing pain or tension, it is also recognized that touching some victims of abuse could trigger their trauma. There is also the possibility that just as touching may cause trauma to reoccur, it may also make some people very uncomfortable, or some may even find it arousing. This may mean it distracts from the purpose of the therapy. The patient may end up transferring feelings and emotions that relate to someone or something else onto the therapist; the reverse is also possible—the therapist places feelings and emotions not directly relevant to the patient on them. Therefore, both the therapist and the patient need to agree that touching is an acceptable part of the therapy, and the patient is willing to investigate and develop an awareness of their body. Not all body psychotherapy courses have been accredited in some countries, as it is considered that they do not meet all the scientific criteria required. Therefore, when searching out these specific types of courses, you do need to be aware of that scenario (Bell, 2017).

DIFFERENT TYPES OF TRAUMA THERAPY

Finally, in this chapter, I will outline some of the programs and procedures you can follow and take part in when it comes to somatic therapy. I will be discussing these in much more detail in the various chapters throughout the book, but this is to give you a flavor as to what might appeal to you or ones you might be specifically interested in—though all can benefit.

Art Therapy

Art therapy can be a useful way to treat trauma. It allows a person to create what they want and at the pace they want. Plus, it includes both visual and physical elements. The art then becomes a release of that trauma while also enabling a person to become more aware of their body and the sensations involved when touching things and creating.

Emotional Freedom Technique (EFT) Tapping

EFT uses similar principles to acupuncture. It believes there are specific points on the body related to organs or other internal parts of the body. Using your fingers and tapping on these points sends messages to the brain. This, in turn, can relieve the tension and pressure that has built up due to the negative experiences and emotions a person may have experienced.

Eye Movement Desensitization and Reprocessing (EMDR) Therapy

EMDR therapy works by the person reliving their trauma slowly and intermittently while the therapist instructs you to move your eyes. The thinking around this is that it is easier to cope with recalling terrible past experiences when your attention is diverted elsewhere. Having your attention distracted like this produces much less of a physical and emotional response to the trauma.

Energy Psychology

EFT is a type of energy psychology. It involves using acupuncture-type methods to tap the body's energy points while the person undergoing the therapy focuses on traumatic events or experiences in their life.

Focusing Therapy

Focusing therapy is all about having that feeling in your body whenever you remember traumatic experiences—focusing on that feeling in the body so that it forms an image. That image can then be used to tell where the trauma is stuck and how to deal with it.

Gestalt Therapy

Gestalt therapy is very much about concentrating on the here and now. It intends to stop a person from constantly thinking only about the past. It encourages a person to be aware of the feelings and emotions they are currently having, and it advises how they can relate that to physical symptoms. There are various forms of Gestalt therapy which I will discuss in more detail later on.

Guided Imagery Therapy

"Imagine you're on a beach, and the waves are lapping at your feet." We have all heard this kind of thing when getting people to relax. That is what guided imagery therapy is: It uses images to help people free themselves from mental anguish and stress.

Mindfulness

Mindfulness is the practice of the awareness of thoughts and feelings as they appear without passing judgment on those thoughts.

Psychodrama

Psychodrama works on the basis that it enables the person to say or do whatever it is that is needed to let them heal from the trauma. This involves reliving the trauma, for which various techniques can be applied. I will discuss this in further detail later on in the book.

Sensorimotor Psychotherapy

This aspect of psychotherapy is centered around the body and how listening to it and understanding it can help heal our trauma.

Somatic Experiencing

Somatic experiencing is also about putting the body at the center—specifically the nervous system—and listening to what it is saying and responding accordingly.

Dance/Movement Therapy

As you can guess from its name, this form of therapy uses movement, often dance. The suggestion is that the person may be able to express themselves through dance and movement in a way they never could verbally; doing this can help heal mental health issues.

2

SOMATIC MINDFULNESS AND EXPERIENCING

SOMATIC MINDFULNESS

Somatic mindfulness is a vital part of somatic therapy. The awareness of your body and what it is doing in the here and now is a big fixture of somatic therapy—not how your body was feeling in the past or will be feeling in the future. Many of us do not listen to our bodies and are oblivious to what they are trying to tell us. You have the ability to remove yourself from what the nervous system is telling you. It may be telling you to feel anxious, defensive, or overwhelmed—whatever behavior you subconsciously feel most comfortable with—even if the reality is it makes you uncomfortable.

Mindfulness started as a Buddhist concept. It then slowly developed over the many centuries into something Western therapists and doctors often use to help with mental health.

There is an excellent example that Andrea Bell tells from her therapy experience. It involves a patient from a challenging background where he could not trust anyone. After a few sessions with him, for reasons that had nothing to do with the patient, she changed the furniture in her office to more, in her eyes, comfortable furniture. However, when he came in and sat down on the new, comfier, and more luxurious chair, he became immediately suspicious, questioning Andrea why she had changed the furniture and whether she was doing it on purpose to mess with his head. Once Andrea had explained the real reasons for changing it, the boy then relaxed and enjoyed the new chair's comfort. That shows you how we are often dictated to by our behaviors and experiences of the past that we forget to enjoy the present and then use it to suggest how the future might go. In this instance, the boy was under the assumption that the therapy sensations with Andrea were going to fail. Andrea then worked with the boy to distinguish what physical sensations he felt when he came into the room. He will then be able to note those reactions when he next gets them and learn to listen to them and think about whether that is the most appropriate response. The more he does that, the more his initial reaction to change should calm down and, slowly, no longer feel like a threat (Bell, 2018).

The other thing about mindfulness is that it teaches us how to stop judging ourselves. Instead of thinking about something we said or did wrong in the past while we are going about our daily lives, mindfulness teaches us not to judge ourselves so harshly. It assists us with trying not to worry about things in the past but concentrate and enjoy only the present.

We know this can work. If you have ever studied athletes before a race, you will see them going through various motions and rituals. All they are doing is practicing mindfulness to be well and truly in the present moment and, therefore, relaxed and calm—not having those doubtful, anxious thoughts run through their mind and show in their body through muscle tension. Those practicing mindfulness the most are usually the ones that win the race.

There is plenty of evidence that backs up the success of mindfulness in assisting with many issues. It can help cut down procrastination. One study showed that those competing in an intensive meditation course showed much improvement in that procrastination than those who did not undergo the course (Chambers et al., 2008). There are also several studies proclaiming the reduction of stress and anxiety as a result of practicing mindfulness. A 2010 study concluded that mindfulness effectively treated stress, anxiety, and other possible mood issues (Hoffman et al., 2010).

It does not stop there either. A 2009 study suggested that mindfulness could vastly improve your attention and focus. Those that took part in specific tests performed much better if they had been practicing mindfulness than those that had not (Moore & Malinowski, 2009).

Furthermore, a study from 2007 showed that those that had practiced mindfulness coped with seeing upsetting or emotionally inducing pictures far better than those that did not practice mindfulness. The study concluded that mindfulness could reduce the impact of things that tend to provoke an emotional response (Ortner et al., 2007).

It seems mindfulness not only has a good impact on yourself but also on your relationships with others. A 2007 study found that those who engaged in mindfulness were far better able to deal with the kind of conflict that crops up in romantic relationships; were more likely to be in a happy and satisfying relationship; and those that practiced mindfulness were able to communicate better than those that did not practice it (Barnes et al., 2007).

One of the by-products of the current pandemic and the many lockdowns occurring around the world is that it has resulted in much stress and anxiety. It has become almost impossible to enjoy the present because we constantly worry about what is just around the corner. However, somatic mindfulness is something you can introduce with ease to your daily routine; therefore, you can reduce the stress and anguish you may be feeling. It is not something that will take up your whole day. All you need are 20 to 30 minutes somewhere in your day to relax and take stock of yourself and the world around you. You can be doing other things while you begin your mindfulness practice. You can be brushing your teeth and thinking about your feet being firmly on the floor, the feeling of the toothbrush in your hand and on your teeth, and the movement of your arm up and down or side to side as you brush.

Many people have dishwashers these days, but I'm not one of them. A good side effect is that I can practice mindfulness while washing the dishes. I can concentrate on the feeling of the soapy water on my hands and the sounds of the cutlery against the dishes. Washing dishes is a great way to become aware of the sights and sounds and increase your awareness. If you are putting your clean clothes away, then take a moment to smell and feel them. You can even take some deep breaths and be aware of your breathing while you fold and put them away. If you are a gym rat (or just an occasional gym-goer), try running on the treadmill instead of looking at the TV on your next visit. Instead of listening to a thumping beat on your headphones, try to focus on the feeling of your feet on the treadmill as you move. Hone in on your breathing and how it quickens as your pace on the treadmill accelerates.

With that in mind, how do you practice mindfulness meditation specifically? Well, the first thing is to get yourself comfortable. Find the most comfortable seat in your house or sit on the floor if you prefer. Don't laugh: I know some people who prefer sitting on the floor rather than on a chair. Wherever you sit, you need to keep your back straight but not so you are stiff. You want to be able to stay relaxed. Your chosen place should be as quiet as possible as you don't want there to be any noise to distract you. You should wear as comfortable of clothing as you can—not too loose and not too tight, as you don't want anything that will distract you from your meditation. To begin with, maybe you want to see if you can fully meditate for five minutes, then try for 10 minutes, then 15 or 20 minutes, and finally 30 minutes.

To begin with, concentrate on your breath. Be aware of your breathing. Notice the feeling of your diaphragm moving in and out. Notice the air coming in and out of your nostrils and mouth. You may even detect the drop in temperature when you let your breaths out compared to when you are breathing in.

The point of mindful meditation is not necessarily to completely stop your thoughts but to be aware of them and take notice as they occur. You don't need to try to ignore them or suppress them, but note them and keep calm, using your breathing to stop your mind from running away with you. You should note each thought and let it go—like factory products on a conveyor belt. You can do this as many times as you need to throughout your meditation.

If you do find your mind going off in different directions and you start to feel anxious or panicky, then take note of your thoughts and what caused you the stress. Then return to your breathing—deep, slow breaths. Don't judge yourself if this happens often. There are so many gizmos and gimmicks to distract us in the modern world. We are just not used to being quiet and in the present and aware, so don't be harsh on yourself. Mindfulness is all about getting back to your breathing and concentrating on living in the moment.

As you can see, you can easily practice this mindfulness at home. You don't need to be in a therapist's office to carry it out. If you are struggling, then there are thousands of videos on YouTube and many apps you can download to help you with your practice.

SOMATIC EXPERIENCING

Peter Levine specifically developed somatic experiencing (SE) to address those suffering from trauma. Levine was inspired after seeing animals that are often preyed upon quickly recover from any potential attack. They went through a physical process to release the nervous energy built up during the threat. Levine suggested that humans don't have that physical release; the trauma remains in their minds and leads to thoughts of anxiety, embarrassment, and many other hazardous feelings. The release that Levine believes nature requires does not occur sporadically in humans. Somatic experiencing is the answer to that—it helps humans process the trauma they have suffered that has become trapped inside them (Osadchey, 2018).

A human's nervous system leaps into action whenever we find ourselves in a dangerous situation, deciding our fight-flight-freeze response. It does this almost instinctively without us needing to think. However, the trouble is that when someone goes through a traumatic experience, particularly if that experience is buried and not released, the nervous system can start to go rogue. It starts to behave as though the person is constantly under threat of attack—every situation becomes a potentially traumatic one. Somatic experiencing believes that burying the trauma results in the kind of symptoms we often see, such as anxiety, shame, and embarrassment. If the body is allowed the opportunity to truly process the traumatic experience it has been through, then these symptoms do not come out to play in the long term. Somatic experiencing is very much about getting the body and nervous system to, once again, self-regulate themselves and find harmony and balance in the body.

Somatic experiencing concentrates on the feelings and sensations that occur in the body—becoming aware of them and understanding them. This can be quite intimidating for many people, as they have never thought about their body in this way; however, it can be very rewarding. Once you have become used to these feelings and sensations, you can start to note them, and when they occur in the future, you can prevent your mind from suppressing them. This is where the harmony between your brain and your body comes into play to allow the physical release of the trauma you need to allow yourself to heal.

As with all somatic healing therapy, research and evidence in this area is still new, so there is no conclusive proof. Still, scientific evidence that SE positively impacts those who have suffered trauma is growing. Although a study from 2017 used only a small sample of people, it found that SE is an effective treatment—specifically for those with PTSD (Brom et al, 2017).

Here are some straightforward and easy-to-do somatic experiencing exercises for you to do at home. You should begin to see if this form of therapy suits you and makes a positive difference. It would be best if you tried to manage at least one minute with exercise—ideally, considerably longer than that.

- **1:** Sit in your favorite comfy chair and take notice of how everything feels. Think about how your feet are planted on the floor; move them to and fro until you feel the floor is just an extension of your feet. Then, think about how your back and bottom feel on the chair or how the chair supports you. If you are leaning forward in the chair, then make sure you lean back and allow the chair to support you. Wriggle around in your chair until you reach your optimum comfort zone. Take some time to appreciate the comfort of the chair, the way it supports you, and the way the floor supports your feet. Take a peek around the room and outside your window, if you need to, and look for something that calms you and makes you feel happy—it could be a painting you have hanging on a wall or the walls themselves. It could be the trees and bushes outside; maybe the birds are chirping and playing in them. Perhaps it's the carpet on the floor. Whatever it may be, take the time to appreciate and enjoy them and the feelings they bring. Now that you've done all this, how do you feel about your comfort, both physically and emotionally? If you take your time with this exercise, it really can make a difference in calming down your nervous system and bringing some harmony to your body and emotions.

- **2:** For the second exercise, take a moment to take everything in—all of your surroundings and how you are feeling. Then, take your right hand and put it just below your left armpit, clutching the side of your chest. Now, take your left hand and put it on your right bicep, elbow, or shoulder—whatever is easiest. At this juncture, take some time to think about how this makes you feel. Is your body cold or warm under your hands? Are your clothes soft, or are they more of a rough fabric? Is there anything else you are noticing? Maybe you can feel your heart beating; perhaps you are aware of your breathing. Do you find doing this satisfying? Does it bring some comfort wrapping your hands on your body like this? Then, see how the rest of your body responds to this kind of physical touch. Try the same thing with your legs. Now, compare what you notice about your surroundings and how your body feels with what you noted at the beginning of the exercise. In times of anxiety or stress, this type of exercise can bring back some comfort and peace to your body through your physical touch.
- **3:** One of the best exercises is to remember a time when someone showed you kindness. Even in the toughest of worlds and lives, there is at least one person who, at some point, shows us kindness. If we are lucky, there are many

people throughout our lives. Try to remember those times when someone demonstrated their kindness to you. Remember the words they said, their hand gestures, their facial expressions, and everything that was part of that kindness act. As you remember this moment, take note of how your body responds to this memory—everything you are seeing, hearing, and feeling. It's almost like you have transported yourself back in time to that very moment. Now, compare what you felt at the time with what you are feeling now as you remember the experience. If any negative memories come through as a result of this remembrance, then try to place them in an imaginary folder and concentrate only on the memory of the act of kindness. At the end of the exercise, note how you are feeling now, how your body is feeling, and how you feel about your surroundings. This is an excellent way of calming yourself and remembering that not everyone is out to get you. You do not need to feel stressed about everyone you come into contact with; there are kind people out there ready to be kind to you.

- **4:** As with the start of most of these exercises, first, take note of your surroundings and your general feelings and emotions. Then, try to remember within the last 24 hours (or longer if you need to) when you last truly felt like yourself or the person you want to be. Recall this moment in as much detail as possible—almost as if you were living through it again. Take note of what you felt during that moment and what was occurring with your five senses. Then, again, remember when you were last most like yourself or the person you aim to be but this time, within the last few weeks. Again, try to recall as much detail as possible as though you were going through it again, and note how your body felt during that moment. Then, as usual, at the end of the exercise, see how you feel about your surroundings, general feelings, and emotions compared to how you felt at the start. This exercise is good at bringing

you back to yourself, away from all the confusion and
madness that you sometimes feel in the world.

- **5:** This exercise involves making some vocal noises, so it
  may be wise to go somewhere where you are truly alone
  before you carry out this exercise. As always, start by taking
  notice of your surroundings and your general emotions and
  feelings. Then, consider the kind of sound that a foghorn
  makes. Take a very deep breath, and attempt to make the
  sound of a foghorn. The sound needs to be a low-enough
  pitch so that you feel it reverberate around your body. See
  how far you can feel it down into your body—perhaps even
  down to the very bottom of your belly and possibly to your
  thighs. As you feel the sound end (it is often described as
  the "voo" sound), then let your next breath occur naturally.
  You can take your time; there is no need to rush the breath.
  If you feel comforted and in harmony, then stay with that
  feeling. For some people, though, making the foghorn sound
  can have an unsettling effect, so if that is the case with you,
  go back to one of the other exercises to regain your sense of
  harmony. If you found the foghorn sound comforting, then
  try it again. Do you feel even more comforted and in
  harmony? I would not suggest doing the sound more than
  three times, though. As with the end of the other exercises,
  how do you feel now? Compare it with how you felt at the
  start of the exercise. This can be an excellent exercise to
  help settle the body's core. As the sound reverberates
  around your body, this can help the muscles relax and
  release any tension you may be feeling.

THE HEALING POWER OF BREATH—SOMATIC BREATHWORK

We all take breathing for granted. It just so happens that we don't have to think about it at all, but that is part of the problem. We are not breathing as deeply as we should; our diaphragms are getting uptight and arent relaxed. By concentrating on breathing, we take care of ourselves both physically and mentally. We can control our breathing; we will breathe at the rate we choose. When we breathe, we also get the opportunity to be aware of our bodies and how they are feeling.

It is believed that breathing significantly impacts your blood pressure, your heart rate, and the arteries' ability to let blood flow through them. No wonder our breathing is one of the first things to get out of control when we are anxious or stressed. It's also believed that breathing deeply can lead to one being in a much better mood. People have also reported having a better night's sleep with fewer occurrences of waking up in the night. It does depend, though; just doing a minute here or there will have much less impact than conducting 30 minutes of breathing deeply day after day. Results for lowering blood pressure were still successful a month later for those that could stay regimented. It is perhaps common sense, but breathing in more oxygen gets the oxygen flowing through your blood cells and nerve tissues. For those that participated in deep breathing, it was reported that oxygen utilization increased by 37% (Hadley, 2017). A 2017 study also found that blood pressure was lowered using deep breathing for those with hypertension (Janet & Gowri, 2017). A 2019 study backed the theory that slow, deep breathing was a better tool for fighting insomnia than hypnosis or some pharmaceutical options (Jerath et al., 2019).

As with all somatic therapy, somatic breathing is all about taking notice of our body and how it works. It's about paying attention to the feeling of your stomach and belly contracting in and out and your rib area and chest as you breathe. Through somatic breathing, you also become so much more aware of your jaw, throat, diaphragm, and shoulders in the movement and motion of breathing. If we concentrate on our breathing and what our body is doing, we stop our minds racing away with all their concerns and worries. We start to truly live in the present moment and stop to smell the roses—or breathe in the aroma.

You can conduct somatic breathing, either sitting up or lying down on your back. You are aware of the breaths you take. This isn't the same as usual involuntary breathing, which happens without you even thinking about it. There is no break between breathing in and breathing out, and the breath can occur through the nose or the mouth. This kind of breathing should allow you to release some of the physical tension within. When you learn to breathe using your diaphragm and to relax when you breathe out, then this has the potential to release much deeper feelings and emotions. I will discuss diaphragm breathing later on in this chapter.

Although somatic breathing can be helpful to those suffering from PTSD, breathing can be one of the things that trigger PTSD symptoms. If you have PTSD and are thinking of investigating breathwork, you need to take extra care and remember that it is at your own risk, and you are responsible for your own health and well-being. If you ever have any doubt, you should seek a medical professional's help.

Here's a straightforward breathing exercise for you to follow:

- Take a normal breath. You should become aware that you want to take a deeper breath, equivalent to when you sigh.

- Breathe out. This should be for six to eight seconds, and you almost completely exhale.
- Gently hold still so that you are holding your breath out.
- At this point, concentrate on what it feels like to need to take another breath. What that sensation is physically, and where you are feeling it in your body. Linger on these sensations and feelings for a moment.
- The more interest you have in these feelings and sensations, the more you will find you can hold your breath.
- Once the need to breathe in again becomes obvious, note the feeling of it, and note that you can give in to it or keep holding your breath out for a few more seconds. Then breathe back in when you want to. Thus, you are now controlling your breathing—not your subconscious.
- Repeat this exercise for five minutes.

You may well have heard of the diaphragm, but you probably don't ever pay attention to it or know precisely what or where it is. Well, the diaphragm is a major muscle that exists just below your lung area, and it assists with ensuring air moves in and out of the lungs. In fact, the diaphragm is used in 80% of breathing. Breathing is much more efficient when the diaphragm is being used than when additional muscles are used (Diaphragmatic Breathing Exercises, n.d.). When a person breathes in, the diaphragm shrinks and heads downward, whereas when a person breathes out, the diaphragm loosens and heads upward, assisting in pushing the air out of the lungs. Considering that the average human will breathe 23,000 breaths a day, which works out to eight million a year, we can see just how important a muscle the diaphragm is (Diaphragmatic Breathing: Everything, n.d.).

When we breathe without thinking, this rarely uses the full capability of the lungs and is known as shallow breathing. However, diaphragmatic breathing uses deep breathing to make full use of this capability. It can also sometimes be known as "belly breathing." This is because it makes full use of the stomach and the abdominal muscles as well as the diaphragm with each breath. This involves consciously moving the diaphragm down when you breathe in, ensuring that the lungs fill with air much more efficiently. A person should realize that their stomach is moving up and down; they should feel their stomach being pulled tighter and relaxing rather than just feeling it in their chest and shoulders as you would with shallow breathing.

If you want to check whether you tend to breathe with your diaphragm or your chest, place your right hand on your chest and your left hand on your stomach and breathe. If your right-hand rises first, you are using your chest to breathe. If your left-hand rises first, you are using your diaphragm. I have noticed that when I am hunched over my desk at home on the laptop and stop to do that test, it is my right hand that rises first. If I sit up straight in my chair, the left-hand rises first. The amount of time people spend sitting in positions with bad posture is a concern of doctors and scientists. It leads to symptoms such as a bad back and causes one to use shallow breathing. This prevents one from getting enough oxygen into the body. No wonder I tend to go a bit light-headed after a while when I'm crouched over my computer.

You only need to practice diaphragmatic breathing for up to 10 minutes, and ideally, this should be for three to four times throughout the day. You should be able to find a moment while at home to lie down and practice your breathing. You want to try and find somewhere free from distractions, so stay away from the TV and leave your smartphone in a different room. Leave your partner/children/pets in a separate room. You want to ensure you will remain free from interruption while you carry out your breathing exercises. As with all somatic techniques, you want to concentrate on what your body is feeling as you experience your breathing.

If you find it useful, you can set an alarm to know when to take a break and carry out your exercises. It is often useful to remember you are always breathing, so this is not exactly going out of your way to do something; you are already doing it—you just need to concentrate and notice it.

There are many different versions of diaphragmatic breathing, but to carry out the most basic version, you need to do the following:

- Find a flat surface on which to lie down. I think for most people, that is likely to be the floor. Place a pillow or cushion under your head and also underneath your knees. The pillows and cushions are not essential, but if you have them, they are good to use as they will help keep your body in as comfortable a position as possible.

- Put one hand toward the top of your chest in the middle area.
- Put your other hand on your stomach, just below the ribcage but above the diaphragm.
- Breathe in through your nostrils only, pulling the air down toward your stomach. The stomach should move up toward the resistance of your hand, while your chest movement should be limited.
- Breathe out through your mouth, but don't open your mouth fully. Keep your lips tight together still. Your stomach should relax and go back in, and, again, there should not be any movement in your chest.

As with anything new, diaphragmatic breathing can feel odd at first, or it may feel like hard work. However, as with anything in life, the more you practice, the easier it should get. You may want to count a number in your head with each breath. Sometimes, this can help a person relax further and can help with knowing how many breaths you have completed. It may also help with keeping you from getting too easily distracted.

When you feel you have mastered this lying down, you can advance to practicing it sitting down or even standing up. This increases your opportunity as to when and where you can practice it. It means you can even do it when sitting at your desk at work, standing in a line, watching TV, sitting on a bus, or anything you can imagine. Once you can successfully practice sitting up and standing up, it opens a whole new world of opportunity and chance for you to carry out your practice. Be careful that when you do advance to that, you must ensure that your head, neck, and shoulders move as little as possible when sitting or standing. Don't be hard on yourself if things aren't going quite as you hoped or the breathing doesn't seem to be working. This is practice. The more you do it and get used to it, the better you will become and feel comfortable. No one else is judging you on how you do, so don't judge yourself. You'll get there with plenty of practice. You have to continue to do it regularly as well. Your body has the memory of a goldfish rather than an elephant when it comes to diaphragmatic breathing, so it won't remember when you did it in the past. You need to keep regularly practicing for it to take effect.

Why would you want to practice diaphragmatic breathing? Well, for a start, the diaphragm is a muscle, so you are strengthening that muscle just by doing this exercise. That alone makes it worthwhile, but other benefits cited include strengthening your core and lowering your heart rate and blood pressure (Johnson, 2020).

The great thing about diaphragmatic breathing is that evidence is mounting to suggest it can positively help alleviate stress and anxiety. A 2017 study noted that it reduced stress hormones in the body, therefore potentially also reducing the feelings of stress and anxiety in a person (Ma et al., 2017). This was further solidified by a 2019 review of studies and evidence that concluded that diaphragmatic breathing can be used as a tool for stress reduction (Hopper et al., 2019).

However, suppose someone with anxiety tries diaphragmatic breathing and finds it does not work. In that case, it may make them more anxious, so always seek out the assistance of a medical professional before embarking on these types of exercises.

EMPOWER YOURSELF BY UNDERSTANDING PTSD AND ATTACHMENT TRAUMA

Post-traumatic stress disorder (PTSD) can occur in individuals after living through or being party to a traumatic event. PTSD usually occurs when people have been involved in truly terrible events and not just minor traumatic occurrences. It is also fair to say that just because someone suffers trauma doesn't mean they will develop PTSD: It depends on each individual. Symptoms of PTSD can include flashbacks, an inability to think about anything other than the event, and anxiety on a very serious level. Sometimes, these symptoms can occur within a month of an event; sometimes, they occur several years after the event.

Complex post-traumatic stress disorder (CPTSD) is best explained as a sufferer of PTSD displaying additional symptoms following a traumatic event. You may find it hard to keep your emotions in check; you may feel very angry at the world; you may find it difficult to trust anyone or anything; you may feel like something is missing, or you feel you are not worth anything, and that nobody else in the world could possibly understand you or the way you are feeling. All this can lead to disassociating yourself from relationships or friendships, and it can take on physical pain, including headaches and chest pain. Complex PTSD includes flashbacks like PTSD, but they are more emotional flashbacks so that you don't just re-experience the event itself but all of the emotions you felt at the time. You then display those feelings in the present, even though the flashback is causing those emotions.

Attachment trauma that occurs early in a child's life, usually from neglect and abuse, can stem from something like separation from a caregiver due to medical concerns or death. It is not always the case that attachment trauma immediately directs back to the parents, and the trauma is the parents' fault. Trauma can come from many different directions and people, so we should take that into consideration. Since we cannot recall memories before the age of four or five, we think we cannot remember the traumatic events. However, our brain and body have remembered it even if our memory cannot. These feelings and emotions can then occur later in life. The trauma will usually show up in things like a fear of relationships, a constant sense of shame, or that the person is unworthy of somebody else's love. As the person may have no memory of why this occurred, it can make it much more challenging to treat than some of the other traumas.

As I alluded to earlier, not everyone will develop PTSD, CPTSD, or attachment trauma from traumatic events. Some will suffer minor trauma, and some will not suffer anything at all, though it is estimated that 70% of adults in America have suffered a traumatic event at some point in their lives (Eckelkamp, 2019). Trauma isn't just something that happens to other people; we are all likely to face it in our lives. Even general trauma requires addressing; otherwise, it can result in mental and physical issues. Trauma can be defined as anything that results in us being stuck in a physical, emotional, or behavioral pattern (Cutler, n.d.). Processing and getting over the trauma often ends up being interrupted; hence the trauma ends up stored in our bodies, and we never truly release it. Stored trauma can often lead to physical pain and the psychological anguish that comes along with it.

That is where somatic healing and therapy come in. Things like deep breathing, somatic experiencing, and movement can help relieve that stuck trauma in your body as you gently and slowly begin to release the tension. Perhaps these methods will allow your brain to process things you had long consigned to your brain's "Recycle Bin."

It's a sad cycle that disability and chronic illness can cause short-term and long-term trauma, but then those who suffer trauma, if not treated correctly, end up developing physical conditions and symptoms. Therefore, someone who develops chronic illness can also be traumatized by it, which in turn, if they are not able to release that trauma, may end up making them feel even more ill and develop further physical pain.

When individuals are diagnosed with a disability or a chronic illness, this can be a very traumatic event. All sorts of overwhelming feelings are likely to be going through a person, and because people start talking about treatment or next steps, the person doesn't always get the chance to process that trauma. It's a worrying estimation that between 12% and 25% of those who develop life-threatening illnesses go on to develop PTSD (Virant, 2019). It is no surprise that people who go through these types of experiences often develop a fear of hospitals or doctors. Most worryingly, it can develop into a complete mistrust of doctors and a wish to avoid having anything to do with the illness. For example, the afflicted individual starts "forgetting" to take their medication or turn up for appointments. Disability and chronic illness will often make a person question their place in the world and what they had always believed to be true. It makes them think about death, how vulnerable we all are, and how helpless we believe we may be. Having to go through emotions and experiences like this, it is not surprising that those with illnesses and disabilities develop trauma.

As mentioned when I began discussing CPTSD, relationships are all too often one of the things severely impacted by those suffering from trauma. It is understandable that a person suffering from trauma may find it hard to form long-lasting relationships. They may well feel danger is around every corner, and trusting either new friends or old friends can become exceptionally difficult. The anger that a person may feel due to losing control over the life they believe they may have lost or the helplessness they feel can link back to chronic illness. This can involve the individual lashing out at those close to them. The person feels under threat from everyone, therefore lashing out and becoming a defense mechanism. They can't hurt you if you hurt them first.

Depending on the type of trauma one is going through and their

SOMATIC THERAPY FOR TRAUMA & SOUND HEALING FOR BEGINN...

traumatic experience, one might go through feelings of shame, feeling as if they are not worthy of another's love, or feeling entirely unlovable. They may even feel guilty about what happened, that somehow the event was their fault, or they deserved it rather than realizing the blame lies with the perpetrator. Having gone through such traumatic events, the person believes nobody else can understand them, so they go through the burden alone and do not share with the people closest to them. Although the following are fictional accounts, I am about to use them as examples. I have no doubt the writers researched thoroughly about trauma survivors in order to make sure their characters behaved authentically. The first example is a plot line from a popular modern drama show. In one example, the character, June, has finally escaped into Canada from Gilead, where all her traumatic experiences occurred. She seems fairly incapable of sharing her experiences with anyone. Still, the person she definitely seems incapable of sharing her events with is her husband, who has been in Canada while she was in Gilead (Miller et al., 2017–present). Another example is from a famous Australian soap opera, where one of the characters, Marilyn, goes through a shared traumatic event with other characters but not her husband. Following this event, she feels the only person she can talk to about it is one of the other characters who went through the same thing. She becomes ever more distant from her husband, who she feels cannot understand what she went through or what she is feeling, eventually culminating in a divorce—although that is not the only reason they divorce (Holmes & McGauran, 1988–present). These two fictional examples are good at highlighting exactly the kinds of feelings and emotions a person who has been through trauma might exhibit. They suggest how trauma may impact their relationships with those closest to them.

Further than that, it may make the person who has encountered trauma ultimately isolate themselves. Sadly, in the current pandemic climate, that is something we are all doing. However, those that have suffered trauma will do it on purpose—putting distance between their partners, friends, families, and colleagues and maybe even become distant from life itself. They're going through detachment and may have no feelings about anything—almost becoming numb to anything around them. Some sufferers may become highly anxious and start showing trauma symptoms any time there is any possibility of them becoming rejected—say, by a potential partner. Others may go the other way and become entirely dependent on someone or become overprotective of their loved ones. If this includes children, then it may start to impact the child's life, as the child is not allowed to do anything that may put them in even the slightest harm. This pertains to just about anything and everything. Getting out of bed in the morning is a risk. There is nothing in life where there is no risk, so this can become problematic if a parent's trauma manifests itself in this way. Some people may find it extremely difficult to have any kind of physical relationship, to be able to place themselves in intimate situations, or find sexual relationships satisfactory. All of the feelings, emotions, and behaviors I have outlined can be bewildering and upsetting, but they are all normal things to think and feel if you have been through trauma. You should not castigate yourself any further. Understandably, trauma can result in these kinds of issues; you should not feel any worse about yourself because you can't make your relationship work after having been through trauma.

THE FIGHT, FLIGHT, FREEZE, OR FAWN RESPONSE

The fight, flight, freeze, or fawn responses are our responses when we encounter what we think is a threat or a danger to us. We do it automatically and subconsciously without even thinking about it. Flight, flight, and freeze are well-known responses, but fawn is also a possible response.

Flight is our wish to run away or flee from the situation that is causing us danger. This is a perfectly acceptable reaction and is not in any way cowardly as some posturing courageous people may view it as. After all, if you're stuck in a burning building, the best response is to get the heck out. Signs that you might be in flight mode include the following:

- Your legs feel very fidgety or restless.
- Your fingers, toes, ears, and nose (or any combination of those) become numb.
- Your eyes move around a lot or become dilated.
- Your muscles and body tense up.
- You feel like a prisoner and feel trapped.

Fight is exactly what it suggests: It becomes an aggressive response to the situation. Some indicators you may be in a "fight" mode include the following:

- You burst into tears.
- You have an overwhelming desire to punch something or somebody.
- You are grinding your teeth, or you feel your jaw tightening.
- You feel like stomping your feet or kicking something or somebody.
- You feel a deep, burning sense of anger.
- You imagine the possibility of harming someone—possibly even yourself.
- You feel pain or a burning sensation in the pit of your stomach.

Fight mode means you typically attack the source of the danger. This can be a very beneficial reaction unless the source you are attacking is capable of causing much more damage to you than you are to them.

The freeze response is best explained as becoming incapable of doing anything in the face of danger and literally freezing. It's like the phrase when a "deer is caught in the headlights." When a deer is in the middle of the highway and sees a car coming toward it, it freezes, and the car either swerves to avoid it or, sadly, hits it. Maybe you've even done this yourself: I know I have. I've stepped out on the road without paying attention, and when I see the car coming toward me rather than running out of the road, I just freeze, and I only survive because the driver stops the car in time. Some indicators you have gone into a freeze response include the following:

- Your body feels cold.
- Your body feels numb.
- You go very white—particularly in the face.
- Your legs feel like lead, and it is difficult to move your body.
- You feel very nervous and anxious.
- Your heart rate decreases, and you can feel it beating.

But what about the fawn response? This is a much lesser-known response. This response is where we will undertake anything or do anything to appease the situation. This can be particularly prevalent among those who have suffered childhood trauma. There was likely someone in their life that they would do or say anything to just to avoid whatever traumatic scenario would play out if they didn't. This type of fawn response is then often carried through to adulthood, and the person could end up in some unhealthy relationships and situations as a result.

Due to the fawn response often first occurring in childhood, it can make it difficult for a person to recognize what is happening when they are an adult. Hence, it is their default response to dangerous situations. However, there are some giveaway signals that you (or someone) could demonstrate with the fawn response:

- To see how you feel in a relationship or situation, you will view how other people feel.
- Even when alone, you find it tricky to work out what you are feeling.
- You feel like you do not have an individual personality, character, or identity.
- You are always trying to please everybody else in your life rather than concentrating and putting yourself first.
- Whenever conflict arises, your first action is to try and please or give in to the angry or annoyed person.

- You disregard your own beliefs or views and instead accept only the views of those around you as being true.
- You may find you provide strange emotional responses to things that, on the surface, don't appear to matter. For example, you could have an angry response to a stranger, or you could suddenly find yourself with a feeling of sadness, which can occur throughout the day.
- You feel guilty and angry at yourself much of the time.
- You find it difficult to say "no" to anyone.
- Everything can become too much for you, yet you will still take on more if requested.
- It is not easy to define boundaries, and you find that you are often being taken advantage of in a relationship.
- You are not happy, unsure, or even scared when asked to give your own opinion.

For those suffering from PTSD, CPTSD, or attachment trauma, there is already a level of self-blame and recrimination that can only worsen if the default response to danger is a fawn response. That is one of the many reasons it is essential to learn why these responses occur and what we can do to switch them off.

There is also talk of a fifth response known as "flop." This is where a person becomes utterly unresponsive to the occurring situation and may even lose consciousness. The term comes from the way the body flops like a rag doll.

All of these responses are perfectly natural, and people will demonstrate different reactions at different times. However, it can become concerning when we perceive threats where there are none, or we make the wrong response to the situation. These types of problems usually occur when we have become stuck in these responses because of past trauma that we have undergone. To get ourselves free from these trapped responses, we need to become more aware of how to feel safe, comforted, and without tension within our bodies. We should use exercises that allow us to safely release some of that trauma, which should mean less dependence on our fight, flight, freeze, or fawn responses.

Peter Levine based his "Somatic Experiencing" theory and work around the fact that he had observed animals in the wild. Despite being constantly in danger from predators, being chased by predators, and sometimes being momentarily captured but escaping, the animals did not suffer trauma. They carried on their life like they always had. Levine noted that animals after such an episode tended to shake and tremble, so he formed the belief that wild animals were able to "shake off" their trauma, whereas humans had lost this ability. As humans have lost the ability to shake off the trauma, trauma can end up stuck in the body, and only with the help of somatic therapy can it slowly and carefully be released (Osadchey, 2018).

I will provide you with a very simple exercise to follow so that you can switch off those fight-or-flight responses and remain calm and rational. It's a simple grounding exercise, and like all somatic healing exercises, it works from the body up to the brain rather than the other way around. This makes sense because we cannot think ourselves out of these situations or out of feeling anxious, but we can get our body to relax, be calm, and tell our brain that all is well.

GROUNDING EXERCISE

As going into fight-or-flight mode can make you feel almost detached from your body or as though your body is incapable of doing what you want it to, one way to get you back to a less anxious state is to reunite your brain with your body. One way to do this is by putting something hot or cold against your body. Obviously, be careful not to scold yourself or give yourself frostbite. If you put something mildly hot or cold on your body, it should reunite you with your body as you let your brain concentrate on what the sensations you're feeling are rather than focusing on false or impending dangers.

ATTACHMENT TRAUMA

I briefly mentioned attachment trauma at the beginning of this chapter, and I'm now going to cover it in much more detail in this section.

Attachment trauma occurs when there is an interruption to the normal bonding processes between a baby or a child and their principal caregivers—whether that be a parent or other guardian. That can be the result of abuse or neglect, but it can just be a general lack of affection or abandonment that was not the caregiver's fault.

Psychology identifies four main styles of attachment that a child may experience early in life with their caregiver. Depending on these styles, they will likely affect the child when they have grown into an adult:

- **1: Security:** People who feel secure grew up with attentive, loving, and sensitive caregivers sensitive to their child's needs. If a person obtains the security attachment, then they are likely to feel comfortable showing and speaking their emotions, will display confidence in themselves in relationships and will be able to face difficult situations and unhappy feelings in a healthy manner.
- **2: Avoidance:** Avoidant attachment occurs when a caregiver does not respond or is not sensitive to a child when hurt or in anguish. Children who experience this type of attachment are likely to grow up not showing their emotions and will not look to their caregiver to provide assurance and comfort. As adults, they are likely to be distant in relationships and not capable of showing or speaking about their emotions.
- **3: Resistance:** A resistant attachment will develop if the caregiver is not consistent or not predictable in the way they respond to a child's anguish or upset. The child may use extreme methods to get the appropriate response from the caregiver. In adulthood, this can display itself as someone who is very needy and clingy in a relationship and is not secure at all in believing their partner loves them.
- **4: Disorganization:** A disorganized attachment will form when a caregiver's behavior is unusual or, in some way, scary. The child does not know what to do to get the comfort and assurance they require. In adulthood, this can lead to relationships full of conflict and arguments.

- The first style of attachment, security, will allow children to develop healthily and become more likely to have healthy relationships in later years. The other styles will result in an incomplete attachment being formed and will likely cause unhealthy relationships and other issues in adulthood.

When the unhealthy styles occur, this can result in traumatic events for a child. Of course, this can include severe events like abuse and extreme neglect, but it can also be something as simple as a child hurting themselves and crying as the caregiver ignores them (whether this is on purpose or not). This can result in a traumatic event for the child. One rare incident in a child's life may not result in attachment trauma, but if this is a consistent pattern, then that can cause long-lasting trauma into adulthood.

However, it doesn't have to be anything the caregiver has done that may cause the failure of the attachment to occur. The caregiver might have unfortunately died, the bond broken, and the secure attachment cannot be developed. It is not always as simple as being the caregiver's fault when attachment trauma occurs.

A person suffering from attachment trauma may find that they are more likely to suffer from stress and anxiety, find it difficult to emote, have trouble sleeping, isolate themselves, or have mental health issues.

If you do suffer from attachment trauma, I will give you an exercise to follow, but please be careful. This exercise can bring up some powerful emotions and feelings. If you think that will be too much for you at this stage, then that is perfectly understandable; you should leave this exercise alone until you are ready or visit a professional therapist.

ATTACHMENT TRAUMA EXERCISE

First of all, find yourself a hard floor if you can. You can do this exercise on carpet, but it makes it trickier. Once you have found the relevant floor, take your socks off. You should then lie flat on the floor so that you are on your belly. Then, think about how you can move forward from that position. You cannot get up on your hands and knees and crawl. No, you must find a way to move while being flat on your belly. You won't have done this since you were a very small child. That is the point of the exercise: to make you think and move in that way once again. Therefore, this may bring up all the emotions of that time. If you are not ready for that, it is not for you. You may feel deep sadness, and you may feel the need to cry. There may be many strong emotions you feel as a result of being back in this position.

TOWERING ABOVE PHYSICAL PAIN AND ILLNESS

I f you find you are always in pain and have tense muscles or aching bones, this could be the chapter for you. You have become so used to being in pain or muscular tension that you feel like it's almost part of who you are. The good news is that physical somatic therapy (officially called somatics) can help you soothe that pain and get back to feeling yourself. Of course, I must point out that somatic therapy is not for healing just any and every physical injury you have. If you have broken your leg, you still need to see a doctor. You are not going to heal a broken bone through somatic therapy; in fact, you may make things a lot worse. However, if you are affected by chronic muscle and joint pain, then that is where somatic therapy can come in. With its ability to get the body to speak to the brain and vice versa, it is possible to alleviate your pain caused by the twists and stuck muscles to which your body has become accustomed.

Here are a few exercises that should really help you with your mobility and general wellness if you are experiencing chronic pain or tight muscles. You can do all the movements in each step 10 times:

- **1:** Lie on your back with your knees bent and your arms by your sides. Inhale, push your pelvis up slightly, and exhale. Inhale, push your lower back down, and exhale.
- **2:** Lie on your back with legs outstretched and your hands stretched out behind you. You are basically going into a star shape. Pretend you can make your right leg grow longer. Inhale as you imagine doing that, and then exhale and relax. Do the same with your left arm: Imagine it is growing or that someone is pulling your arm to make it longer. Do the same with the left leg and finally with the right arm.
- **3:** Lie on your back with arms outstretched sideways, your knees bent, and then cross one leg over the other. Inhale. Then, move your legs over to the left. Make sure this part is just your legs—everything else will remain central and exhale. Switch legs and do the same, bringing your legs down to the right and back to the center. Then, do the same but with your right arm pointing up and your left hand pointing down. While moving your legs, move your head to the left and vice versa.
- **4:** Get into a sitting position and just rotate your head and torso to the left. Then do the same to the right. Now, do the same but put your right hand on your left shoulder, and after you have rotated, move your head gently back to the center. Then return everything to the center. Do the same for the other side.

SENSORY MOTOR AMNESIA

Sensory motor amnesia (SMA) is a phrase that the pioneer Thomas Hanna, a visionary in the world of somatics, introduced (Warren, 2019). It describes the pattern of physical behavior that your body's muscles carry out without you even thinking about it, which often does you a disservice. For example, day after day, you slouch at your desk over your laptop. Your back muscles become used to this and adapt accordingly so that something bad for you actually becomes normal for your body, and you do nothing to correct it because your body does not tell you to. In fact, quite often, the opposite occurs. Now, sitting up straight becomes painful, and slouching becomes very comfortable. This pattern can then lead to chronic physical pain. In this example, you are likely to end up with severe back pain or maybe even a hump, and you will be forever crouched over, even when standing.

It is easy in the modern world to develop SMA. We are forever slouched over desks, slumped in chairs, and sitting in cars or public transport. We do not move as much as we should, so our body adapts accordingly. It no longer bothers with all that twisting, running, and flexibility you used to need: Our muscles instead focus on what they need to do for slouching and slumping. In turn, muscles can become habitually stuck in unwanted positions, even pulling bones out of place over time.

Another way you can develop SMA is if you have some kind of injury. Then, while your injury heals, it affects how you are moving. This is particularly true if you injure your foot—it affects the way you walk. Then, once your injury has healed, you're still walking in the way you were when you were injured. This is doing you harm, and your body has forgotten how you used to move about normally. Another example would be an injury such as a twisted pelvis.

If you have SMA, you may notice that sometimes, your body is hesitant about its movement; maybe there is a slight shaking or jerking of the affected areas, or there may even be a shudder when your body has let go of some of its tension.

You can do a very simple exercise if you believe you have SMA and would like some confirmation. I advise you that if while doing this exercise you come across pain, take it very slowly and only move within what is acceptable to you; don't try and force anything, as you are only likely to do yourself further damage. It is good to do this exercise slowly to give your brain the chance to comprehend what you are doing. If you do things quickly, the automatic part of your brain will start taking over.

Sit down with your arms down by your sides. Turn your head to the left. You will need to stay looking left throughout the exercise, so make sure your head turn is within your comfort zone and not too painful or stretched. Now, you are going to look up toward the ceiling and move your right shoulder up toward the back of your head. Then, slowly release that position and go back to the position you were in before. You can try this on the other side as well. How did it feel? A bit hesitant or shuddery or shaky? If it was, then you probably do have SMA.

A practice known as pandiculation can help bring about the link between the brain and the muscles and help you to ease your SMA problems.

SOMATIC PANDICULATION

Pandiculation may sound like the most complicated word in the world, but it's really quite a simple concept. Pandiculation involves intentionally (or sometimes, subconsciously) moving muscles to link the movements to our nervous system. The morning stretch and yawn is a perfect example of this. It's a recalibration of our body with our nervous system to further etch movement patterns into our being. We often do this unintentionally and subconsciously when we wake up, but pandiculations can be done on purpose at any time to bring about a myriad of desired results. There are countless somatic pandiculation videos online that target different muscles for different reasons. This act may be more significant than you realize. Bad posture, tight muscles, and unagile movement may become habituated if we don't engage in pandiculation.

Pandiculation is best explained as the nervous system setting off our internal alarm and saying to the body, "Get ready for some movement!" Humans and any animals with vertebrae tend to automatically perform pandiculation when they wake up or if they have been stationary for a very long while. You probably notice that a baby performs this when they wake up, or you may have seen your pet cat or dog arch their back and stretch out when they have woken up from a doze. All of these are examples of pandiculation. In fact, it is said that animals pandiculate 40 times a day ("Pandiculation—the Safe Alternative to Stretching," 2010). You don't see them all slouched over with bad posture or twisting their ankles just because they had to go and chase a mouse or a stick.

Pandiculation lets our nervous system know the level of tension in our muscles and regulates and resets that muscular tension so we don't end up with muscular pain in the long term. It has been suggested that a fetus can perform pandiculation while in the womb, showing what a primitive and vital action it is (Warren, 2019).

Sadly, with all the bad habits and patterns of physical behavior we so easily get ourselves into in the modern world, automatic pandiculation is just not enough to rid ourselves of all that muscle tension. Sometimes, if our posture is pulled out of alignment, our nervous systems can simply forget to do much pandiculation at all.

Thomas Hanna studied pandiculation in great detail and came to the realization that pandiculation addressed muscle tension and most of the underlying causes of people who had posture issues, movement issues, and chronic pain. He devised some exercises that people could do themselves, rather than relying on automatic pandiculation. He would ensure people were much more equipped to deal with their muscular tensions and free themselves from much of their pain by encouraging voluntary pandiculation. Voluntary pandiculation must be carried out very slowly and intentionally so that the nervous system takes on board what it is being told and updates itself in response (Warren, 2019).

Any pandiculation exercise will require three main aspects:

- **1:** Contract the muscle.
- **2:** Have a slow, intent lengthening of the muscle.
- **3:** Relax as you let your brain and nervous system comprehend what you have just done.

The psoas [**soh**-*uhs*] is an exceptionally important muscle in the human body. Without such muscles, you wouldn't be able to even get yourself out of bed in the morning. That's how important it is. The psoas muscle is also relevant to the way you breathe, so it can have a psychological impact—not just a physical one. Whatever you are doing—running, riding a bike, sitting on the sofa, or dancing—your psoas muscle is required and will be doing work to enable you to do these things. The psoas is so important because it's the muscle that connects your body to your legs. These muscles are otherwise known as the hip flexors. They are extremely vital when it comes to your posture and supporting and regulating your spine. Since the psoas muscle is also connected to the diaphragm, it's prevalent in walking, breathing, and even responding to fear and excitement. If you are under stress, your psoas muscle actually contracts. Essentially, it has a direct impact on your fight-or-flight response. If that stress goes on for long periods, then your psoas muscle is contracted for long periods, leading to a myriad of health issues. That same contraction can happen if you sit down for a long time, run or walk too much, fall and stay asleep in the fetal position, or do a huge amount of sit-ups.

A tight psoas muscle can lead to any number of health issues and complaints, including digestive issues, exhaustion, sexual dysfunction, lower back pain, pelvic pain (which can impact sexual practices and appetite), sciatica (which can cause intolerable pain), a limp, a difference between the length of your legs, curvature in the spine, and a weak core.

You may think that stretching the psoas muscle may be enough, but the psoas muscle takes its instructions from the brain. No matter how much you stretch it, it will be doing what the brain tells it to, and if that is to contract, then contract it will. You could, therefore, end up doing more harm than good by stretching. The best you can achieve is that you may be able to loosen the muscles for a little while after stretching, but soon after, the brain will reset the nervous system, and the psoas muscle will go back to how it was before stretching. Any potential long-term tension can still occur.

I'm going to give you two very simple pandiculation exercises that you can easily complete at home. If you are having trouble with your psoas, these will help you release that tension and trauma and help you open up your life to a world that is free of pain. (Please note: if your psoas doesn't release or re-contracts after pandiculation exercises, then you may be suffering from a twisted sacrum, also known as sacral torsion, a twisted pelvis, or SI joint dysfunction. You'll need to fix a turned sacrum first. I recommend the program "comforting your SI joints" by somatic educator Lawrence Gold.)

- **1:** First, lie on the floor. A flat surface is preferable to a carpet. If you have an exercise mat, that may provide extra comfort. Lie on your back with your knees up and your feet firmly on the floor. Make sure that you can easily slide your foot and leg along the floor (hence, carpet is not such a good surface for this). Put your arms and hands behind your head.

Now, take a breath in and arch ever so slightly so that your pelvis moves toward the ceiling and your back contracts; then breathe out and relax.

- Then, when you next breathe out, bring your head and back forward and have your elbows pointing toward your leg. Then, bring one of your legs toward your elbow, then slowly move everything back to where it was: Your head and back to the floor with your elbows and hands behind your head, and your knee and leg back to the floor with your foot planted firmly on the ground.

- Then, do the same with the other side. Take a breath in and arch very slightly, then breathe out and relax; on your next breath out, move your other knee toward your elbows and then slowly move everything back to where it was before.

- Next, do the same exercise, but when you put your foot back on the floor, slide your leg and foot all the way along the ground and flex your toes. Breathe in and out as you require. You can also slightly vary so that when you next bring your leg up and put it down, it comes up more naturally so that your leg and foot are curved outward rather than straight. You can repeat the exercise several times with both legs. It will be interesting to see if you notice any difference between each side; maybe one side feels less tight than the other. Whatever you notice, after doing these exercises for a while, you will see that your psoas is not as tight, and you have managed to release some of that tension out of your body.

- **2:** Do the same exercise, but this time, keep your arms by your side when you lift your knee up. Then, when you slide your leg out this time, bring your arm over your head from your side—as if when you swim, you are doing the backstroke. Do one stroke, put your arm over your head, and relax. Go back into position, repeat, and then do the same with the other side of your body. This exercise will help with the muscles toward the upper part of your back; if

your psoas is tight, you should feel that along the side of
your body.

There are also some straightforward exercises you can do to ensure
all the various muscle groups undergo pandiculation.

- This one will help work your biceps. You can do this
  standing up or sitting down. Just bring your forearm toward
  you slowly as though you were lifting a dumbbell, and then
  let it slowly go back to its position and relax. If you need to,
  you can lightly place your first two fingers of your other
  hand onto your arm just to put a tiny bit of resistance there,
  and that helps your brain and nervous system work out what
  is going on and not cause any SMA possibilities.
- I definitely have a problem constantly pushing my head out
  in front of me, particularly when hunched over my laptop.
  An exercise to help remedy that is the following: Kneel
  down, arch slowly, slowly pull your belly and head back, and
  then relax. Again, if you need a little bit of resistance to
  help, you can place one hand under your chest and one hand
  on your belly. Your spine and the front of your body should
  feel more in harmony after doing this exercise. Rather than
  being hunched over with your head forward, you should be
  able to sit up straight with your head sitting nicely on the
  top of your body where it is meant to be.

These exercises should really help you in the long term in a way
that stretching simply cannot. You are performing pandiculation on
your muscles that will work wonders for you. With some luck, the days
of never-ending pain, inflexibility, or struggle in your movement will be
gone. All helped with something that you can easily do at home for
free.

6

A TREASURE TROVE OF
SOMATIC PRACTICES

In this chapter, I am going to outline some of the most powerful somatic practices. It really is a treasure trove of a chapter. All these years have been like digging for diamonds or panning for gold without any luck—until now. You are going to find that treasure you needed—your pot of gold at the end of the rainbow. These are easy-to-follow practices that you can do in your own time and space. They do not require special equipment or great expense to be able to take part in them. Best of all, there is genuine scientific evidence backing up these practices, so I know they work; soon, you will, too.

POLYVAGAL THEORY AND THE VAGUS NERVE

The polyvagal theory was developed by Stephen Porges and helps us to better understand our nervous system. It came out of his studying of the vagus nerve. The vagus nerve is involved in the calming element of the nervous system. This balances out with the active element, so if there is more calming occurring, then less activity is needed. If more activity is occurring, then less calming is needed. Polyvagal theory describes a third element, what Porges labeled as the "Social Engagement System"—a combination of both the active and the calming aspects (Wagner, 2016).

As the name suggests, it is the social engagement aspect that assists us in working our way through relationships and to better cope with any conflict that may arise.

The nervous system has two main elements when it comes to feeling like we are in grave danger: the element that deals with our fight-or-flight response and the part that deals with shutting down completely (think back to the "flop" method of dealing with danger). In order for the social engagement system to become engaged, there has to be a sense of being safe.

It is the vagus nerve that helps calm the body, and it has two main aspects to it, which behave in very different ways. The shutting down aspect occurs through one part of the vagus nerve. When this shut-down occurs, a person will usually feel very tired and maybe quite giddy—rather like if you had the flu. This can affect a person's heart, lungs, diaphragm, and digestive system.

The other part of the vagus nerve affects things above the diaphragm. This is the part that services the social engagement system. This part of the nerve helps to control our nervous system. For example, if you are letting someone rock climb, you let the rope down slowly for them to work their way down safely; you don't let the rope go all at once. That is kind of what the vagus nerve is doing here: keeping your nervous system regulated and stopping it from becoming hyperactive. Whereas the fight-or-flight response can take seconds to take place and recovery can take anywhere from 10 to 20 minutes, the vagus nerve's response to calm takes mere milliseconds. Therefore, we should be able to calm our responses in the same way you let down the rope slowly for a rock climber to control their ascent down the face of a cliff.

A good example of social engagement in action is if you go down to your local park and observe the dogs. Some dogs will be aggressive toward other dogs or will run away, and their owners have to chase after them—these are the dogs in fight-or-flight mode. But if you see the dogs happily playing, wagging their tails, wanting a stick or ball to be thrown, and jumping up in a friendly way at their owners, these are the dogs who feel in a safe space and are employing the social engagement system.

If a person has trauma that they have not managed to release, then they can find themselves forever in a world of fight or flight; instead of happily going about their daily activities with their social engagement system fully in tune, everything becomes a task of dread and fear.

The vagus nerve actually impacts the middle ear, which can help us focus on human voices and remove all the unnecessary background noise. It also impacts our ability to make facial expressions—another essential for communication. Finally, it also impacts our vocal cords and the noises we may make to each other—again, to communicate in a calming manner. It is the longest nerve in the body, and if you are wondering how it got its name, it's because, in Latin, *vagus* means "wandering." You know it's a long nerve when it's named the "wandering" nerve.

Ultimately, if we can find ways to reset that vagal nerve or exercise it so that we feel happy, safe, secure, and playful, then life can be so much better for us.

EXERCISE #1

First is a really simple exercise. Start by sitting up and moving your head slowly to the left, back to the center, and then to the right. Is there any difference between each side? Do you find it more difficult to move your head to one side compared to the other? When I first discovered this exercise, I found it slightly more difficult to move my head to the right side compared to the left side. After this, lie down on your back with your knees up and your feet firmly on the floor. Once you become experienced at this exercise, you can do it sitting up or even standing up, but you should lie down for it for the first few times. Place your hands behind your head, with your fingers interlocked and your elbows pointing out so that you are holding your head in your hands. Then, move your eyes to the right—not your head: just your eyes. Use your hands to support your head so you don't move it. You only move your eyes. Hold your eyes in that position for 30 seconds. Then, relax and let your eyes come back to the middle. If you notice that you may need to take a breath or have the urge to swallow, those are vagus nerve responses and signs that the exercise is working.

Now, do the other side: Move your eyes to the left, with your head not moving and staying central, and hold your eyes there for 30 seconds. Then, relax and let your eyes come back to the middle. Take a moment, then return to your sitting position and move your head side to side to see if your mobility has improved. By the way, 30 seconds is the minimum time to hold your eyes in position. If you are not getting any of the signs, like a deep breath or swallowing, you can hold your eyes in position for 60 seconds or more. When I first discovered this exercise, I found it slightly more difficult to turn my head to the right side. Once I had done the exercise, then I found I could move my head without restriction equally on both sides. This exercise works.

EXERCISE #2

The second exercise you can do is to just sit down. Whether that be on the floor or in a chair—as long as you are comfortable, that is the main thing. Place your right hand on the top of your head, and then tip your head to the right. Move your eyes and your eyes only. Hold that position for 30 seconds. You can relax after that and resume your normal sitting position. Now, you will do the same but for the other side. Put your left hand on your head, and tip your head to the left. Move your eyes up and to the right. Hold the position for 30 seconds. Again, you can hold the position longer if you are not feeling any effect.

EXERCISE #3

For the third exercise, again, be in a sitting position, take your right hand, and put it on top of your head, tipping your head to the right. However, this time, take your left hand and reach around to clutch your right side. Then, move your head to the right side, and use your left hand to pull your side. Again, move your eyes only, up and to the left, and hold the position for 30 seconds. Then, release yourself from the position and relax. You should notice yourself feeling a bit calmer having performed that exercise. Do the other side: left hand on top of your head and tip your head to the left. Use your right hand to reach around to your left side and pull your side. Then, move your eyes up and to the right side and hold the position for 30 seconds. Once again, release yourself from that position and relax.

EXERCISE #4

For this next exercise, you need to find somewhere comfortable to lie down. If you have an exercise or yoga mat, that is probably best. I found lying face down on a carpeted floor isn't much fun, as it usually just reminds me I need to get the vacuum cleaner out! Once ready, you are going to prop yourself up on your elbows, hands pointing out in front of you and flat on the floor. Then, you are going to turn to your left and look over your shoulder. As per usual, hold the position for 30 seconds. Release that position and relax; lie face down if you want to for a few moments. Now, do the same thing but look over your right shoulder this time. Hold the position for 30 seconds, then release yourself from the position and relax. As you are using your neck muscles in this exercise, it can be really good for those who have tension in that area and, as a result, suffer from headaches and migraines. Do this exercise, and you should release some of the tension and be able to get some relief from the pain.

Believe it or not, breathing can also have an impact on your vagus nerve and your vagus nerve on your breathing. That is something known as "vagal tone," which basically represents your vagus nerve activity (Fallis, 2021). The higher your vagal tone is, the easier you will find it to return to a relaxed state after a moment of stress. If we can find a way to activate our vagal nerve and increase our vagal tone, then we should feel less stressed, less anxious, and generally happier. A 2010 study found that those with a high vagal tone were generally positive in their feelings and had good physical health (Kok et al., 2013). There have even been studies that suggest that if mothers are anxious and stressed during pregnancy (giving them a low vagal tone), this actually gets passed on to the baby when it is born, and the baby also shares a low vagal tone (Field & Diego, 2008). There has even been a device that can be planted in you that will activate your vagus nerve every so often, but that is an extreme way to go. Deep and slow breathwork can activate your vagus nerve and increase your vagal tone.

Therefore, at this point, it would be good to give you some breathing exercises to activate your vagal tone. These exercises all have different purposes. This first one is to enable you to relax.

BREATHING EXERCISE #1

You can start by sitting down and putting your arms around your rib cage and your belly, or you can use a pillow to put in front of you and use that. You are basically putting yourself into a hug position. Then, breathe in until you have a full feeling and hold for four seconds; after, breathe out for longer than you breathed in and hold for six seconds. You can "hug" yourself a little harder when you breathe out if you like because that is what is activating the vagus nerve. You can then transpose this exercise to the floor to make it even more relaxing. You can lie on your back or your front. If you are on your back with your knees up and feet firmly on the floor, you can put pressure on your belly and your chest with your hands. If you are lying on your front, you can lie down stretched out, and you can put a pillow or cushion under your belly or chest to add some pressure.

You then breathe in for six seconds and hold it for four. See if you can feel your heartbeat rhythm and use that as your count of four. Breathe out for eight seconds and then hold that for four seconds; keep repeating. If you feel you can increase the time you exhale, try to do that. It is that exhaling length that really alerts the vagus nerve and gets you to a place of relaxation. One last thing you can do to relax even further is to lie on your back with your knees up and feet firmly on the floor. Place something under your buttocks and lower back. This is to ensure your pelvis is raised up higher than your head. When there is too much blood flowing toward your head, this immediately alerts the vagus nerve and starts slowing down your heart rate and relaxing you. Breathe in until you feel full. Swallow and breathe out for longer than you breathed in. After, just take a momentary pause until you feel the need to breathe in again. Then, breathe in until you feel full. Swallow and breathe out for longer than you breathed in. Pause until you need to breathe in again. Keep repeating. This should see you enter a state of deep relaxation and calmness.

BREATHING EXERCISE #2

This next exercise is a nice and easy one you can use whenever you want, which will activate the vagus nerve. Vocalizing sounds can be really beneficial—that's why singing usually feels so good to you. The first sound to make is an "mmm" sound. Take a deep breath—with your belly, not a shallow breath with your chest—and when you breathe out, make that "mmm" sound for as long as you can. Take a deep breath again, and when you breathe out, make an "ahhh" sound this time. Take a deep breath, and when you breathe, make an "ooh" sound. Finally, take a deep breath and make all three sounds in a row until you run out of breath: "mmm, ahhh, ooh." Making these sounds is a really good way to activate that vagus nerve for those times when you are feeling stressed.

GUIDED MEDITATION

I'm now going to provide you with a guided meditation for vagus nerve stimulation. As with all the vagus nerve exercises, this should help you relax, feel calm, and release any tension. For this, you need to make sure you are sitting up comfortably.

- **1:** Make sure you breathe from your belly and diaphragm, and you're not shallow breathing from your chest. Breathe in for six seconds and hold for four seconds.
- **2:** Breathe out for eight seconds and hold for four seconds.
- **3:** Keep repeating.
- **4:** The most important thing to remember is that your breathing out should last longer than your breathing in. Even if you become relaxed enough to stop counting, you need to make sure the exhale is longer than the inhale. That

long breath out stimulates the vagus nerve, leaves you feeling calm, and releases any tension.

- **5:** You can stop your breathing, become aware of your whole body again, and when you feel ready, you can open your eyes.

PENDULATION

Pendulation is a term devised by the king of somatic experiencing, Peter Levine. As you could probably guess from its name, it describes something similar to a pendulum, but what is swinging, in this case, are your feelings, emotions, and nervous system. You are swinging between that state, which is fear and fight or flight, and the calm and relaxed state where your vagus nerve is stimulated and your vagal tone is high. If a person can learn to move between those two states, then when a person gets into a state of anxiety, stress, and feels tense or in pain, they can learn to swing to the other state and stand a chance of becoming more relaxed, peaceful, and at ease. Of course, it is never quite that simple. Sometimes, all you can do is move to a less painful or less anxious state, but that is still a better place to be than where you started. It also means that you can do so in small pieces when you go to those dark and worrying places. You are in control, so you don't have to go through everything all at once. You can deal with it and then get back to your safe and secure space. After all, how can you really know what feeling happy is unless you have felt sad as well? How can you know what calm means without feeling stressed? Both states have to exist, and we have to understand and learn to appreciate the negative as well as the positive.

Peter Levine compares it to contraction and expansion: The basic rhythm of life is contraction and expansion. However, when a person becomes traumatized, the rhythm becomes contraction and nothing else. Through pendulation, the contraction can slowly be opened up to an expansion. Then, there will still be a contraction—the rhythm of life—but there will be an expansion until the person becomes able to tolerate the contraction, knowing that a bigger expansion is coming. Those who are happy with life and living it to the fullest learn to respect and appreciate the contraction, knowing it leads to expansion when they are calm and open (Somatic Experiencing International, 2019).

In a moment, we'll look at a pendulation exercise. This first exercise is particularly useful if you are in pain or feel tension in one specific part of your body.

PENDULATION EXERCISE

For this exercise, you are going to think about two places on your body. First, think about the part of your body that is in pain. We have to acknowledge the pain in the body before we think about anything else. I often find my upper back can be quite painful if I haven't been sitting properly at my desk, so for this exercise, I may focus on that and acknowledge the pain there, but, at the same time, maybe give it a rub and let it know I care for it. Then, think of a part of your body that isn't in pain and doesn't give you any problems. Maybe it's your hair; perhaps it's your big toe. Whatever it is, think of that and how good it is, how it's free of pain, and how it helps you achieve what you want. Then, switch between the two—thinking about the pain and then the good part of your body. Going back and forth is the pendulation aspect. Contract pain, and expand part of your body that is good. As I say, this exercise is good if you have a particular part of your body in pain or if you are anxious and that has manifested as a physical symptom. You focus on that—maybe it's an upset stomach, a headache, or maybe your arms feel itchy. Switch to thinking about a part of your body that is not impacted and switch between the two. Your anxiety should gradually ease as you acknowledge the anxiety but also acknowledge a part of your body that is working well for you. You may want to slow down your breathing as you do the switching to help give you that extra level and activation of your vagus nerve to help calm you down.

SOMATIC TITRATION

Titration may have a complex-sounding name, but it is not a complex concept to understand. It is the process of slowly tackling the trauma. If a person were to consider their trauma all at once, it would be too much, and they would become overwhelmed. It is the process of slowly remembering and becoming comfortable with your trauma. It is not just the slowing down of the trauma but slowing down to take time to appreciate how your body is feeling, the sensations you are picking up, and the world around you. It could be said that pendulation uses titration because you don't just focus on the part that hurts: You focus on that for a bit, then on something that isn't hurting and come back. You are slowly thinking about the trauma. You don't just focus on the part that hurts forever until it completely overwhelms you.

The name "titration" comes from a chemistry term that describes slowly dripping potentially dangerous chemicals into a beaker so that the chemical change—turning these chemicals into a harmless substance—occurs safely. The unsafe option would be to put the chemicals in all at once, causing an explosion.

COGNITIVE BEHAVIORAL THERAPY

Cognitive behavioral therapy (CBT) is a type of therapy specifically aimed at those who may have mental health difficulties. It is based on the theory that people have ways of thinking that are not beneficial to them, and these unhelpful ways of thinking become a habit or a pattern of behavior. By teaching people more helpful ways of thinking about things, they may be able to cope much better with their anxiety, depression, or whatever issues they may be having and maybe even relieve themselves of those issues.

As CBT involves changing the way you think about things and your thinking behavior patterns, it will usually include getting a person to realize where their thinking is exaggerated or less moderated. Try to get the person to recognize the reality of that situation and change their thinking accordingly. It may provide certain issue resolution skills to assist the person with particularly complex situations. It may also include providing the person with confidence in themselves and their instincts.

I have had close family members go through CBT. While I realize and appreciate its ability to get a person to cope better with what they are going through—providing them with the tool kit to apply whenever they feel things are spiraling out of control—It doesn't always address the root cause of the problem. It often overlooks the actual cause of their depression or anxiety.

However, I can't deny the evidence that exists to support the view that CBT can make a big difference in someone else's life and help them contain and control the difficulties they are going through. A study of analysis from controlled trials concluded that CBT was effective when dealing with major depression, though its effect was not huge (Lynch et al., 2009). A similar study dealing with previous data concluded that CBT effectively dealt with many cases of depression, anxiety, panic disorders, social phobias, and PTSD (Butler at al., 2006). As there is empirical evidence to support the effectiveness of CBT, this has led to its use as an official treatment for those with mental health issues.

You may think CBT is something you have to do in conjunction with a therapist, but, in fact, what the therapist does is give you the tools to use yourself in your daily life to help combat your worst thoughts and feelings. Overall, it is possible to do exercises yourself. I will outline an excellent, simple CBT exercise to follow here. This one is particularly for those who may often find themselves depressed or possibly anxious.

CBT EXERCISE #1

First, write down the negative thoughts you have in your head. Maybe it's, "No one likes me," "I am useless," or whatever destabilizing thought it could be. Then, write down the opposite positive possibility: "I am likable" or, "I do have use." Initially, it can be very hard to accept the second statement. Still, over time, the more you repeat the exercise and feel comfortable with yourself, the more you will start to accept the second statement as fact.

CBT EXERCISE #2

Another exercise you can engage in is if you naturally think negatively about something. Try to ignore that negative thought and concentrate on five positive things instead. Imagine you don't like a room because you hate the carpet; try to think of the five positive things about the room—you like the large windows, you like the large doors, you like the paintings on the wall, you like the roundness of the table, and you like the light coming through when it's sunny outside. Try to think of five good things about whatever you are feeling negative about. If you can find someone else to do this with, then even better: You will be able to work off each other and get some enthusiasm for finding positives.

ENERGY PSYCHOLOGY

What is energy psychology? Well, David Feinstein, an early advocate of energy psychology, described it nicely as "acupuncture without the needles" ("Energy Psychology," 2017). Although that simplifies it somewhat, this is an accurate description. Energy psychology involves tapping various points on your body, which will then send messages back to the brain to regulate your emotions and feelings and help calm and relax you. Usually, the tapping is carried out in tandem with becoming aware of the body and the feelings, thoughts, and behaviors that may need to change. Someone having this type of therapy may be asked to remember a traumatic event while the body tapping is carried out.

If trauma is trapped in the body, then using tapping can be the way to release that trauma and bring relief and peace to a person. There are various types and techniques of energy psychology that are practiced. ("Energy Psychology," 2017) These include :

- **Thought Field Therapy (TFT):** This type of therapy requires body tapping to occur in a very specific order. A person will be required to recall a traumatic event, and then the tapping will occur in the required sequence. This form of therapy was developed by Dr. Roger Callaghan, who claimed to have formed algorithms that pertained to the correct order in which to perform the tapping.

- **Tapas Acupressure Technique (TAT):** The word tapas makes me hungry. However, this technique has nothing to do with bite-sized Spanish food. The title of this technique takes its name from the man who invented it: Tapas Fleming. This technique requires someone to use their fingers to apply pressure to areas around the eyes, above the nose, and on the back of the head. The person may then need to focus on images that have caused them distress in the past and to then focus on more positive images. They might then focus on what they believe may have caused their issues and then focus on healing and forgiveness.

- **Emotional Freedom Techniques (EFT):** This technique is not unlike the others. It requires a person to recall a traumatic event and then for tapping to occur on 12 points on the body in a specific order while the person declares affirmations. This technique was developed by Gary Craig and is a variant of "Thought Field Therapy."

These may sound like the kind of practices you would need a therapist to perform on you, but they are all techniques that can be self-taught and carried out by an individual. Like all the therapies and techniques in this book, it is easy to find time to incorporate them into your daily routine.

As with many new therapies, the jury is still out on genuine scientific evidence to prove the true value of energy psychology, but research is emerging that suggests it can positively impact those who have trauma, anxiety, and stress. Feinstein carried out research on all the studies that had taken place and concluded that energy psychology did make a valuable difference when treating those with emotional and psychological issues (Feinstein, 2012). Of course, Feinstein is a big advocate of energy psychology, so to be fair, one has to take what he says with a pinch of salt. However, he references many independent studies from all over the world, so one can also conclude that there must be something in it if so many people are noticing the positive difference it can make. Personally, I am a huge advocate of EFT tapping and make sure to practice at least three sessions per day. I have noticed a profound positive difference in my anxiety, OCD, and countless other traits.

ENERGY PSYCHOLOGY EXERCISE #1

Ready to try an energy psychology exercise? Let's go for it. First, make sure you are sitting somewhere comfortably. Now, find an area on the left side of your chest or just above that maybe feels a little sore or tight. Give that a little rub using your fingers—make circles with your fingers over that area—and then you can say some affirmations at the same time. Maybe try saying, "I love, respect, and cherish myself—even my flaws." You can continue to say that as you rub the sore area. Then, breathe in deeply and breathe out very slowly. Pause momentarily and consider how you feel and how your body feels afterward.

ENERGY PSYCHOLOGY EXERCISE #2

For this next exercise, you need to cross your left ankle over your right and put your arms in the air out in front of you—facing outward so that your thumbs are facing down. Do the opposite with your hands as you did with your ankles. Clasp your hands together so your fingers are interlocking, and roll your hands in. Then, put your hands on your chest in the most comfortable way possible. Now, inhale through your nose and exhale through your mouth. Do this five times. You can relax after that. Uncross everything and pause again to consider how you and your body feels. Then, do the same exercise, but this time, put your right ankle over your left and your left hand over your right. Turn your hands and arms in again, and, as with last time, inhale through your nose and exhale through your mouth five times. Once you've done that, relax and uncross everything. Take a moment to think about how you feel and how your body feels. Finally, just to round things off, put your five fingers from both hands together and up, so you are making a kind of pyramid with your hands. Feel present and aware in that moment. Breathe deeply using your belly and not your chest. After a few breaths, relax and think about how you feel again.

ENERGY PSYCHOLOGY EXERCISE #3

Once you feel confident with the ankle and hand-crossing exercise, there is a slightly more complex version you may want to take on. This involves looking up toward the ceiling or sky when inhaling and looking down at the floor when exhaling. Then, just to make things even more complicated for you, move your tongue to the roof of your mouth when inhaling, and move your tongue to the bottom of the mouth when exhaling. There is quite a bit to remember with this version of the exercise, so start with the simple exercise, and once you have that down to a tee, perhaps you can move on to this more complex version and see how it goes. After, relax and uncross everything. Once again, make the pyramid shape with your hands and take some time to be in the moment and aware of how your body feels. As you can see, there's no tapping your forehead or having to lie down and get in difficult positions. This is something you can easily fit into your day—maybe when you wake up or before you go to sleep. Any moment you get a few minutes to yourself, aim to do these exercises.

SENSORIMOTOR PSYCHOTHERAPY

The people responsible for naming therapies love giving difficult names to them, don't they? Sensorimotor psychotherapy comes from the sensory motor, which we had previously encountered in this book when discussing sensory motor amnesia. This type of psychotherapy, like most in the somatic therapy arena, concentrates on the body to unlock and release trapped trauma.

Pat Ogden first came to develop this kind of therapy after working in a psychiatric hospital and realizing that patients there never linked their physical ailments with their mental health issues. She noticed that those who attended therapy tended to relive and trigger their traumatic experiences, and it didn't really help heal them. Ogden set about rectifying this situation by combining elements of psychotherapy with elements of somatic therapy—something that would emphasize the link between the body and the mind: not ignore it. Ogden joined together with Ron Kurtz, and together, they formed a training institute known as the Sensorimotor Psychotherapy Institute (Sensorimotor Psychotherapy, 2015).

Like most somatic therapies, sensorimotor psychotherapy believes that trauma can become trapped in the body if not dealt with fully at the time, so it can result in both physical and mental problems. It tries to close off that trauma in a safe space. It does not necessarily believe that a trauma's exact specifics need to be recalled to effectively release it.

Although how sensorimotor psychotherapy is applied can vary depending on the practitioners and the issues it is addressing, there are three main elements that need to be focused on:

- **1: Creating a Safe Space:** Doing this enables a person to feel comfortable and allows them to really be aware of their body, their feelings and sensations, their movements, and their breathing patterns. Having a place where the person feels protected really helps them be aware of their body and what it is feeling both in the moment and when related to past experiences.

- **2:** As a person recalls their traumatic experience, both **what they feel** and **where they feel** it is noted. For example, if a person says they feel anxious, where do they feel it? Does their stomach feel tied in knots? Is it causing a headache? Do they feel the need to scratch their skin? This can then help with trying to reimagine any traumatic events by incorporating those bodily feelings.
- **3:** The person needs to **complete the required action** that will allow the trauma to be released. This should give the person a sense of satisfaction as they finally do what needs to be done and put the trauma to one side. The person should be able to find that calm and peace that exists when trauma is finally put into the past and stays there.

Sensorimotor psychotherapy aims to give people the ability to control their reactions to traumatic events and an awareness of how trauma can impact the body—not just the mind. It also looks to provide the tools to tell the difference between the past and the present. It helps with being able to consider thoughts and feelings—both in mind and in the body—rather than becoming overwhelmed by a traumatic event.

There is still not much research on the effectiveness of sensorimotor psychotherapy. However, one study was carried out on ten women with a history of child abuse. They took part in 20 weekly group therapy sessions based on sensorimotor psychotherapy. The study concluded that there had been significant improvements in awareness of bodies, disassociation, and acceptance of peace and calm (Langmuir et al., 2012).

One aspect often employed in sensorimotor psychotherapy is grounding. When you feel like you've lost your footing in the world and are unsteady both mentally and physically, grounding is required. Grounding exercises are described as being able to firmly plant your feet on the ground and taking the time to be aware of your body and everything around you. Here are a few elementary grounding exercises you can practice anywhere:

- There are a few variations you can do. You can place a hand on your forehead and a hand on your heart, a hand on your forehead and your belly, or a hand on your heart and a hand on your belly. Pick your combination, or give them all a go. Once you are in position, apply a tiny bit of pressure with your hands and then breathe deeply.
- Rub your hands together, specifically the palms. Think of it almost like you had a stick between them, and you needed to create fire. Once your palms have warmed up from the friction, place them over your eyes, apply a tiny little bit of pressure, and breathe deeply.
- Cross your arms over and grab your upper arms, so your left hand will be on your right upper arm, for instance. Squeeze gently and continue to do that all the way down your arms and back up again.
- Put your right hand on the left side of your chest and stroke (like you would a cat) down from your shoulder to your heart. I must say I find that one particularly comforting, but then they say stroking a cat can be therapeutic; maybe it's the stroking that I find comfort in.
- Put one foot on top of the other and apply a little pressure. Change over your feet and do the same.

These are just some simple exercises that you can do at home. Generally, sensorimotor psychotherapy is a form of therapy that needs a therapist to guide you and interpret for you more than some other therapies. Still, it is nothing you cannot teach yourself. With the grounding exercises, I have already given you a head start on activities you can easily practice at home.

GESTALT THERAPY

Gestalt therapy is about concentrating on what is happening right now and not basing the present on what may have occurred in the past. Those undergoing gestalt therapy are asked to reimagine those past experiences. Through the various techniques and tools, they become aware of how their own thought patterns and behaviors are negatively impacting their life. If they can change those ways, they can find a fulfilling life.

The word "gestalt" can mean whole, and the psychotherapist who developed this type of therapy, Fritz Perls, was very much a believer in people being treated as a whole—mind, body, and soul/spirit. He also believed people could only truly be understood when they viewed things through their own eyes, not by mentally going back to the past and staying there, but by bringing the past into the present. Gestalt therapy advocates that it is no good just talking about how a person feels in the past but by reenacting those feelings in the present. If one fails to bring out feelings in the present, this can lead to mental and physical health problems. Peris was a firm believer that we were not put on this earth to try and live up to other people's expectations, and, equally, other people are not obliged to live up to ours (Clarke, 2021). By providing people the ability to become self-aware, they will appreciate the connection between mind and body and find much better ways to deal with all the bows and arrows everyday life can sling at you.

Does it work, though? Well, a study carried out in Hong Kong regarding anxious parents found that after four weeks of gestalt therapy, the parents had lower anxiety levels, were less willing to avoid inner experiences, were kinder to themselves, and demonstrated more mindfulness compared to those that did not go through the therapy (Leung & Khor, 2017). A study carried out on women with depression found that the depression was reduced effectively using gestalt therapy (Heidari et al., 2017). Why these studies seem to concentrate on women, I'm not sure. Still, a study conducted on divorced women concluded after 12 sessions of gestalt therapy, the women showed much more self-belief in their abilities (Saadati & Lashani, 2013).

I would say that gestalt therapy is a form of therapy that is best practiced with a therapist rather than alone. However, there are simple and straightforward gestalt therapy exercises you can do at home if you want to explore this area.

GESTALT THERAPY EXERCISE #1

This exercise is known as a body scan meditation, and it helps us connect with our bodies—an essential part of gestalt therapy and somatic healing therapy. Make sure you find a comfortable and quiet place to lie down. Close your eyes and become aware of your breath, how the air is coming in and out of the body, and how your belly rises and comes down. Take a few minutes to focus on how you are breathing and what your body is doing. After those few minutes, start to focus instead on the toes of your left foot, and imagine your breath rushing all down your body, down your leg, and into those toes. Concentrate on any feelings you may have in your toes, and stay with those feelings—be curious about them. Now, move your focus along your foot—from your toes down to the heel and ankle of your foot. Take your time in moving down. Each time, refocus on that part of the foot and imagine your breath flowing down to that part of your body and what your body feels as a result.

Move through your whole leg right up to your pelvis, doing the same thing. Then do the same with your other leg. Now, focus on your belly and lower back, then through your upper back and chest, and up the rest of your body until you reach your shoulders. After that, focus on the fingers of both hands simultaneously, and move up both your arms until, again, you reach the shoulders. Now, shift your focus to your head, moving up through your neck, chin, mouth, nose, eyes, and everything else, over the back of your head, and finish at the top of your head. Now, switch your focus to the whole of your body, and feel your breath come in through the top of your head and go out through the tips of your toes. Then, feel it come in through your toes and out the top of your head; keep doing this for a few minutes. Then, slowly become aware of your belly rising and falling with each breath again. Begin to move some of your body, such as your hands and feet, and when you feel you are ready, slowly open your eyes. You may want to remain lying down for a while before you finally get up off the ground and start moving around again. You can take the opportunity to note down any particularly strong feelings you had during the meditation or comparisons on how you felt before and after.

FOCUSING THERAPY

Focusing is exactly what it sounds like. You focus on yourself and learn to hear those innermost feelings that your body is trying to tell you. Focusing can be practiced by anyone who has learned the procedures. It can be used as often or little as the person doing the focusing desires. The person doing the focusing is the one that is in control of what goes on.

Focusing was first developed by Eugene Gendlin in the 1950s when he researched what in particular made psychotherapy beneficial to people. He discovered that those that seemingly got the most out of psychotherapy were people who had feelings that were not easily explainable. Still, such people were able to put descriptions or images to these feelings. This resulted in people finding what had yet to be discovered, which allowed the psychotherapy to continue moving forward. Gendlin also noted that this was normally accompanied by a sigh or deep breath from the person, which signified a release of some kind. For those in somatic healing, they may well say it is trauma that is being released (Jordan, 2016).

Gendlin came up with focusing to help those who could not so easily access the ability to excavate these nameless feelings so deeply hidden. Initially, he wrote how focusing consisted of six main steps:

- **1:** Make a space.
- **2:** Find those unknown inner feelings—which Gendlin described as a "felt sense."
- **3:** Find a description or title for your "felt sense."
- **4:** Repeat those titles or descriptions to ensure they correctly match the "felt sense."
- **5:** Try asking: This is where the person focusing will ask themselves questions that can't simply be answered with a "yes" or "no," such as, "What was so difficult about that? Why can't you move past that? What was so lovely about that?"
- **6:** Have a release in your body, which Gendlin termed a "felt shift." It is obviously very beneficial to the person doing the

focusing if they do experience a "felt shift," but it is not essential. Focusing is an ongoing process, so where the person doing the focusing may start out and where they may end up can be two very different places (Jordan, 2016).

A study of 87 people found that focusing may be effective in providing support to those who have undergone severe trauma (Zweircan & Joseph, 2018). Some would say the evidence is in Gendlin's own research when he developed the idea of focusing.

Now let's walk through the six steps that Gendlin identified in the form of an exercise, and you can see whether focusing is something you think can make a difference in your life. This exercise can take up to 20 or 30 minutes, so you need to clear some space in your itinerary. Instead of watching a TV show in which you already know what is going to happen, perhaps you can do this exercise instead. You can either lie down on a bed (perhaps do this when you first wake up or before you sleep) or on the ground. You can also sit in a chair with your feet firmly on the ground if you prefer.

- **1:** The first step is to clear the space so that we can do a quick relaxation exercise. Get yourself comfortable and take a deep breath. Notice the weight of your body either on the floor, bed, or chair. Make sure any clothing that may be too tight is loosened, and close your eyes. Breathe in and out, and notice your breath as you are doing this. Do this several times and just be aware of your breathing. Take note of anywhere in your body where there is tension. Picture that tension as a river of water that is running through your body and out your fingers and toes. Continue to breathe, letting that tension run off your fingers and toes. Now, find a place within your body where it feels peaceful.
- **2:** Slowly, move to the next exercise and find that "felt sense." Keep your eyes closed and think about the center of your body. Try to remember an experience in the past week that was of concern or difficulty for you. Think about that experience and try to form an image of it in your mind. Try

to put to one side all the thoughts you have had about it and search for that "felt sense"—that feeling you had when that experience occurred and not how you felt about it after. Put aside your thoughts and just try to get the feeling of that experience in you.

- **3:** Now you need to find a title or description or image for that "felt sense." Keep your eyes closed, keep breathing, and see if any words or images come to mind.

- **4:** Repeat that word or image and see if it resonates with you. See if it truly does match that "felt sense" you had in the center of your body about your experience. Keep checking one against the other. You'll know when you have it right, as you'll feel your body be in agreement with you.

- **5:** What do you find you are asking yourself? It depends on each experience what kind of questions may crop up, but maybe you are asking yourself things like, "What is so difficult about this experience for me?" Between each question, you should wait a minute or so to determine what your "felt sense" is telling you. Then, see what words or images come to you to label that feeling. Now, try to get your body to feel what it would be like if that situation or experience you have been pondering was actually all okay. Take a minute or so to feel that. Then, ask yourself, "What is it that's stopping the experience from becoming okay?" Don't answer from your mind. I must say I always find this one difficult to resist but do try. You need to feel it in your body again. As with the other points, this may take a minute or so for something to come to light. Once again, listen to that "felt sense'" in your body and come up with a word or image that can represent what it is that's stopping the experience from being okay. Finally, try to see if you can come up with what might be able to get you from the negative experience to it becoming positive or at least a lot more bearable. Again, don't answer with your mind: Let your body do the talking. Here, you can do some more asking. "Does it feel right to do that?" If your "felt sense" is saying no, then you need to reconsider; if your "felt sense" is saying, "Yes, that's right," then you can stop there.

Hopefully, at the end of that, you feel you have some kind of answer to your problem. Even if not, solutions can crop up later. For the moment, take some time to pause and just appreciate yourself. Appreciate the "thinking" your body has done in connection with the issue you are having.

Then, when you feel ready to do so, open your eyes and start to become aware of the room and everything around you. If you were lucky, you might well have had that release of tension at the end of the fifth step. If you didn't, that's okay. As I stated before, that is not the whole point of focusing. The main point is getting to know your body and understanding and listening to it so that you truly know what you are feeling and what's the best way forward to resolve your issues.

PSYCHODRAMA THERAPY

Don't worry. This doesn't involve Anthony Perkins in a wig from *Psycho* or anything like that. Psychodrama Therapy is a form of therapy that requires a person to engage in actions in order to resolve their problems. This can include role-playing and group therapy.

Psychodrama came into fruition in the early 1900s thanks to the psychiatrist Jacob Moreno, who held his first psychodrama session in 1921. He came to believe in psychodrama because of his appreciation of group therapy and his own interest in the theatrical arts. The idea behind psychodrama is that by using dramatic techniques, a person will find the truth. That they will be able to see the way they behave with others and in situations and help people be able to deal with the emotional issues they may have in their lives. It may be used to act out past, present, or future episodes. Attacking issues in this way may give people a fresh outlook on their issues and the best way in which they can be addressed ("Psychodrama," 2016).

Psychodrama is usually performed as group therapy with one person's experience being acted upon and the others in the group taking on other roles within that situation. However, you can perform aspects of psychodrama on your own, though it is not as simple as some of the other therapies to slot into your daily life.

There are usually three main sections to psychodrama therapy: warm-up, action, and sharing. The warm-up section is there to encourage trust and safety and ensure participants feel willing and comfortable in their surroundings and in their therapy. This may include participants introducing themselves while performing a role of some kind. In the action section, an experience in a person's life will be acted out. There are usually certain methods used to achieve this, which include:

- **Role Reversal:** A person does not play themselves but plays someone else of importance in their lives. This can bring a better understanding of why the "someone else" may behave as they do, therefore creating empathy; it may better help the person understand their relationship with the "someone else."
- **Mirroring:** The person becomes an onlooker while other people act out an experience from the person's life. This can be useful if a person is feeling quite detached from their

being, is not in touch with their emotions and feelings, or if a person is feeling exceptionally negative about the experience.

- **Doubling:** Someone else takes on the person's role and expresses what they think the person's thoughts and feelings may be. This method can be used to either build an understanding of the person or to challenge, in a nice way, the manner in which the person is behaving in this scenario.

- **Soliloquy:** In a group therapy situation, this would be performed to the other members of the group or to a therapist. However, this is one you can do on your own, and if you need an audience, you can always do this with your partner, family member, or close friend—as long as whatever you are speaking about does not directly concern them. You can even use an empty chair at which you can express your feelings.

The sharing section is when the person walks through and tries to better understand what has just happened and why, how to better resolve things in the present, or how to better resolve the same types of scenarios in the future.

I think psychodrama is one of the least comfortable therapies for a person to put themselves through—particularly if you have been through traumatic events. However, for those who either really struggle to bring out their emotions or for those who, perhaps, need to reign in their emotions, it can be one of the most rewarding therapies.

A study on the effectiveness of psychodrama on middle school girls who had undergone trauma found that it reduced anxiety and depression, and the girls became less withdrawn (Carbonelli & Parteleno-Barehmi, 2016). Another study reported that psychodrama could be an effective treatment for adolescents with trauma (Mertz, 2013). Research carried out on people at an addiction center who had PTSD found that after undergoing psychodrama, there was a 25% reduction in their PTSD symptoms (Giacomucci & Marquit, 2020).

As we've seen, psychodrama is primarily a group therapy, but it is possible to conduct exercises on your own. All you need is an empty chair; the chair represents the other person in your life that this scenario is dealing with. Move the chair appropriately; place the chairs close together if you feel close to the person. If you feel distant from the person, place the chairs far apart. Then, sit down in the chair that represents you, pretend the other person is sitting in the other chair, and say everything you feel you need to say to that person. It could be there are questions you want to ask—not just express a feeling. Once you have done this, get up and go sit in the other chair and play the role of the other person, perhaps giving answers to the questions or responding to what you have said. Then, finally, go and sit back in your chair and be you again, and respond to what the other person has said. You can then carry on back and forth until you get to the resolution you need. You may want to record the conversation, as sometimes, it can be quite a shock what you may say either as yourself or the other person. This should only go on for a matter of minutes, though. This type of exercise can be so helpful if there are feelings or situations that have become unresolved. Often, it can be useful when the person you have those unresolved feelings toward is no longer with us, as you would never have the opportunity in real life to have that conversation. Whatever the situation, this exercise can be really helpful in addressing those unresolved issues and feelings, helping you feel better about yourself and other people, and making you determined to move forward in your life.

EYE MOVEMENT DESENSITIZATION AND REPROCESSING (EMDR)

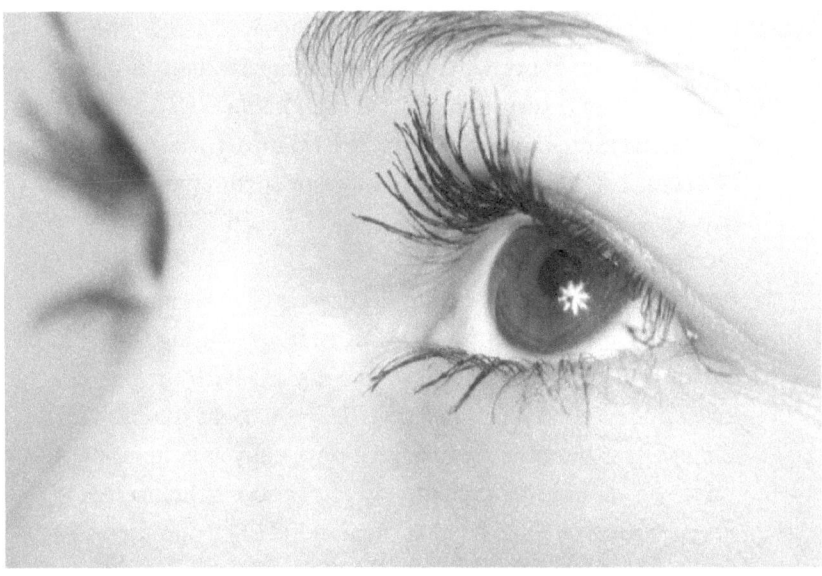

EMDR is a therapy that looks to heal people from trauma. EMDR works on the theory that just like the body would try to heal a wound, the brain, too, needs to heal from a traumatic event. When it doesn't get to heal and process properly, that is when mental health issues occur. EMDR helps reactivate that healing process.

As the name strongly hints, eye movements are used during the therapy. A person undergoing EMDR will think about certain things related to an experience while making specific movements with their eyes. Doing this helps the person begin to process these memories and feelings. Rather than feeling negatively toward these memories, they begin to feel positive at having gotten through such experiences. Eye movement works because of the similar function that occurs in your sleep with rapid eye movement (REM). Yes, that is where the band took their name from if you didn't already know that.

EMDR concentrates on the past, present, and future. It looks at the traumatic experiences of the past, the issues of the present, and the resolutions that can be achieved in the future.

There are eight phases that take place during EMDR. These are:

- **1: History Taking:** The individual works out which experiences can potentially be treated with EMDR. They may also think about what skills or changes in behavior they may need in the future to address such issues.
- **2: Identifying Tools to Cope With Emotional Distress:** A person may learn different techniques and strategies to help reduce stress between each EMDR session.
- **3, 4, 5, and 6: The EMDR Therapy:** An experience is identified and put through EMDR therapy. During this, a person will recognize an image to associate with the experience, the person's negative feelings about themselves, and any associated feelings—both physically and mentally. They will then develop positive feelings about themselves. The person will consider that positive feeling compared to the negative feeling. The person will then concentrate on the image, the negative feeling, and the bodily feelings while undergoing EMDR. This may include taps and listening to tones. The person will note how they naturally respond to these things. After each section of movements, taps, or tones, the person will try to let their mind go blank and take note of whatever first comes into their mind. The outcome of that will determine what kind of EMDR is next employed.
- **7: Close:** The person keeps a log throughout the week detailing anything relevant that occurs. It is used to reaffirm the activities the person developed to cope with things in the second phase.
- **8: Progress Report:** The final phase is reporting on the progress made.

A study of 24 trials concluded that EMDR has positive effects with regard to the treatment of emotional trauma. Seven out of the ten studies found it more effective than CBT (Shapiro, 2014). I do need to add that the study was written by Francine Shapiro, who conceived and developed EMDR, so you need to bear that in mind when considering the findings. There are further studies, though. One systematic literature review identified that EDMR improves trauma symptoms (Valiente-Gomez et al., 2017). Another analysis of all the data regarding EDMR trials concluded that EMDR therapy reduced the symptoms of PTSD significantly (Chen et al., 2014).

EMDR is another therapy where it can be best to find a therapist to work with, but it can still be worked on by yourself in the comfort of your own home. Here is an exercise to prove it:

EMDR EXERCISE #1

If you sit down somewhere comfortably, cross your hands over your chest so you are making a butterfly shape with your fingers pointing up. Then, link your two thumbs together. Use your hands to tap alternately on your chest's left and right sides. You are doing this so that your brain's left and right sides form a connection. Take note of your surroundings and anything going on. All of this should help calm you and give you a feeling of peace. It should also help you cope with and process whatever your current issue causing you stress might be.

7

SHAME TRAUMA: HEALING THE INNER CHILD AND CREATING BOUNDARIES

The trauma of shame is something that, sadly, occurs far too often and is usually linked to experiences that took place in someone's childhood. It can be hard to seek help and deal with the emotions and feelings that often manifest. But if you do, somatic healing therapy can help alleviate some of the pain.

HEALING THE INNER CHILD THROUGH SOMATIC THERAPY

Shame, like any trauma, gets "stuck" in a person. They find it hard to move on from that moment and release the shame, so it remains within, causing tension in the same way any trauma does. Shame, though, tends not to be caused by one specific incident like a car crash or a war but occurs slowly, over time, incident by incident, making the person feel like there is something wrong with them and they have no worth in the world. They start to believe that everything that goes wrong in their life is down to them. All their problems are nobody's fault but their own. Sometimes, of course, a small helping of shame can be a good thing. You did something embarrassing when you were drunk, and you wake up the next day feeling ashamed, so you call those you impacted and apologize. Shame, in that respect, helps us reassess our behavior and relationships with people, but toxic shame is not like that. It is larger in scale and a repeated incident chipping away at us until our bodies and minds can no longer deal with it. It often feels as though there is no process to reassess or take any action to move on from the shame.

For a person to deal with their shame trauma, they need to feel like they are in a comfortable, safe space. This is important for trauma generally but even more so for shame. Often, the person may have to deal with their deepest, darkest feelings, and that can only be done in a safe space where they feel comfortable enough to open up about such things.

There are a number of reasons why somatic healing therapy, in particular, is effective for shame. One is that it's very much rooted in dealing with the present, getting a person to think about the here and now, and being aware of their bodies. It's about listening to their bodies and not just their minds. With shame, it is easy for a person to become disconnected from their bodies and stop paying much attention to the details of what is happening around them. Somatic therapy is good at breaking that habit.

The other thing it's useful for, which we covered in a previous chapter, is pendulation. It's getting a person to go back and forth, from one state of being to the other, and not getting stuck in just one state. Those dealing with shame are most definitely stuck, and pendulation can help them move out of that state slowly and safely.

While there is a built-in feeling of shame within us, it is not really possible to feel shame unless someone has shamed us. It is exceptionally important for anyone going through this type of trauma to realize that the shame is being put on you. It is not your fault in any way, shape, or form. This feeling of shame is most commonly put upon us by people in power, whether that be family, friends, relationships, or work, to name a few. In fairness to those in power in our lives, they often do not realize what they are doing, but nevertheless, it is them putting the shame upon us. Equally, any neglect or an easily dismissed child can grow up with feelings of shame, which can easily be triggered later on in life.

One of the strange elements of shame is that often when people feel shamed, they then try to shame others. We may shame somebody because they have reignited the shame in us. However, the solution to losing that feeling of shame is often to go back to the original reason for it. Sadly, that can routinely be shame passed down from guardians or caregivers. They don't always think about the consequences their behavior will have and how long that impact can last for.

Many believe that the best way to finally relieve yourself of the shame is to hand back the shame to those that shamed you. They also believe this needs to be done forcefully as, more often than not, the shame was handed out forcefully (Lyon, 2017). This doesn't have to be all at once; it can be tentative at first and build up to being forceful, but it does usually need to be forceful to have the desired effect. I must be clear as well: You do not have to give it back to the person in real life (though that can be a separate option from somatic therapy) but do so in an imaginary way. This can be difficult just as an action, but many people become hesitant because they actually feel ashamed to hand back the shame—particularly if it is to a family member or someone close. However, it needs to be made clear that there is a massive difference between calling out things when they are wrong and shaming somebody. It is also important to say that the person you are giving your shame back to, in all honesty, probably did not mean what they did or did not truly understand what they were doing and what the effect of that would be. Maybe they felt ashamed and tried to pass their shame on. The shame can also pass down many generations; maybe the caregiver that shamed you had been shamed by their caregiver. The receiver of the shame gives it back to the giver of that shame and feels a release and peace within themselves because of it.

The family we grow up in and even the society we grow up in mold our impressions and early beliefs. If they are not always positive experiences, they can become limiting beliefs, as in, "I am not good enough for this," or "I do not deserve this" type of thinking. If someone tells you often enough, "You will never amount to much," well, sure enough, you start limiting your own belief in yourself. If everyone says, "Your brother is so much better than you," you may end up believing it. That can go to society as well. If certain groups of people do not receive positive messages, is it no wonder they start questioning themselves and whether they have anything to offer the world. Once you become aware of these things, it can become such a relief. That the shame and guilt you felt wasn't genuine: It has been placed on you by those around you and by society itself. Once a person realizes this, it really can be a freeing moment.

This can even extend to the culture you are brought up in. Say you are brought up in a culture where everyone must be very macho. Everyone is saying "man up" or "boys, don't cry." Suppose you grow up in a macho culture like that. In that case, it's no surprise you will probably struggle to ever show any kind of emotion or feeling to anyone else and may be somewhat aggressive in most situations you find yourself in. All of these types of things can influence our inner child and make life difficult for us when we are older. Seeing as the Taliban have just taken back over Afghanistan, perhaps you live in a culture and society where the education of women is not valued. Perhaps over time, some individuals are brainwashed into believing this absurd doctrine. Someone asks you, "Why don't you do what it is you really want to do with your own life?" You reply, "No, that is not what I'm meant to do. I am not capable of that," but you are. Society has placed a limiting belief on yourself, and you start to believe it. You end up doing things that you never really wanted to do because you believe that is right for you, and if you follow a different path, you will feel shame.

Even if we consciously reject those values and beliefs that we thought were once true and we now realize are false, there is still the issue of our subconscious mind. It is estimated that the subconscious mind is responsible for 90% of our feelings and behaviors and that a conscious decision or action is usually preceded by an unconscious one (Meyer, 2020).

The subconscious mind is extraordinary, really. If you think about when you are a baby, this is the motor that is running you. We don't really have a conscious mind until we are around five or six. It is the subconscious mind that is entirely in control of what we do up until that point. It's like a sponge soaking up everything that is going on around it and then processing it. It is inevitable that it has a heavy influence over the conscious mind.

When we are very young, our minds will normally take on any new information and take it at face value because we do not have a set of values and beliefs and lived experiences at which to judge it against. This is why those early years are so important and can have a lasting impact on us for the rest of our lives. Once we get to five or six, we now have a value and belief system to judge any new information against, and that is what our subconscious does. Hence, it is often the way we see the world at this stage in life that impacts how we see it later in life.

The inner child, then, can be seen as part of our subconscious mind. The experiences and, possibly, trauma we went through during those early years don't just get forgotten about—never to be seen again. It all gets bundled up into a small part of who we are and influences our health and happiness throughout life.

However, if that inner child is hurting or angry, and that is having a negative impact on our lives, it doesn't mean we can't do anything about our subconscious and our inner child. This is where somatic experiencing really comes into play. Previously, all this stuff was going on, and we weren't even aware. But through somatic experiences, we become aware of ourselves and our bodies. We are listening to ourselves and our bodies. Therefore, we can make a conscious effort to reprogram our subconscious with positive and loving thoughts. This can be the way we talk to ourselves, the people we surround ourselves with, and even things like social media. For all those negative thoughts and feelings you either have about yourself or hear from other people, we have to think of the positive instead. If you call yourself stupid, try to think a more positive thought. The conscious can override the subconscious if we just tell it enough times; eventually, our subconscious will start to be aligned with our conscious. Combined with all the many somatic techniques that there are, the inner child will start to feel the love, attention, and comfort it needs, and the healing process can begin.

Going through all the experiences that we do usually results in us carrying around emotional baggage. We don't mean to, but it is our way of saying, "Look at what happened to me: so many things!" It is only once we let go of our emotional baggage that we realize just how much it was weighing us down. We need to let go of that as well. Life is just too short to carry that baggage around and take it into every new situation, experience, and relationship. It is exhausting. We need to be lighter on our feet and freer in our thoughts and feelings if we are going to get anywhere near living the dream life that we want to.

We don't just need to clear out our emotional baggage, but we need to clear away those limiting beliefs. While they are still hanging around, we have no chance of healing ourselves because our minds will always be giving us reasons we can't do things. "I'm not good enough for this, so why try?" "I'm not good enough for them, so better to end it now before they realize," or "I'm just not a very sociable person, so I don't need friends." All of these kinds of thoughts and more put us off from achieving our potential as our limiting beliefs try to sabotage whatever opportunities may be out there for us. They are not the truth. To become truly self-aware, you have to realize these beliefs for what they are. Help is at hand, though. The subconscious mind producing all these thoughts of inadequacy can be reprogrammed using the emotional freedom technique (EFT) tapping. This involves tapping on various points of the body where it is believed energy fields are residing, combined with specific words or phrases to give a new message to your subconscious and reprogram it.

The conditioning and programming you go through as a child can come back and continue to haunt you through your teenage and adult years. If your role models are telling you that you are not good enough, then it wouldn't be surprising if, in your adult life, feelings of inadequacy and worthlessness start to manifest themselves. Equally, if all people around you worry about money, then in adult life, you too will probably spend your time worrying about money and chasing money. What we go through as children during those all-important stages can define us for the rest of our lives.

However, there are plenty of somatic practices that can help you to reprogram your subconscious, heal your inner child, and slowly begin to undo all that bad work that started when you were a very young child. The breathwork that has been discussed in this book can help you start to get in touch with your inner child, feel in the moment, and listen to what your inner child is saying. Things like journaling or writing a letter to your inner child can really help with dealing with this. EFT and other tapping exercises can help reprogram that subconscious and get you to say positive things about yourself and slowly remove all those negative thoughts and limiting beliefs.

One aspect of somatic therapy that has come out of looking at the inner child is the theory of "reparenting." You now have the opportunity to give yourself things you didn't get as a child that you needed by reparenting yourself—perhaps it is self-belief or compassion or any number of things. It doesn't mean your parents or caregivers were terrible at parenting, by the way: It just means they were acting out on their own beliefs and value system, and maybe they didn't give you everything you needed through no particular fault of their own.

There are forms of reparenting psychotherapy that require a therapist who will take on the role of the parent, but the essence of reparenting you can do yourself: Love yourself unconditionally. You need to be compassionate to yourself; don't judge or criticize your thoughts and feelings but legitimize them and appreciate that they are part of who you are. You give your inner child plenty of positive affirmations to remind yourself that you are loved, you are worthy, and what you think and feel is valid. If taking yourself back to your inner child and thinking about those things is too overwhelming, then you should seek out a therapist so that the exercises can be conducted in safety. But the general principles of reparenting—that you get in touch with your inner child, address the needs, and fulfill those needs—you can carry out on your own.

Learning to heal your inner child can make a world of difference for you. Having that self-compassion and the knowledge of how to take care of yourself can lead to many improved relationships—whether it be personal, family, friends, or work. You'll actually like yourself; enjoy being in your own company and the company of others, and find you enjoy life and want to live it to its fullest. You'll have confidence in yourself and your abilities, and you will have released all that pain and tension that had been holding you back for so many years. In some cases, you may have completely detached yourself from feelings and emotions, so healing the inner child will put you back in touch with yourself, and you will once again feel things like joy and love.

If healing your inner child is something you believe you need and are interested in, here is a straightforward EFT tapping exercise to set you on your way:

- **1:** First, tap the side of your hand—the side with your little finger on it rather than the thumb side—at a fairly regular pace. While tapping, say to yourself, *"I love my inner child. I accept my inner child. I unconditionally and without exception love myself."*
- **2:** Now, tap the top of your head, tap your forehead above your inner right eyebrow, and tap your right temple, repeating the following phrase (or a phrase you made up that fits you better) on each area: *"I love the inner child that did not get everything they needed. That child was and is incredible."*
- **3:** Tap your cheekbone, just below your eye and to the side of your nose: *"My inner child is capable of anything and has the potential to achieve anything."*
- **4:** Tap your top lip—the part in between your nose and mouth: *"My inner child does not know any limitations."* Tap your chin: *"and I love my inner child no matter what."*
- **5:** Tap below your armpit, on the side of your ribs; tap the top of your head; tap your forehead above your inner right eyebrow; and tap your right temple, repeating the following phrase on each area: *"If my inner child makes mistakes or errors, it really does not matter. I love my inner child regardless."*
- **6:** Tap your cheekbone; tap your top lip: *"I fully accept my inner child in a way that was not available at the time."*
- **7:** Tap your chin: *"I envision holding my inner child and telling them how amazing they are and that everything is going to be alright."*
- **8:** Tap the area where your heart is—toward the left of your chest: *"I will always protect my inner child and always provide protection to my inner child."*

- **9:** Tap below your armpit, on the side of your ribs: *"My inner child has my full support and acceptance."*
- **10:** Tap the top of your head; tap your forehead above your inner right eyebrow: *"I love my inner child exactly as they are."*
- **11:** Tap your right temple: *"If anyone says anything bad against my inner child, then I will stand up to them."*
- **12:** Tap your cheekbone; tap above your top lip: *"I will show my inner child that they are of value, they are worthy, and they will always be wanted and loved."*
- **13:** Tap your chin; tap your heart area: *"I really want to encourage my inner child to show just how incredible and dazzling they are."*
- **14:** Tap below your armpit, on the side of your ribs; tap the top of your head: *"By healing my inner child, I am also bringing healing to myself."*
- **15:** Tap your forehead above your inner right eyebrow: *"I no longer require the programming and conditioning that I was brought up with. What I tell myself now is the truth."*
- **16:** Tap your right temple; tap your cheekbone; tap your top lip: *"My inner child is and always will be a part of me, and when I am taking good care of myself, then I am taking good care of my inner child."*
- **17:** Tap your chin: *"When I am demonstrating love to myself, I am also loving my inner child."*
- **18:** Tap your heart area; tap below your armpit on the side of your ribs: *"When I show myself compassion, I am also being compassionate to my inner child."*
- **19:** Tap the top of your head: *"I am releasing the trauma and tension in my body and mind."*
- **20:** Tap your forehead above your inner right eyebrow: *"Release it from every bone and muscle in my body."*
- **21:** Tap your right temple: *"No more will I have to carry this emotional baggage around. It is gone forever."*
- **22:** Tap your cheekbone; tap your top lip. *"I feel so free when I release all of the pain and tension."*

- **23:** Tap your chin: *"I can't wait to see what the future holds. I am excited about the days in front of me now that I understand myself better and am in touch with myself and my inner child."*
- **24:** Tap your heart area; tap your armpit: *"I am no longer fearful, I am no longer doubtful of myself, and I look forward to seeing how the new me will take on the world."*
- **25:** Then, stop and just take a moment to relax. Take a deep breath in, and then let the breath out.

That is your tapping exercise which hopefully has been very helpful. If doing these exercises becomes too overwhelming, then seek out a professional therapist to safely help you through the process. It often helps if you can visualize your inner child when you are doing this. If you have a photo of yourself as a child, that can sometimes assist with visualization. Then you can imagine loving that child and wanting to protect that child. The next time you feel like being harsh with yourself, overly judgmental, or hypercritical, you can look at the photo and the child's innocence. Those feelings of wanting to love and protect that child, guide them, support them, and encourage them should return. It would be advisable to repeat the exercise as often as possible. Doing it just once likely won't have the extraordinary compounding effect that daily practice will. Just find a comfortable, peaceful place for a few minutes in your day, and go through your tapping exercise. Be excited about the powerful positive results EFT tapping can provide. Remember, you can tailor the phrases to match your particular situation.

SHAME

It's scarily easy to find yourself feeling shame. You feel like you do not belong among the people you interact with. You feel like nobody understands you or could ever understand you. Shame can also come about from much more serious situations like abuse or neglect where the victim ends up feeling ashamed (when it should be the perpetrator who should be ashamed of their actions) of what has happened to them and that they let it happen. Even though, realistically, they could not have done anything to stop it. People who get ostracized at school or find themselves being bullied can often develop feelings of shame. In order to heal from shame, we need to recognize the underlying needs behind that feeling of shame.

It doesn't just happen on its own, either. Shame develops through the interconnections with others and the environment we live in. That means realizing we are not alone in the world. We are all going through a journey, working out what it means to be human. None of us really understand it or have it down perfectly. It's important to stop and appreciate that.

Shame most often occurs when our expectations of joy and happiness are not matched. For example, a child does something to a parent, and they show no interest whatsoever, or you tell a joke to your friends and nobody laughs (no wonder comedians are known to sometimes have mental health issues). Shame can surface in the forms of blushing and shyness and can include humiliation and embarrassment. Hence, such things as bullying and belittling can result in shame. As previously mentioned, shame can definitely result from something as harrowing as abuse or neglect, but it can also be from the buildup of smaller (but no less authentic) episodes.

That is not to say we should ever be without shame. Shame holds a purpose. Without it, we may never realize when we have done something wrong and would not be able to carry ourselves in society. But when shame becomes trauma, it does not serve the purpose it exists for. If it remains untreated and is left to fester in a person, then it can end up in addiction and depression, among other things. Those feeling such extreme shame usually struggle with relationships as they are expecting rejection anyway, so they try their best to get the other person out of their life first. Also, sufferers may feel very angry. So an individual trying to maintain a relationship of any kind with a sufferer whose first response is to get seriously angry, maybe even indulge in violence, is not generally a priority in life. Shame can obviously lead to feelings of insecurity and inadequacy, so this can result in things like self-harm and suicidal thoughts. Maybe someone constantly criticized ends up trying to be the perfectionist who never can attain the perfection they are after, or maybe they end up displaying symptoms of obsessive-compulsive disorder (OCD). Not only does shame cause mental issues, but it causes physical issues as well. A person with heavy shame may have bad posture, always look down and not look anyone in the eye, suffer things such as tiredness or a tightening in the chest, feel like they need to vomit, or have digestive or stomach problems.

That is, of course, where somatic therapy comes in. It can help with both the mental and the physical symptoms of shame. By becoming aware of what your body is telling you, you are likely to realize that the tension in your body relates to the shame you are feeling in your everyday life. As you think about and deal with those episodes of your life that may have contributed to this shame, release them, and let go, these episodes become signals of strength for you rather than something making you weak and fearful.

Shame nearly always relates back to what occurred in your child-hood. Those insecurities, doubts, fears, and low self-esteem you feel now are likely rooted in your childhood. If you are constantly scolded for the slightest misjudgment, then it is hardly surprising if you grow up thinking everything you do is wrong or that there is something wrong with you. If you get bullied, you can develop feelings of "Why me? There must be something wrong with me." Obviously, truly trau-matic experiences like abuse and neglect can bring these feelings out in a much more extreme way.

If we know that our adult feelings of shame are deeply rooted in our childhood, then we know that healing the inner child can, in turn, heal our shame. Some of the best techniques and therapies to help with this include CBT, where we learn to try to control and change our thought behaviors and patterns. Therefore, instead of thinking of insults to ourselves, we can learn to think positive thoughts and reaf-firm the reality that we are good and capable of good things.

Prolonged exposure (PE) can be a good form of therapy to address this issue. Slowly, a person pays attention to things that stimulate them and makes them deal with the issue. Maybe you start with a photo of yourself as a child, then discuss your shame as a child. Then you imagine yourself somewhere that reminds you of that shame. Slowly but surely, it will remove the power the shame has over you.

Stress inoculation training can be a good therapy to employ. Rather than stress itself, it uses the same training to contain and control your shame. It can include breathing and muscle relaxation techniques, role-play, and taking note of negative thoughts and amending them. There is also such a thing as compassionate mind training (CMF), which can help a person who speaks negatively about themselves change their behavior and be compassionate and kind toward themselves and their inner child.

EMDR is another good one to follow. Thinking about your shame and all that hurt your inner child has experienced while undergoing the eye movement actions may well help to alleviate your shame and start to heal your inner child.

However, one of the most powerful techniques for healing shame and your inner child is EFT tapping. It is one of the best techniques because you don't necessarily have to relive those memories when you were shamed over and over. You just need to remember them enough to release them. EFT is, in its essence, a healing process and not a memory jukebox. Combining the positive affirmations with the tapping of the energy points on your body can be exceptionally powerful and provide a true sense of relief and release from your shame, making you realize your inner child needs love. As your inner child is part of you, it is you who can best provide that love and support.

Here's a specific EFT tapping exercise to help you learn to heal not only your shame but also your inner child. You don't have to repeat the affirmation if it does not relate to you. We all went through different experiences, so if the affirmations aren't right for you, just replace them with what you think is more appropriate to the experience you went through and the shame you feel.

- **1:** Start by tapping the side of your hand and saying, *"I may not have received the love and belief that I needed as a child, but I still love and accept myself. Although I may feel that I am not worthy and insult myself and doubt myself, I still wholeheartedly love and accept myself."*
- **2:** Tap the top of your head, your forehead above your inner right eyebrow, the side of your temple, your cheekbone,

your top lip under your nose, your chin, your heart area, and under your armpit at the side of your ribs. Do this cycle approximately eight times while saying the following:

I may not have felt supported when I was a child or felt like there was someone there for me all the time. I may not have felt there was anybody to protect me, and I may have suffered terrible consequences as a result. I always thought there was either something wrong with me or that everything I did was wrong. I always felt I deserved the bad things that happened to me. I just didn't know any better back then.

I say negative things about myself. I sometimes get so embarrassed by myself that I detest myself. Sometimes, I see myself in the mirror, and I really do not like what I see. When I think about my life, I feel like I have achieved nothing, and everything I have done amounts to nothing. I give myself unrealistic expectations and targets to meet. It makes me feel like I don't see the point of anything. These are all things that I have built into my being since I was a young child. Although this is what I learned as a child, I have now learned that my belief that I am not worthy is utterly false.

As a child, I did not know any better, though, so I believed it to be true for many years; that lie still influences my life today. When these thoughts enter my head, it makes me feel very low and unhappy. I must have the strength and courage to change these thoughts as I know. Now that I am an adult, I know these thoughts are not the truth. My mind may now realize this, and the tapping I am now doing will tell it to my heart and the rest of my body. I know all these thoughts I had about myself are wrong and untrue, but they made me feel like there was something wrong with me and like no one could possibly love me.

I could never be good enough for someone else. All untrue. I no longer have to carry around the emotional baggage that my caregivers handed to me. The shame that my caregivers possessed and passed to me goes no further. It stops here. They can keep the shame. I reject it. It is acceptable that I am not perfect in every way, and I have flaws. This is what being human is. I love myself, and I accept myself—flaws and all. The shame I once felt no longer has any hold over me. When I release the shame, I feel free, and I feel relieved. I look forward to the new relationship I have with myself.

- **3:** Take a deep breath in, breathe out, and relax.

SETTING HEALTHY BOUNDARIES WITH SOMATIC SKILLS

Setting boundaries can be essential in helping yourself heal and recover from trauma. They are the mechanisms that separate you from other people. It is what helps define you as you—where you begin and where you end. Boundaries are meant to be flexible, though. When you feel safe, you are more likely to extend those boundaries, and when you don't feel safe, you will restrict and pull those boundaries in. You can see how this is important. If your boundaries are too free, you end up giving yourself to others, and it can be easy to lose yourself. On the contrary, if your boundaries are too restricted, then you can become isolated from the rest of the world and become lonely.

Like most things, our boundaries were learned from how our caregivers responded to us when we were children. They should engage with us when we need engagement and leave us alone when we need space. It is not always a problem if caregivers don't engage: This can help the child strengthen their resolve and ability to cope. However, there are three main areas where if caregivers overstep the mark, it can cause issues:

- **1: Invasion:** This is where the caregiver, rather than letting a child have their "alone" time, will do the opposite. Maybe because they need their comfort, not for any malicious reasons, but this can lead to a child growing up and installing very closed-off boundaries, withdrawing, and therefore, potentially becoming isolated.

- **2: Abandonment:** This is the opposite of invasion. Caregivers do not respond to a child's needs or wish for engagement. In adulthood, this can result in boundaries that are too free. A person will end up trying to please everyone, maybe always trying to do things to gain attention, and they can lose themselves within that.
- **3: Both Invasion and Abandonment:** In this scenario, the caregiver inconsistently alternates between the two. This can really cause issues because sometimes a person may end up trying to overplease people, and sometimes, they will end up pushing everybody away. It is hard enough maintaining any kind of relationship with an individual who consistently does one of these things. But, if they are doing both, sometimes randomly, it can only make life a headache both for them and those around them.

I don't really like to label people. I've always thought there is probably some truth in Becker's labeling theory, but for the sake of being clear, I am going to refer to "toxic" people—though I am sure they are good people at heart, and they just haven't had their own boundaries set for them. We all know people like this: People who have negative thoughts and feelings are the ones who always seem to find a way to bring us down or let us down. Setting boundaries is one way of not having such people in your life if you don't want them. If you have set healthy boundaries, these types of people should be nowhere near you. Equally, the kinds of conflict or awkward situations you can find yourself in can be avoided with boundary setting. If those boundaries are there, then you and everyone else know where you stand, and conflict should not be a daily occurrence.

Having somatic skills can be extraordinarily helpful in setting and maintaining boundaries. For a start, you will start to develop your body awareness. You will start to discover that "felt sense." That will help enormously in telling you whether things feel right or not and whether you need to strengthen your boundaries. You will also have that self-awareness about your own thought processes. Whereas before, you may have automatically done or said something which would have allowed someone to take advantage of you or cause you to withdraw when someone was only trying to help you out, now, you will be aware of what you are doing and how you are behaving. This may stop you from making those same errors when it comes to your boundaries.

One of the most important skills to learn for setting your boundaries is learning the ability to say "no"—not just in a half-hearted way but in a way where the other person knows you are not going to budge from that. Don't just automatically say "yes." Always think through your response, and remember to listen to that "felt sense" of yours as well. You can start off with small things like saying "no" to coming out on Friday night because you are worn out and you really just need a night in. Or saying "no" to loaning the person money when they never pay you back. That's not a loan: You are just giving them money. Next time, don't do it. Of course, people are disappointed when you say no —that is inevitable, but that doesn't mean you have to give in. You will disappoint people, but that will make them respect you more, and the next time you say "yes," they will know you really mean it, and they will stop asking you unnecessarily in the future.

This brings us to what you do need to say a definite "yes" to, and that is your commitment to healing and looking after yourself. If you are putting your needs first, respecting yourself, and loving yourself, then saying "no" to others becomes easier. Say "no" to others but "yes" to yourself.

Here's an exercise to help with your boundary setting, which will help you in saying "yes" and "no" and ensuring your body is saying the same thing.

BOUNDARY EXERCISE #1

First, see what happens to your body when you say "yes" out loud. Repeat it several times and see what you notice. Now, try saying "yes" with your body instead. What changes? Maybe it is your breathing or your posture. Is your movement free? Do you feel tense? Think about and note down the situations in which you would like to be able to say "yes." For example, do you want to do a boundary-setting exercise? "Yes!"

Next, do the same but for saying "no." Take note of how your body responds to you saying "no" out loud several times. Then, try saying "no" just with your body and see what changes there are in your body. Think about the situations in which you would like to be able to say "no." For example, "Are you coming out again tonight?"

Take one of the situations where you said you would like to say "yes," take on the body posture of saying "yes," and note down what occurs when you imagine that scenario. Then, do the same with a situation you want to say "no" to.

At the end of that, you should be aware of how to ensure your body and voice are saying the same thing and being really clear about what you are communicating.

8

ANXIETY, SELF-LOVE, SELF-COMPASSION, AND CRUSHING DEPRESSION

Everything that is mentioned in this title, somatic therapy can address and resolve. If you find you have anxiety, then this is something that somatic therapy can treat. If you have depression, then this is something that somatic therapy can crush into the dust. If you are in desperate need of learning how to show love and compassion to yourself, somatic therapy can show you how and help you achieve that. Do you want to be able to forgive yourself for doing things that you perceive to have been wrong? Somatic therapy can help you find that release of negativity from your soul. Somatic therapy is like finding a water fountain in the middle of a desert. You have a thirst for healing yourself, and somatic therapy is going to quench that thirst for you.

It's hard to move on, though, if you don't give yourself a break. You need to be able to forgive yourself. No one is perfect, and that includes you. You made some mistakes and errors in life, but we all have. That's all part and parcel of the human experience. If you don't find room in your heart to forgive yourself, you will never get past the first obstacle. You will always feel resentment. You will always be prone to anger and lashing out at your nearest and dearest. You will never achieve what you want to in life or reach your maximum potential. You need to clear your heart and forgive yourself; then, you can start to look at all the exciting opportunities there are for you in life.

You also need to practice detachment from outcomes. Once you do that, it will help you clear your heart, forgive yourself, and stand a chance to reach your maximum potential. Best of all, you might actually enjoy life rather than worrying about it all the time! I found when I practiced detachment, it really did free me up from so much stress and worry that I was previously focused on. Realize that you cannot control everybody else. People will let you down, and people will do things you don't agree with. That, I'm afraid, is life. You can't fix those people. The only person you can "fix" is yourself. You don't need fixing because there isn't really anything wrong with you; you need healing. The only person's actions that you are ever in control of are your own.

Find your own version of happiness. Don't take any notice of other people telling you whether you should be happy or not or trying to define your achievements or lack of them. It's down to you to decide what true happiness looks like—not anybody else. However, you also need to detach from the idea that everything has to work out a certain way because it doesn't. Look how often you plan an event only for something completely out of our control to change that. The pandemic is a prime example of that. Out go all our plans due to something out of our control. Accept it: Things do not need to be a certain way or the perfect way. Once you can accept that, you will find you truly feel free to enjoy and appreciate life. Also, you probably won't be as hard on yourself in the future as well. You won't just enjoy and appreciate life, but you will enjoy and appreciate being you.

Let's give ourselves some self-love right now with a quick EFT tapping exercise:

- 1: Start off by tapping the side of your hand as you say: "I accept myself for who I am. I love myself for who I am. I respect myself, and I expect others to respect me as well. I love myself fully. I do have value. I do have worth. I am good enough. I do deserve to have love and to be loved. I honestly do love myself, and I promise to love and respect myself. I accept myself as the person that I am."

- **2:** Tap your inner forehead above your right eyebrow; tap the side of your temple; tap your cheekbone: "I completely love myself. I respect myself, and I believe I am of great value."
- **3:** Tap your top lip; tap your chin; tap under your armpit on the side of your ribs: "Loving myself is a magnificent thing to do. Thinking that I could not love myself is no longer an option."
- **4:** Tap the top of your head, your forehead, your temple, your cheekbone, your top lip, your chin, your heart area, and under your armpit: "Some of my behavior was probably because of this incorrect belief that I could not love myself. But now, my mind and heart are open to the potential of self-love. Maybe I was scared to love myself previously, but I reject that notion now. I am not afraid. I am ready to love myself."
- **5:** Tap the top of your head; tap your forehead; tap your temple; tap your cheekbone: "I find that, actually, the more I love myself, that I love myself even more."
- **6:** Tap your top lip; tap your chin: "By loving myself, I find it makes it easier to love others."
- **7:** Tap your heart area; tap under your armpit: "This makes me happy. That's why I love loving myself."
- **8:** Tap the top of your head; tap your forehead; tap your temple. "I reject all the thoughts I previously had that made me believe I could not love myself."
- **9:** Tap your upper lip; tap your chin; tap your heart area; tap your head: "I clean my heart and forgive myself in order to be able to love myself."
- **10:** Tap under your armpit: "I love and value myself. I deserve respect. I will love myself because I deserve love."
- **11:** Take a deep breath in, breathe out, and relax.

To go alongside self-love, you need self-compassion, so here is an EFT tapping exercise for self-compassion. I suggest you complete the tapping cycle approximately three times while saying the words below:

I will be compassionate toward myself. I love and accept myself for who I am. I love myself; therefore, I will be compassionate toward myself. Since I am compassionate toward myself, I will look after myself and care for myself. I love myself wholeheartedly. I clear my heart—ready to take on the compassion I now have for myself. All the thoughts and reasons I held before that made me not be compassionate toward myself I now reject. I release those negative thoughts and feelings from my mind and from my body. It's great for me to show compassion toward myself. It will make me healthier both in mind and body, and it will make me a better person. If I am compassionate toward myself, then I am more likely to show genuine compassion for others as well. I refute talking negatively about myself or putting myself down. I realize now that that was not a healthy way to be. The next time I make an error of judgment or I make a mistake, I will show myself compassion. I deserve to be compassionate toward myself, and I will be compassionate toward myself.

Take a deep breath in, breathe out, and relax.

We've given ourselves some self-love and self-compassion, and now it's time for some self-forgiveness. If we don't practice this, we will always be angry at ourselves and the world. Let's begin the healing and forgive ourselves. Repeat the tapping cycle approximately three times for this while saying:

I want to forgive myself thoroughly. I feel ashamed about things I have said or done in the past. I want to release the guilt and tension I have and feel free. It is alright for me to forgive myself. In order to let go and be free, I need to forgive myself. I wholeheartedly love and accept myself, and I forgive myself. If I love myself, then it follows that I can forgive myself. If I want to look after myself, then it follows that I forgive myself. I deserve forgiveness even if I fight against that belief sometimes. I love myself unconditionally;

therefore, I forgive myself. Whatever I have done in the past, I accept the blame. I learned from those mistakes I made in the past. Now, I forgive myself, and I move on from it. I'm looking forward to beginning afresh now that I have forgiven myself—to live a happier and healthier life and to be able to forgive myself and forgive others with ease. I accept myself as I am, and I forgive myself. I fully forgive myself. I am a good person. I forgive myself, and I am at peace with myself.

Take a deep breath in, breathe out, and relax.

I know that the words "self-love" can either bring out images of people with round, purple sunglasses and flowers in their hair or make you think it is a euphemism of some kind. Yet there's a reason the phrase, "You can't love somebody else until you love yourself," exists. The fact is that until you love yourself, it makes dealing with the rest of the world a lot harder. If you hate yourself, it is almost inevitable that you will feel angry with yourself and everyone else because there has to be some kind of outlet to get that anger out. If you don't love yourself, then you don't respect yourself, so you will always put someone else's needs and wants before your own. If this is in work, it will probably lead you to face complete burnout. If it's relationships, your personality and individualism will probably become completely subsumed by your partner. If you love yourself, then when those bad things in life happen (which they will—there's no escaping some of them, such as the death of a loved one), then you are so much better equipped to deal with situations in a healthy way and not resort to unhealthy ways to get through them. Once you develop self-love, then everything else comes from it: respect, value, confidence, and belief; those other things we talked about, like compassion and forgiveness for yourself, become so much easier.

Of course, it's not easy to get to that point. There are so many blocks and obstacles that we put in the way of ourselves getting to that point. It's all the negative talk and limiting beliefs that we place before ourselves, believing we are not good enough, not worthy of love, and will never amount to anything. We need to clear our hearts and minds of those thoughts and feelings to progress to self-love.

Once we love ourselves, then the opportunity to forgive ourselves becomes possible. Although, we need to take responsibility, own up to, and apologize for genuinely bad things we've done and said. However, if you're looking in this book, then the likelihood is you are blaming yourself when it really wasn't your fault. As the saying goes, "It takes two to tango." Whatever the situation is—you think you hurt someone or upset someone—it took two to make that happen. You can't just do it all by yourself, so it can't all possibly be your fault. Unless you were in a tango dance, and then you stepped on your partner's foot, then that was your fault. No, hang on: "It takes two to tango."

You are not alone either; we all have made terrible errors and judgments in our lives. We make thousands of decisions every day, so it is inevitable that some of them don't go as well as we would hope. That's life. If you can make that step to forgiving yourself, it truly is transformational. Once you realize not everything is your fault, not everything is down to you, and not everything is based on what you do, that can really change things for you. Until you do that, sadly, you are probably going to stop yourself from living the best possible life you can. There is always going to be an element of self-sabotage, but once you forgive yourself and let go of all that self-doubt and self-blame, then anything becomes possible.

Let's do an EFT tapping exercise to clear the blame. You know the score by now. Start with some tapping on the side of your hand. Then move through the cycle from the top of your head to the side of your ribs. Tap for as long as feels right, or as long as you need to. Say the following:

> *I'm embarrassed about what I have done and said. It was so silly of me to do. I regret my actions very much and feel very guilty about it. I would like to be able to forgive myself for it, but I still feel it is all my own fault. Thus far, I have not been able to let go of the guilt and forgive myself. Today that changes. With this tapping, I am starting my journey of releasing the guilt*

and shame from my mind and body. Today, I forgive myself,
and I no longer hold on to the guilt. I love and accept myself, so
I know I can make that step to forgiving myself. Not every-
thing is my fault; not everything happens because of me and
the way I am. I know that now. I didn't before. Hence, I was
unable to forgive myself. I will now forgive myself. If I could
turn back time, I would have done things differently, but I
know I am human. Whatever was causing me to behave the
way I did took place, but it is human to err. For that, I can
forgive myself. All this guilt, shame, and regret that I have
been holding in all these years, I now give it permission to
clear. I am releasing it all from my body and my mind. Slowly
and safely, I release it all. I am ready to forgive myself. I let go
of all my guilt. I clear my guilt from my head and heart.

Take a deep breath in, breathe out, and relax.

Even with all these promises of forgiveness and self-love to ourselves, it can be challenging to move past a certain point. That is because we sometimes have internal conflict going on within us. We want to forgive ourselves, but something stops us and says, "No, you don't deserve forgiveness." Generally, internal conflict can sometimes just mean things don't feel right within us. We are not at peace with ourselves or with someone else. If that internal conflict is not resolved, it can turn into much more serious afflictions such as despair and depression. You need to be able to clear that inner conflict within yourself in order to be able to progress.

Everything around this chapter—and the entire book—is about exploring yourself and finding out about yourself. It's about how you've been programmed over the years and how you have had limiting beliefs put on you. It's about how you can learn to love yourself, accept yourself, and forgive yourself. Through this self-discovery, it will become clear why you have behaved the way you have and why you have had these feelings and emotions over the years. Maybe you will even discover new emotions and feelings you didn't even know were in you. Up until now, you have, at best, been treading water, barely keeping your head above the water. You have not had that opportunity to really grab life's opportunities and think about what it is you are really meant to be doing. There is a word in Sanskrit—*dharma*—which takes on the kind of meaning of what your soul's purpose is. Well, in your journey of self-discovery, this is really the chance to find what the purpose of your soul and your life is. This is the chance to give your soul all the nourishment and goodness it could possibly need as you explore yourself and love yourself more. Now is the chance to find out what it really is that you want to do and what it is that will make your soul sing. Grab life's microphone and belt out the number your soul is longing you to. This can all be achieved with the help of somatic therapy. It can heal you, it can help you discover yourself, and it can help you move away from anxiety and depression to a true place of happiness and peace. Somatic therapy can help you achieve all of that and more.

DEPRESSION AND SOMATIC THERAPY

Depression can last for days, months, and even years. It is a challenging thing to cope with and struggle through when it's happening. It can be brought on by anything. Maybe something in your life dramatically changes, or you go through a traumatic event. Sometimes, it comes on when there doesn't appear to be a reason—your body is probably just catching up years after the event, or something small is the thing that has tipped your body over the edge. Depression is what occurs when our body goes into permanent "freeze" mode or even to its "shutdown" mode. Women tend to experience depression twice as much as men ("Depressive Disorders," n.d.). This is perhaps not that surprising considering everything their bodies and internal dynamics have to go through compared to men—combined with the pressure women often put on themselves to "have it all": a pressure that is thoroughly absent from most men's lives.

I remember the one time in my life when I really struggled with depression. It was my late teenage years to my early 20s. I can remember it very well because, although I have not had any episodes like it for many years, I am always on the lookout for the same feelings coming back. It used to be a massive effort just to get out of bed. If I got out of bed before noon, it was a miracle. Once I was up, I could not be bothered to shower, brush my teeth, or get dressed. I always wanted to be alone, as being in the company of other people became excruciating. You don't think anyone would want to be around you, so it becomes a self-fulfilling prophecy as you isolate yourself from anyone who would want to help and support you. Though I could never have carried out a suicide attempt, I just didn't have that kind of action in me; it didn't stop me from having the kind of thoughts where you don't think anyone would miss you if you weren't there, and the world would probably be a better place if you weren't there. Possibly, you'd be happier if you weren't there anymore because life is just too painful and too much effort for you. In my case, I don't think there was one event that triggered it off; I think it was many things over a long period of time that brought me to that point, and I think it was because it was a part of my life where everything was changing as well. I was questioning who I was a lot of the time. Putting it into words doesn't even begin to describe how dark and lonely depression is, but I don't feel like that now—that's the positive. If you can address it, depression does not have to last forever. There's a reason our bodies and minds go into depression, so that means there's a way out. That way can be via somatic therapy.

We already know from the previous chapters that there are many somatic therapy techniques you can try if you feel depressed. You can use CBT to challenge your thinking patterns. You can inquire into all those thoughts you are constantly having that describe the worst possible outcome or state. Let's think about how realistic that thought actually is and see if we can change the thinking pattern. Vagal nerve stimulation can be a good one as well. There are more extreme versions of that where electrodes are used to stimulate the nerve rather than just your fingers, but just doing some simple vagal nerve stimulation will get your social engagement system going. Then, you can get into a more playful mood where maybe you can play around with the expressions your face makes, the tone of voice you have, and try to get that black cloud hovering over you to move on, allowing the sunshine to burst through.

You can follow some straightforward techniques that really help with depression specifically. One is to put yourself in postures or positions where you lengthen the spine. The next chapter mentions somatic yoga practices, which include postures that are helpful to this. When we become depressed, our body tends to hunch over, and our chest caves in a bit, so doing things to lengthen your spine helps to improve your mindset and outlook. It's not a permanent cure, but it can be beneficial among all your other somatic work.

Movement is also a great thing to help you if you feel depressed. Just getting out of your chair and standing up can make a small difference. Still, if you do some basic exercise, some small yoga movements, some Qigong, or just some muscle tense and release exercises—both of which are covered in Chapter 9—it can really help lift your spirits and get you feeling a bit better about yourself.

Sensorimotor psychotherapy, which I walked you through in Chapter 6, can be a handy tool in any fight against depression. Take the time to feel your body and ask those questions to yourself about how you feel about things. Just taking the time to know your body and the world around you can perk up your nervous system and help it output some positive energy.

ANXIETY, TRIGGERS, STRESS REDUCTION, AND SOMATIC THERAPY

Anxiety is a form of extreme worrying where you feel exceptionally stressed, your breathing may become shallow, you may feel as though you will have a panic attack, you feel sick in your stomach, or your skin is itchy. Different people have different physical reactions to anxiety, but the mental anguish is similar: You are scared or worried about something or some situation. Triggers are what your memory associated with the danger—be it a person, event, or object. For example, I had a friend who used to be a landlord, and one tenant caused her a major headache. Once that tenant left, my friend became very fearful of anything to do with the apartment. She started imagining all kinds of problems with the apartment that didn't actually exist, but it wasn't the apartment that was the actual danger—it was the behavior of unpredictable people that had been the real danger. The apartment in itself was perfectly fine.

I know someone who was having chemotherapy. They celebrated their completed first round of healing by eating fish and chips—not realizing that the chemo was likely to make them sick later. Sure enough, they "were ill" after the fish and chips. Thereafter, they could not face fish and chips for a very long time—not just because it had made them sick but because it ultimately reminded them of chemo and, therefore, of cancer. These triggers can work for very ordinary objects and things, but because they relate to the danger the person encountered, the brain gets scared and links the two together, jumping to the wrong conclusion.

I should be clear: triggers are not a bad thing. Their job is important by making us aware of impending danger. An issue only starts to arise when your brain and body go into overdrive, and you start to get triggered to danger when, in fact, everything is perfectly safe. This can become a spiraling issue, where, in the example of my friend's apartment, they become fearful of it, so the best way to escape that fear is not to go near it or not talk to anybody about it. However, then your mind starts making the association that what saved you from your (imagined) danger about the apartment is not going near it. Then, you can become anxious just generally about apartments. Any apartment now is a trigger for the danger. Now, you're afraid to go out because you might see an apartment, and you try not to talk to anyone because they might mention that they live in an apartment. Although this may sound a little silly, this kind of thought cycle is not uncommon. When the triggers reach this level of sensitivity, they become the danger. You can get caught in a spiral of anxiety that only ever travels down.

Here are some straightforward and easy-to-follow somatic therapy exercises that you can use to heal your anxiety and dampen those triggers:

- 1: You are going to get yourself into a good "grounded" position. Make sure you are sitting comfortably in a chair or on a sofa with your feet placed firmly on the floor in front of you. Try to get your shoulders, neck, and arms to relax. Place your hands and arms on your thighs so that you are in a good position to breathe. Breathe as you would normally and try to concentrate on where you are feeling the anxiety physically. Identify those areas. Is it your stomach? Is it that your chest feels tight? Is it your hands that feel sweaty? Is it that your skin feels itchy? Is it that your heart is pounding? Wherever it is that you are feeling the anxiety, concentrate on that area and imagine your breath coming from that area. You can touch the area so that your mind and body make the connection of where the anxiety is and that you want to heal it. You should be in that situation of breathing, concentrating, and healing for approximately 30 seconds to see what happens, and then you should experience that for a full minute. Hopefully, the area shoud feel less tense, and your anxiety will begin to reduce.

- **2:** Every so often, just sit down and touch base with yourself. How are you breathing? Are you breathing with your chest? Then make sure you focus, and breathe with your stomach instead. Taking away that shallow form of breathing should start to impact your feelings of anxiety and start to lessen them.

- **3:** When you are feeling tense, scrunch up that part of your body, make it as tense as possible, and then slowly let it out gently. As strange as it may seem, making the area where you are feeling the anxiety as tense as possible and then letting it go can actually reduce the anxiety. This is because your body and mind recognize an issue and address it. Once you have done this, your body may feel more relaxed. Without this method and by just trying to relax alone, your body feels like maybe you are trying to ignore it. By recognizing anxiety and scrunching up as tight as possible in the relevant area and then letting go, your body notes you have recognized it is having difficulties in that area. Now, you have recognized that it is happy to forget it and move on.

SOMATIC ANGER RELEASE

Anger is sometimes reacted to as a maligned emotion. We view it with suspicion and fear. If someone is angry, we sometimes see that as a weakness; for example, we may hear, "Oooh, what's wrong with them? Touched a nerve, did I?" and other such comments. Of course, like all emotions, anger does serve a purpose. If we are angry, it is because something is wrong. When someone is always angry, there is something wrong that's much deeper. It's not just an issue at work or irritation because your partner didn't do what you asked them to do. It can also lead a person into trouble. Constant anger could lead to violence and threats or saying unkind things to people that aren't meant to be. For some people, it can result in silent treatment or a never-ending sulk. When it comes down to it, whatever the outcome, it is just not pleasant feeling like that—being always at odds with everyone and everything. It is exhausting on top of everything else, and a person will probably not be left with many friends or family that can tolerate that permanent anger. However, I want you to remember something: It is okay to be angry, and it is not something to be ashamed of. It is a normal human emotion that we all go through. It can be dangerous to suppress emotions and can lead to health issues, so being angry is fine, within reason. We just need to be careful when the only emotion we ever seem to feel is anger.

Somatic therapy and experiencing can be such a great help to those who need to understand, release, and let go of anger in a healthy way. It will help release all those emotions buried deep inside that a person has been unwilling to recognize and accept. Using somatic techniques over a long period of time can assist greatly in managing and regulating anger, which in turn can have the health benefits of reducing digestion issues, more relaxed muscles, better concentration, and a better night's sleep (Friedman, 2019).

As anger is such a powerful emotion, it is essential to deal with it in a safe and healthy way. Engaging in cathartic methods where someone is encouraged to let it all out with screaming or more physical releases is one way but may not be healthy. However, by using somatic experiencing and other such practices over time where you learn how to listen to your body, you can start to understand your anger. You can let it out little by little in a controlled and healthy way and in a safe space. Just letting it all out in one go in an uncontrolled manner may not have such a safe effect on you—particularly if you have PTSD or other trauma symptoms. It can actually be quite harmful to you, and any anger is only going to be released temporarily—it is not going to have the long-lasting effect you require.

Let's get into a somatic anger release exercise to see how easy it is to do; once again, it is safe to do in your own home, and you can go into a room by yourself and practice when the emotion becomes apparent.

First, as always with somatic practices, get to know your body. Take some time to feel where in your body the anger is. Take some deep breaths in and out and feel where that anger is. Now, wherever you are feeling that anger, shake your body. You can use your hands to apply some light pressure if you want to. Shake your body and imagine yourself shaking that anger out so that it is gone and you are free and ready to move on. This is a really simple, straightforward exercise for you to manage when feeling angry or frustrated.

Another option is to find something that you can squeeze very hard: a towel, some clothes, or you can even squeeze the forearm of a partner or friend. Just be careful: It is the forearm and not the wrist or elbow joint. Make sure it's something that gives you a burst of letting the anger out, so you can carry on with your day.

Combining these exercises with your general somatic experiencing will allow you to get to know your body, understand where and why the anger lives, and allow you to slowly but surely release and let it go so that you can resume and get on with your life healthily and safely.

9

DISCOVER NEW ROADS TO RECOVERY (FURTHER TECHNIQUES TO HEAL TRAUMA)

While not part of somatic experiencing, there are many further techniques that are somatic in nature, and you can incorporate them into your healing and therapy routines. They all help with the brain's flexibility and spark its ability to adapt and change for the better.

QIGONG AND SHAKING PRACTICES

The translation of "Qigong" is "energy work." That's because, in its essence, what you do when you practice Qigong is to try to channel energy through your palms. Usually, this is done while standing up. This is usually combined with certain breathwork as well. The key to it all is the coordination of the eyes with the movements you make, combined with your breathing and the concentration of your mind. A review of the many studies on Qigong and Tai Chi (another practice) concluded that they had many health and psychological benefits (Jahnke et al., 2010). If you think back to what Peter Levine said about animals shaking off their trauma, it makes sense that engaging in energy practices, including shaking, can be good for our physical and mental health.

The good thing about Qigong, like so many somatic practices, is you can do it anywhere; as long as you can find a quiet and peaceful place, you can easily practice it.

To give you a flavor, here is an easy shaking practice for you to follow:

- Begin by standing up with a good, upright posture. Close your eyes and feel yourself breathing; feel yourself and your body in the present moment. Then, when you feel ready to do so, open your eyes, but be careful not to lose that feeling of being in the present; wake up the energy within your body. Start by shaking your right arm, but be sure to keep it in a relaxed state: Don't tense it up when shaking. Then, shake your right leg. You will need to lift your leg up slightly off the ground in order to do so. When you feel it is ready to move on, put your right leg down and shake your left arm. Then, when it feels right to do so, move onto your left leg.

- Once you feel it is okay to move down, put down your left leg and shake your whole body: arms, legs, body, head—everything. Again, be mindful to keep your body loose and relaxed—don't tense it all up. You can close your eyes if you want to. Unlike when you were shaking your leg, you should keep your feet on the floor. However, you can lift your heels up and down but don't actually lift your leg off from the floor. Try shaking yourself even harder, give yourself up to the act of shaking, and see if you can really release that energy from inside of you. You can lift your arms up if that is what your energy is directing you to do. Your mouth should be completely relaxed, so if this guides you to making noises, that is fine. You are letting energy out, so making some noise is fine if that is what you are directed to do. Very slowly, start to shake a little less hard—do this slowly until you are back into a static standing posture.

SOMATIC YOGA

Somatic yoga is, as the name suggests, a mixture of yoga with the mind-body principles of somatics. It uses the somatic awareness of the body to help you rewire your brain and give your muscles a workout to release that tension and stress that may have built up due to trauma. You aren't just following what a yoga teacher is telling you and copying the movement. You are actually doing that movement and thinking about how your body feels and what your body is telling you.

One aspect of the somatic yoga practice is ensuring there is an element of grounding included. As you may well remember from previous chapters, grounding gives us that feeling of safety and calmness, which is so important if we are to listen to our bodies. For many of the previous practices, grounding meant sitting down with your feet firmly planted on the floor. For yoga, that is slightly different, as you can imagine. Grounding in this context consists of sitting on the floor, cross-legged, with your arms outstretched resting on your legs. Then you lift your hands up in the air, make the peace sign with both hands, and then place your hands (still in the peace sign mode) on the floor, letting your shoulders relax. You may feel the need to close your eyes.

In this situation, the floor is the earth, so this grounding is us making our connection with the earth. As with all grounding, this is where you start to feel your body in the present and in the here and now. Then, you can take a deep breath in and let the breath out; then, you will be ready to begin the rest of your yoga practice.

The various poses you can do in yoga have specific reasons and benefits. I'm just going to walk through a few of them here, so you know their benefits:

- **Child's Pose:** This pose is meant to calm you down and can be known to reduce stress and increase energy. To carry it out, you need to get into a kneeling position. Your big toes should be touching, and your knees need to be apart. Take a deep breath in and try to lengthen your spine. Breathe out and bend forward—moving your head toward the floor. If you want to, you can use your hands to rest your head on. Open the backs of your shoulders up and allow your stomach and your chest to expand. You may want to move your knees further apart. Let your arms relax and place them by your feet, with the palms facing up. Breathe and relax. You should feel the position become more pronounced when breathing. As it is a pose for relaxation, take a few minutes to stay in that position and relax. When you are ready to come out of the pose, move your hands up to your knees, breathe in, and move your hands around to use them to push into the floor and lift yourself up. Move your chest and shoulders up slowly so you are back into a kneeling position, sitting upright.

- **Standing Cat-Cow Pose:** These are actually two different poses that have been combined to make an even more effective pose. It can help with the flexibility of your spine and, therefore, your posture. However, best of all, for our purposes, it helps calm a person and can reduce stress. To do this, you need to start off on your hands and knees, with your head in the center of your body looking down. First, do the Cow Pose, so breathe in and move your stomach toward the floor while raising up your chin and chest and averting your gaze up. Try to move your shoulders outward and away from your ears. Then, you move into the Cat Pose. Breathe out and move your stomach up toward your spine. Imagine a cat when it gets up from its nap and stretches its back. That is basically what you need to look like. Move your head toward the floor, but be careful not to put your chin into your chest. Breathe in, moving back into the Cow Pose, and then breathe out by moving into the Cat Pose. You can repeat this at least five times. When you need to come out of the poses, lift yourself up and sit back on your heels with your body in an upright position.

- **Forward Bending Pose:** This is one you can start by standing up. Basically, you bend over (forwards) and see if you can place your hands flat on the floor. Don't worry if you can't; don't force it and give yourself an injury. Just bend over as far as you can.

- **Relaxation Pose:** I'm sure you can guess what the benefit of this one is! Lie on the floor on your back with your hands by your sides, slightly outstretched, your palms facing up,

and your legs slightly apart. Feel your body and feel the
contact you have with the ground. Take a deep breath in.
It's that simple.

Here's a yoga exercise for you to practice. Start with the grounding
exercise I provided earlier. Then, once done, bring your hands up to be
in front of your chest—almost as though you were saying a prayer.
Breathe in, and then lift your arms up as high as you can. When you
breathe out, drop your shoulders down—almost like you are shrugging.
Repeat that: arms up/breathe in and shoulders down/breathe out four
or five times. Then, when you reach up this time, put your palms
together and look up if you can. Then, breathe out, let your hands
come down to the "prayer" position, and put them down to where you
had them in your grounding position.

MOVEMENT-BASED TECHNIQUES

As well as shaking practices and yoga, there are other techniques that
involve somatic movement—that is, not so much worrying about what
you look like while you are doing the movement but concentrating on
what it feels like. Somatic movements are usually slow to give our
bodies and brains a chance to learn them, performed with our
complete concentration on our bodies' feelings and sensations. They
usually have some purpose, whether physical or mental benefits or
both.

These techniques include tense and release (conditioned) relaxation, where you tense and release each muscle in your body. These
techniques should leave you feeling very chilled out and are easy to do
whenever you want to anywhere in your house.

Here is a quick and simple tense and release exercise for you to
practice. Please do be careful not to injure your muscles. If you get
sharp pain at all, please stop.

Concentrate on a group of muscles; for instance, let's say your calf.
Take a deep inhalation and tense that muscle until the point you feel
some pressure on it; hold that for around five seconds. Then, you
release while breathing out at the same time. It can be a good idea to

visualize the muscle letting the tension out like air coming out of a burst tire or something similar—whatever works for you. Take note of the difference in how you and your body feel when relaxed compared to being tense. You should stay relaxed for approximately 10 seconds and then move on to the next muscle. Once you have completed all the muscle groups, relax, take in and enjoy the feeling of relaxation. All in all, it should take you 10 to 15 minutes to complete the exercise. The main muscle groups are your foot (curl your toes down), your calves, your thighs, your hands, your biceps, your butt, your stomach, your chest, your shoulders, your jaw, your eyes, and your forehead (raise your eyebrows).

You can also do this as a muscle relaxation exercise where you hold the tenseness for around 15 seconds and then let go and relax. For this, you just breathe normally—it doesn't matter when you inhale and exhale.

TRAUMA CLEARING SHAKING

Trauma clearing shaking exercises are designed to release the tension and trauma from the muscles deep inside your body. They involve a safe way of shaking that releases both tension from your muscles and calms your nervous system and you. You don't need a lot of time— maybe 20 minutes at most—and anybody can do it. It doesn't require you to be in any physical shape in particular. This very much ties in with the theory that the way animals cope with trauma is by "shaking it out," so to speak. When this safe way of shaking is engaged with, it suggests to the body that it returns to its normal balanced state. These types of exercises should leave you with a feeling of peace and tranquility.

For example: lie down on your back and place the soles of your feet together with your knees bent out. Then, raise your pelvis an inch or so off the floor and gradually pull your knees inward an inch or so every 30 seconds. After some time, you should reach a point where you begin to shake. If you are taking a long time to shake naturally, then this is because your muscles are very strong. You may need to hold the pose for longer. When ready, you can place the soles of your feet and pelvis on the ground and relax to let the trauma release through shaking. If you need to stop shaking, then you can just lengthen your legs out. Once you have finished, just lie down on your back and let yourself calm down and feel tranquil. It is quite a strange feeling to suddenly find your legs and body shaking, but that is what your body is designed to do when your muscles get fatigued, so it is all perfectly natural. It is very therapeutic as you shake out some of that trauma.

SOMATIC ART THERAPY

Don't worry. You don't have to be Van Gogh or Picasso to take part in art therapy, though they may have benefitted if they had done. Your art skills do not matter, but it is the therapeutic nature of it that matters. It is not just painting either; art means music, dance, sculpting, drawing, writing, and other art forms. The main point is that we learn about ourselves and our minds and bodies. It is not what your artistic finished product looks or sounds like. We know that we often express our innermost thoughts and feelings when we are creative. Look at any number of songwriters who deal with personal tragedy by writing a song about it. Look how we use someone else's art to express ourselves. I know there was a particular song I used to play which would help me grieve my mom's death. Playing it helped me break down, cry, and go through the grieving process. Without it, I had a stiff upper lip and kept everything inside, which, as we know, is rarely healthy.

It is said that because art engages our mental and physical capacities, it means we "forget" about whatever physical pain we may have. It is not simply something to take our mind off the pain, but it is something that relaxes us and, like some of the movement techniques, can set the body back to its normal state. Essentially, those suffering from severe chronic pain can greatly benefit from being involved in art therapy. A great study showed that 200 people in hospital either for surgery or a medical issue engaged in art therapy for 50 minutes. On average, they showed an improved mood and reduced their feelings of pain and anxiety (Shella, 2017).

We know that our soul, spirit, or psyche plays a huge part in our physical healing. That is why people will say "mind over matter" and the like. It is not your actual brain telling your body to be well, but the part of you that produces your feelings and thoughts. Art is the ultimate for expressing and engaging that subconscious part of ourselves, so it is no wonder it can help those who have constant pain—whether physical, psychological, or trauma-related. In this way, art therapy can be used alongside and in conjunction with traditional medicine to help people with any number of physical and mental health problems.

A quick art therapy exercise you can do is the following. Unfortunately, for art therapy, you need more than just yourself. For this, you need some crayons, coloring pencils, or pens. If you have paint, you may want to paint. You will also need some paper. Any paper will do— it doesn't need to be a special paper of any kind. Before you begin your art, just take some time to close your eyes and take a few deep breaths in and exhale with a longer breath. Just be in the moment and be aware of your body and what it is feeling and sensing. Once you feel ready, take your pen or pencil and draw a large circle on the paper. Now, inside the circle, draw how you are feeling at the moment. I know that's a hard thing to interpret, but go with what shapes and colors you are being pulled toward to represent your emotions. The circle represents a safe space, and therefore, you are free and able to express yourself within that circle. To learn what your drawing means, you can then do a writing exercise in which you ask the drawing questions, and the drawing, as though it were a person, can answer. Start off with some general questions and then work up to the specific questions about what the drawing's needs are and how the drawing intends to satisfy those needs. Don't feel like you have to follow a script; let the conversation go where you want it to go. Let whatever comes out of that dialogue just immerse itself into you. Don't try to force any conclusion or try to analyze what you have drawn and discussed. Just let it go into you, and by being in touch with your body and mind, what needs to happen or be addressed will work its way out in a natural way.

10

DO THESE PERSONALITIES
SOUND FAMILIAR?

During our lifetime, we will come into contact with a number of different people, all with their own unique identities and personalities. However, there are certain personalities that, if we come across them, are very capable of causing psychological damage and trauma. If we learn how to deal with these personalities and heal ourselves when we do come into contact—and it has an impact—then we could send our ability to self-love and self-compassion rocketing high. When we come into contact with these types of personalities, they cause us damage. It is not our fault: It is the other person who has the problem, not us. Unfortunately, they never resolve their problem, so we are often left with the weight of their unconsciousness as we try and recover from the trauma they cause. No more. After this chapter, you will be ready to forgive yourself and move on from past encounters with these personality types and be more prepared for when you come across them in the future.

NARCISSISTIC PERSONALITY DISORDER

This is quite a topical subject because there are commentators hinting that certain celebrities fit this personality type. All we have are rumors; none of us actually know the individuals in question, so it is a little bit much to point the finger. However, there are those who say that the reports of certain celebrities injuring staff, being aggressive toward staff, estranging family members from friends, and the need to give interviews about it all point to a classic narcissist. We're on the outside looking in, so we don't really know what is true and what is not, but it is an interesting premise.

Those that genuinely have a narcissistic personality disorder usually display an inflated sense of their own importance, a constant need for attention and respect, have problems showing any kind of empathy for other people, and most of the time, they have very difficult relationships. It can cause major issues in all areas of a person's life, such as their work, relationships, and financial stewardship. If someone with this disorder does not get the attention they need, they will be prone to becoming very unhappy and frustrated. Others will, more than likely, not enjoy their company and will steer clear.

Other signs of this disorder include wanting to be recognized as better than other people—even though they have not achieved anything to suggest that they are. They inflate their achievements and concentrate on illusions of grandeur about how powerful, rich, and beautiful they are. They may also exaggerate how they will find the perfect partner. Due to their own sense of superiority, they believe they can only socialize with those of equal or greater importance and will look down on anyone else. They will try to dominate conversations and often cut off or make sarcastic remarks toward those they consider not of the same standard. As they believe themselves to be higher than other people, they expect anyone inferior to treat them as such and that any such person would always be willing to answer any request. They may display signs of jealousy toward other people, and they would believe there are people who are jealous of them. They will always want the very best of everything—the best TV, best car, best phone, best house, and so on. Hence, the financial difficulties they can sometimes find themselves in.

Due to all of this, narcissists do not react well to any perceived criticism or suggestions on how they might want to improve their behavior. They can become very angry and frustrated if they do not receive the kind of compliant behavior they expect from other people. They will often get angry and try to put a person they see as inferior down, so they can feel better about themselves. In relationships, this type of behavior can end up as abuse—often psychological and sometimes even physical if the person cannot control their anger. You would never know where you stood with the person; the relationship would be the opposite of the safety and security you would be looking for. You can end up in a constant state of distress, wondering what is going to happen next and how your partner is going to behave or respond to anything and everything. If you do recognize these patterns of behavior in your relationships and believe you have suffered abuse as a result, please understand it was nothing about you that the abuser disliked or took exception to: They would have behaved that way to everybody. You may end up thinking there was something wrong with you. No, there was nothing wrong with you; they were the ones with the sickness. Don't feel like it was down to you to have tried to change their behavior. There really was nothing you could have done. They need to take responsibility for themselves.

It is not just in romantic relationships that narcissistic abuse can occur in; it can occur with members of your family or your colleagues or managers at work. Dealing with this type of disorder in those types of situations can also cause great trauma. Having a manager or colleague who sees you as inferior and expects you to happily meet their every demand can be exceptionally exhausting and demoralizing, to say the least. They are likely to fly off the handle at you if you do not comply with their demands. When it is a family member who you love, and they will not accept any criticism and do not have any empathy for you and your feelings, this can be heartbreaking. There is obviously plenty of opportunity for psychological damage that could take years to recover from, especially if this occurs when you are a young child.

Somatic therapy can be a helping hand to any narcissistic abuse. It is almost inevitable that with this kind of trauma, it does get stuck inside of you, and it is not something you are going to easily feel comfortable talking about. Therefore, just having talk therapy, though it may be helpful, is unlikely to get to the real crux of your trauma, whereas somatic therapy will be able to do that. It will help you release the trauma that is stuck deep inside of your body. This way, you can begin to heal. The boundary work we covered in a previous chapter can also be a great help should you find yourself in that kind of scenario ever again as, of course, is all the work on self-love, self-compassion, and self-forgiveness. None of this was your fault, and it is exceptionally important that you realize that and begin to love yourself again.

Another great method of helping to heal yourself from abuse is to take part in some EFT tapping. Tapping those vital energy fields and saying positive affirmations about what you went through and how you are going to heal from it can do wonders for the body and soul. Here is a short exercise for you to follow:

Inhale a deep breath and close your eyes. Make your body aware of the times in your past when you have come across narcissistic behavior. Maybe it is a situation that is occurring in the present. Take note of where in your body you are feeling the trauma. Inhale a deep breath and open your eyes.

- **1:** Start tapping the side of your hand. Say, "Despite the hurt and pain a narcissist has caused me, I still love and accept myself fully. A person in my past or in my present has caused me damage through their narcissism, and it is not easy to recover from that experience. I find it a struggle to move on and truly feel free from the pain. Despite the hurt and pain a narcissist has caused me, I still love, respect, and accept myself wholeheartedly. I hope the narcissist finds their own peace and manages to heal themselves and free themselves from their damaging behavior."
- **2:** Tap your forehead above your inner eyebrow, your temple, your cheekbone, your top lip, your chin, your heart area, under your armpit on the side of your ribs, and on the top of your head. Continue to repeat that cycle while saying the following:

The hurt, pain, and damage inflicted on me by narcissism. All the days, I was fearful because I did not know what to do or how to behave. I will heal from all of this. I may have been scared in the past to let myself heal. It was easier not to have to deal with the pain I was feeling and to believe that there was something wrong with me rather than with them. If I heal myself and love myself again, then it opens up the possibility of becoming hurt again in the future, so it is easier to do nothing. I love and accept those thoughts and feelings. Even though I know better now, they were natural thoughts and feelings. Now I am ready to heal myself from that experience.

I deserve to have calmness and serenity in my life. I deserve to love and be loved. The behavior shown to me was not actually about me, although that felt like the reality at the time. That's why it was so hard to let go of the hurt and pain, but I now know their behavior was not personal—it was just the symptoms of their sickness and not anything to do with me. I'm ready to heal. I am safe and secure. I am looking after myself. I have learned to set and respect boundaries. They belittled me and made me feel inferior, but I reject that notion. They are no better than me.

My life will not be dictated by this experience. Everything the person said was just their illness doing the speaking. It is not reality. I know the truth. I am an amazing person who is worthy of love and respect. I am ready to heal. I will heal. If someone truly loved and respected themselves, they would be able to love and respect me. People who are cruel to other people usually don't love and respect themselves to begin with. I acknowledge that, and I am moving on from that. I am healing from all that they have said and done. I love myself in ways that person never did, and other people will love me. I fully love and respect myself.

- **3:** Inhale a deep breath and close your eyes. Breathe out and open your eyes. Hopefully, those places in your body where you were feeling the trauma have now felt some relief, and you have let some of that tension and trauma go. Rinse and repeat as necessary.

Remember that it is okay and perfectly natural to be angry about this type of abuse. You were mistreated by partners, family, friends, or work colleagues. It was not due to anything you did: It was because they were sick. However, just because they were sick does not excuse what they did to you and what they put you through. You do not need to justify their behavior on their behalf. What they did was wrong—plain and simple. If you are angry about it, that is your right, and that is okay. Do not try to suppress your emotions or keep them bottled up inside of you, as that is not healthy. It is okay to be really angry at the person and what they did to you.

BORDERLINE PERSONALITY DISORDER

Borderline personality disorder will demonstrate itself in a person with wide-ranging moods and behavior. This will often result in some very impulsive decision-making and actions. BPD sufferers may have periods of severe anger, depression, or anxiety that can last several days.

The symptoms of this disorder can also include extreme mood swings and difficulty identifying with themselves and their place in the world. This means their likes and dislikes can change in an instant. They tend to see everything as one of two things: good or bad. This can make it difficult for those around them, as one day, they may think someone is their best friend, and the next day, they may believe them to be their worst enemy. Clearly, this can lead to some very unhealthy and volatile relationships with partners, friends, family, and work colleagues.

Those who have this illness may have issues of abandonment (whether they are real or not) and try to move relationships on too quickly or completely cut them off, so they are not the first to be abandoned. As mentioned in the first paragraph, impulsive behavior can be a result of borderline personality disorder. Therefore, the sufferer may go on expensive shopping outings, drive too quickly and without due care, have unprotected sexual relationships with many partners, may take to drugs or alcohol excessively, or even eat far too much in a short period of time. It is not unknown for sufferers to engage in self-harm or thoughts of suicide.

It can be the case that those that develop borderline personality disorder underwent traumatic events during their childhood, such as abuse or abandonment. Therefore, just as somatic therapy can heal those issues themselves, it can also help heal someone with borderline personality disorder. If we can heal the trauma within the person, that in turn should start to heal the mental illness. In addition, you can include CBT which will help a person be more aware of their thought patterns and how to change them. You can start to see how somatic therapy can help heal those with borderline personality disorder.

ABUSIVE PARTNERS IN RELATIONSHIPS

An abusive relationship can include physical or sexual abuse, emotional abuse, or neglect. Clearly, anyone who has to go through that kind of relationship with a person is not going to come out unscathed. It will more than likely cause trauma. It is likely to affect future behavior, and it may cause triggers so that ordinary things in life can cause a person to become fearful. The abuser may even cause you to doubt your own thoughts and feelings. They may have found a way to cut you off from your family and friends, so you no longer have anyone to tell you that your partner's behavior is wrong and you need to get out of the relationship. Once you've been through all of that, it makes it really difficult to ever trust anyone to be that close to you again.

In order to help you try to avoid ever getting involved in such relationships, these are the kinds of personalities and people you need to avoid. It is never easy, though, because part of the abuser's tool kit is to be able to charm you in those early stages of a relationship, only for their true colors to come out much later.

The most likely personality types to inflict abuse upon a person are the narcissist, which we have already covered, the sociopath, and the psychopath. Some of the character traits of all three can overlap.

Sociopaths tend not to be able to have empathy for anyone else, may indulge in impulsive behavior, will try to control other people usually in an aggressive manner, can be charming and charismatic, never learn from their mistakes or accept any punishment they may get for their behavior, will lie without a second thought, can often try to get into fights, may threaten harm to themselves without any intention of carrying it out, and may have issues with holding down a job or may get themselves into debt.

Psychopaths are not too dissimilar. As with a sociopath, psychopathy is not an actual psychiatric diagnosis. Someone who aligns with these traits may actually be diagnosed as having antisocial personality disorder (ASPD). The antisocial aspect comes not from them being unsociable—as like sociopaths, they are capable of great charm and charisma—but from their tendency to not care too much for the rules of society (Lindberg, 2019). As well as not being too concerned with society, they are not going to be concerned about anybody else's safety or well-being. They will not have much of a moral compass, they will be a consistent liar, and they may engage in very reckless and dangerous behavior. They are more than likely to demonstrate great anger and generally be quite aggressive.

Somatic therapy can be a healer for anyone who is going through or has come out of an abusive relationship. It really can lessen those emotional scars. It can ease the trauma out of your body in a safe and secure way. It can help you get to know yourself again, realize the truth of the situation—that it was not your fault—and help to love yourself again and to forgive yourself.

Let's do a quick exercise that will start you on your way to healing from an abusive relationship. Sit comfortably and close your eyes. Be aware of what your body feels when you remember this abusive relationship. Take note of what it feels. Practice your deep breathing, and as you are doing this, say the following: "I am accepting of this feeling. I love myself. I am healing myself. I was fearful, but now I am safe and secure. I want to heal, and I know I can heal." Just keep breathing and saying these sentences, and you should start to feel your body heal over time.

WHERE TO GO FROM HERE—
HOW TO KNOW YOU'RE
HEALING

I t's one thing to take part in somatic therapy, but how do you know it's working? That's what this chapter is all about— knowing when you are healing. You will be able to spot the signs that tell you the healing is taking place. It will make it clear to you how to tell what you have achieved thus far and what you still need to work on and improve. It also helps to manage your expectations in terms of how long it may take you to fully heal and recover. The main thing to remember above all is that even if you are finding it difficult to heal and love yourself at this moment in time, you are not alone. I have been through some of the experiences in this book, so I want you to know that you have my support, love, and respect. It's all wrapped up in the words on these pages—hopefully as a constant source of comfort to you. It's also always wise to seek outside support from others that may have been through what you have.

HOW TO KNOW WHEN YOU ARE HEALING

One thing to bear in mind is that healing is not something that is going to occur after just two minutes of breathing practice. It is something you have to adopt as a major part of your life in order to achieve.

It's not like a broken leg—you wrap it in plaster, leave it alone, and it heals—that's it. No, you have to keep on practicing somatic therapy and really integrate it into your life for it to be a complete success.

So how do you tell the therapy is working? First of all, it'll show through your nervous system, which as you go through therapy should become much more regulated and much more in harmony. Your fight-or-flight response should be becoming more settled, and your heart rate should be at a normal rate. You should be sleeping well, and your digestion should be good. Your immune system should be stronger. Your blood pressure should be normal. Of course, not all of these things are going to change overnight. If you were having specific issues in any of those areas, over time, you should start seeing minor improvements. Maybe you noticed you slept a bit better, or you are able to go to the restroom on a more regular basis. This isn't just the physical side of things either—maybe you notice you were able to set a boundary whereas before, that would have scared you greatly. Whatever it may be, you should see those slight changes occur the more you do the work.

The other way you may notice a difference is in your ability to let more into your life. When the trauma is stuck in your body, and it is having all these negative effects on your life, you find you don't really do a lot, and you don't really want to have too many people in your life, as you are anxious or stressed about so many situations and people. It could be that something triggered you, and you go into retreat. Or something happens, and you get angry and can't calm down from it. When you are healing, you start noticing that you can take more on. Fewer things make you anxious and stress you out, so you have more time to spend actually living life. Whereas you were getting angry and couldn't calm down, now things are happening. It's like water off a duck's back: You just get on with it.

Those are the two main ways you can monitor and notice whether the healing is working. If you're reading this after conducting somatic therapy for a while and you are noticing some of those improvements, well done! You are healing, and may you continue to heal. If you are just at the beginning of the journey, you can now look forward to spotting these types of improvements over time so that you can live life to the fullest and be the best version of yourself that you possibly can. I look forward to seeing you achieve that as well.

WHAT TO LOOK FOR IN A SOMATIC THERAPIST

Although we have concentrated on exercises you can do at home, to truly have access to everything involved in somatic therapy, you are probably going to want to find a somatic therapist. You might want to review the therapist's qualifications, experience, and whether they are licensed: If they aren't, cross them off your list.

With a therapist, you have the added indicator that you need to feel comfortable with them. You need to feel that they understand you, and they are in agreement with the issues you are looking to address. One way to fathom this out is to ask the very simple question of whether they can help you. From their response, you should get a good feel for whether you are going to be comfortable with them. You can always ask some follow-up questions as well. I would hope this book has given some confidence and plenty of knowledge to have the confidence to ask those questions. You are probably going to want to ask what their plan of action is: What exactly is the treatment they are likely to be recommending for you? This will help give you a really good idea of whether this is someone you can trust. Have they understood you and based on your trauma be able to apply a rough plan for you? Equally, are they big enough to admit that things may change as you go along? As things come up in sessions, they may need to adapt their plan. It's good to know if they are humble enough to admit that is a possibility. Equally, don't trust someone who says following their plan will definitely heal you in a specific amount of time. They don't really know how things can turn out. They may have a good idea, but no one can know for sure until you start doing the work. Therapists making definite promises are probably not to be trusted. Based on all of this, you probably don't want to find a therapist who is going to make you commit to a long period of therapy for a huge amount of money, given that any plan made for this type of thing could well change. You want them to be as adaptable and flexible in their outlook as possible.

It's not just about feeling comfortable as well: It's about whether you actually like the person. You could imagine them as someone whose company you like to be in. In a sense, one way leads to the other, as you are unlikely to ever feel comfortable in the presence of someone you didn't like. However, it's not just about being comfortable, particularly as having been through trauma, you may not feel comfortable with yourself, let alone anyone else. Start to use that somatic sense already, and see whether you feel you like the therapist as a person or not.

When it comes to qualifications, at the very least, you are going to want a therapist who has had training in somatic experiencing. Ideally, you probably want them to be qualified with something else—a slightly different field to somatic experiencing so that they aren't just focused on the one way to do things. It's always nice to see someone who is progressing as well. They haven't just trained at one thing and stopped: They have continued to learn and grow as a therapist. One of the biggest qualifications can be if they have done the work on themselves and if they used their own somatic therapy to heal themselves. It suggests what they did worked, and they should have some experience of what you have been through. Ultimately, they should be able to understand and have empathy for you.

Remember that as long as you haven't signed some dodgy contract that states you can never leave, you don't have to do anything. If, after a while, you feel it isn't really working for you, then there is nothing to stop you from ending the therapy there. You are never under pressure to have to stay doing something that is making no difference to you. You can always seek out alternative therapists and alternative therapies.

FINDING MEANING AFTER TRAUMA

It can be hard when you've been through trauma, even if you are healing or have begun to heal. You know you want to move on, but you don't know where you want to move on. Below are some tips to assist you in finding yourself and finding meaning after trauma.

One tip is to try and lead a fulfilling life. I know that's easier said than done, but after everything you've been through, you probably feel like there is a big hole in your life. What do you want to fill it with? Think about what it is you want that means you look forward to waking up tomorrow and seizing the day.

If there are things stopping you from fulfilling your life, then it's time to admit they exist—not as a bad thing or as something to feel guilty about but in a pragmatic, accepting way. All this trauma has actually caused me to be, let's say, "distant" in relationships. Now, I accept that it is the case, and this is now an opportunity for me to slowly change that. It may be painful, and it may be difficult, but if we can accept there may be things that stop us from progressing, rather than see them as a negative, we can see it as a chance to try better this time and turn it into an opportunity.

An important thing to remember is that by getting through this and still being here, you are an exceptionally resilient person. That means you can probably get through anything. You are a strong person, even if it sometimes doesn't feel like it, and that really is an important lesson you have learned. Through your somatic therapy, you will only grow even further as a person. Although what you went through was terrible, and you would much rather have never gone through it, it will have made you stronger in the long run. This is a way of saying, also, that we need to find meaning in life. Without that meaning, we usually drift along without knowing where we are going. It's important to do the things and see the people that bring meaning to your life. If you can do that, then you can fill the hole that trauma has left you.

THE SOMATIC DAILY RITUAL FOR EMPOWERED HEALING

Throughout the chapters, I've tried to give you some examples and exercises to work on and see what impact they have. However, the best thing is to bring much of that together into one daily ritual to get an enhanced healing experience. I've included aspects from various chapters in this book. All in all, the ritual should take you around 30 minutes, so you should still be able to fit this into your day. I think this ritual works particularly well in the morning, as it has elements of both releasing tension and relaxing you but also getting you ready to face the day ahead.

Once you've got the hang of this one, you can easily write your own ritual with the knowledge and experience you have built up. You can even put it up on your wall or fridge for that constant reminder and inspiration for you to complete it each day.

1: Breath Work (Five Minutes):

- Find a comfortable place to sit. You don't need to sit up completely straight, but your back does need to be supported.
- Close your eyes.
- Take three deep breaths: Inhale through the nose and exhale through the mouth.
- Put one hand on your belly and one hand on your chest. Take 10 deep breaths. You should be able to feel the air start off in your belly and work its way up toward and into your chest.
- Take 10 deep breaths: inhale and exhale out of the nose.
- Take 10 deep breaths: inhale out of the nose and exhale out of the mouth.
- Take 10 deep breaths: Inhale and exhale out of the mouth.
- Inhale one last deep breath. Hold it for seven seconds. Exhale and relax.
- Relax for 30 seconds, breathing normally.
- Open your eyes.

2: Mindfulness Exercise (Five Minutes):

- Make sure you are in a comfortable position.
- Close your eyes.
- Become aware of your body, and see if there are any specific areas that feel relaxed. Focus on one part of your body that

is feeling good and relaxed. Concentrate on that one place and the feeling.

- Think of a word that best describes this feeling.
- Take note of any changes to your breath when focusing on the relaxed and happy places in your body.
- To end the exercise, start to slowly take note of the sounds and smells around you.
- When you are ready, open your eyes.

3: EFT Tapping (Five Minutes):

- The cycle will include tapping on the side of your hand for a minute, followed by a continual cycle of the top of the head, inner forehead above the right eyebrow, temple, cheekbone, top lip, chin, heart area, and under the armpit on the side of your ribs.
- Say the following while tapping: "I love and accept myself wholeheartedly. I am ready to heal. I found it difficult in the past to accept the truth or that I had done nothing wrong and that I am a good person. I now know that to be true. I can't forget my past, but I can move on from it. I accept myself for who I am. I am a beautiful, loving human being, and I deserve to be loved. I respect and accept myself. I am ready to heal, and I will heal."
- Take your time doing the tapping. You do not need to rush from one stage to the next. Take your time saying the affirmations. You can choose not to say them if you don't feel they apply or add in anything you feel to be more appropriate.

4: Qigong (Five Minutes):

- Take a standing position. Make sure you are nicely relaxed and stand with your feet slightly apart.
- Take a breath in and reach up with your hands.

- Breathe out and bring your hands down to the center of your body. Have your hands facing each other with palms down—almost like you are pushing something down with the air below the hands.
- Rub your hands together like you are trying to start a fire with them until they start to feel warm.
- Once they are warm, close your eyes and place the palm of your hands on your eyelids. Keep them on there for approximately 30 seconds.
- Take your hands away from your eyelids and rub them all over your face. Rub your face 10 to 30 times.
- Now, stroke your fingers through your hair. This is dependent on how much hair you have. It may just be a short run, or you may be able to run your fingers through your hair for quite some time. Do this 10 to 30 times, depending on how much time you have to spare.
- Rub your ears. You are basically giving your ears a massage, so you can rub your ears or pull your ears—whatever feels good to you.
- Put your hands gently on your neck and press on the muscles. Gently is key: You don't want to give yourself an injury.
- Find the part of your spine that sticks out just below your shoulders. Gently tap it with one hand, then tap it with the other hand. Do this for five seconds with each hand.
- If you are still feeling any tension after that, just do a quick shake of your whole body. As you have been using your arms a lot, particularly shake off the tension from your hands, arms, and shoulders.
- End with breathing in, reaching up, and breathing out—bringing your hands down.

5: Somatic Yoga Exercise (10 Minutes):

- Start with a Forward Bend Pose.

- Move slowly into a Standing Cat-Cow Pose with your knees bent, moving your hands up to your knees and gently raising your back and head.
- Go back into the Forward Bend Pose and repeat, going into the Standing Cat-Cow Pose and back to the Forward Bend Pose a couple of times.
- Move into a standing position crouched over, but put your elbows into the top of your thighs and gently and slowly move your elbows down your thighs until you reach your knees. Do this three or four times.
- Do the Standing Cat-Cow Pose with your knees bent. Moving from a Cow Pose to a Cat Pose. Do this five times.
- Stand with your legs apart and swish your arms from one side to the other, one arm at a time. Start off slowly and speed up the movement. Do this five times.
- Do the Standing Cat-Cow Pose on your hands and knees. Do this five times.
- Go into Child's Pose. Hold it for a few moments.
- Go on your back with your arms outstretched behind you. Swing your leg over from one side to the other. Do the same for the other leg. Do this five times.
- Stay on your back and put the soles of your feet together with your knees bent. Hold this for a few moments.
- Pull yourself up to sit cross-legged with your arms resting on your legs. Hold it for a few moments.

AFTERWORD

Well done! I wish you incredible power on your somatic adventure. You've made it through to the end. That in itself is something to be proud of. You can congratulate yourself for taking that first step in becoming curious about somatic therapy and reading about it. I am confident that with your curiosity, combined with the advice and practices in this book, you will be well on the way to healing from the trauma you have undergone in the past. Just reading this book shows your bravery in wanting to heal from the trauma, and you will need that bravery as you continue on your journey.

Trauma is an all-encompassing event that we go through. For so long, people have surmised that it is something that only happens in the brain. Now we know so much more—that it happens in the brain, the body, and the spirit. One of the only ways to reach all those three things and truly heal is from somatic therapy. I'm not saying "talk therapy" isn't useful because, of course, it can be. Still, talk therapy alone won't always get to the root of the trauma in your body, and, sometimes, talk therapy can be the worst thing for someone with trauma to go through as they are going to be asked to bring up their traumatic experiences. There is little titration practiced in talk therapy, but working with somatic therapy helps you release that trauma little by little—not just through talking and using your mind but by becoming in touch with and aware of what your body feels and senses.

The trouble with trauma is that it also ends up causing other issues such as chronic pain, depression, anxiety, addiction, digestion issues, and lack of sleep, but all these things can be addressed and worked through with somatic therapy. Another wonderful thing about somatic therapy is that there are so many elements that you are not stuck with just doing one method or another; there are a variety of techniques and exercises that can be employed. Sometimes, it can be trial and error, but you should find something that suits you and works for you.

Through the concepts that somatic therapy teaches us, we really gain an understanding of our body, how it works, and how we can best get it to work for us. Grounding is a great exercise for just getting yourself settled and becoming aware of your body and what it is feeling. If ever you find your mind is racing away with you or you are becoming a bit panicked or anxious, one of the best things to do is to take a few moments to sit down with your feet firmly on the floor and go through some grounding techniques. I nearly always feel calmer and more at peace having done that and gotten in touch with my body and listened to it. It's almost like my body thanks me for listening to it.

Setting and maintaining boundaries can be an essential exercise for many—particularly those who have submerged themselves into others' lives or those that have been in abusive relationships. It also helps to keep things in the present and the here and now, which is where we all want to live.

As I touched upon in the last chapter, going through somatic therapy helps you start to self-regulate your nervous system, and over the long term, this can have such an important impact. Your emotions are self-regulated. No longer do you get upset at someone for seemingly no reason. Well, I'm not saying ever: We all get tired and grumpy sometimes but not because you have trauma that is still trapped in your body. Your fight-or-flight response becomes more regulated, so not every single thing will send you into a state of panic and anxiety. Slowly, your decision-making process becomes more in line with what it should be. Your digestion, sleep, and so many things can become more regulated, and all of it leads to your recovery, healing, and having the kind of life you imagine having for yourself. Self-regulation is such a vital part and goal of somatic therapy.

The use of movement can also be considered a cornerstone of the somatic experience. This doesn't have to be dance (though that is available in art therapy) or anything overly energetic. It can be as simple as a few postures in yoga, some shaking in Qigong, or some muscle tensing and releasing. These can be as energetic as you want or as serene as you want, but that movement is another part of getting to know your body, being aware of your body, and listening to what it is saying to you. All of these movements address the fact that trauma is in your body—not just in your mind.

There is no doubt in my mind that you have made the right decision. Somatic therapy is one of the best ways for you to heal yourself from your trauma. I'm proud of you for taking such a monumental step. I wish I could be there with you by your side as you go through your somatic journey, but hopefully, you feel I am there with you, cheering you on in the form of this book. You can transform your life and lead a life so much less full of pain and hurt than is currently the situation. You can start to look forward to life. You can start to be excited to wake up in the morning—not wake up with that horrible feeling of dread in the pit of your stomach. You actually can't wait to see what the day has in store for you.

You are no longer controlled by the trauma, and you have taken control of your life. This is such a powerful statement and one that will be true. You have the rest of your life to live; go and enjoy it.

It's so easy to incorporate so much of this into your daily routine as well. Even the ritual I provide only takes 30 minutes out of your day. So much of it can be done when you wake up or just before you go to bed that you can easily make sure you accomplish it. All you need is a quiet space in your house (sometimes easier said than done, I know), and away you go.

This is your body. This is your life. Go and make it the best it can possibly be. All the best and, as the whole of this book encourages you to, take care of yourself.

❧ II ❧
SOUND HEALING FOR BEGINNERS

SONIC MEDICINE FOR THE BODY, CHAKRA RITUALS, AND WHAT THEY DIDN'T TELL YOU ABOUT VIBRATIONAL ENERGY

INTRODUCTION

You are energy and energy only. This energy is arranged in a particular form that makes you the human being you are. Your particles are always moving within their assigned form, always alive with possibility, and vibrating at a frequency that keeps the entire system alive and functioning in the necessary configuration. This movement is known by many different names, a few being qi, prana, and spirit.

Anything that upsets the optimal frequency at which the particles of your being function can bring about disease and discomfort. This disease can manifest in any part of your body, including organs and systems, and also includes your mental and spiritual well-being. In such instances of disease, our particles are no longer operating as harmoniously as they could be, and the music of their collective movements manifest a dissonant orchestra of frenetic, haunted musicians, in contrast to the desirable symphonic masterpiece in which all instruments are in direct support of one another.

Introducing the right sound at the right vibrational frequency to bring your particles back to their optimized frequency can more simply be described as sound healing. Simply put, we can manifest well-being in our body, mind, and spirit by targeting particles (the body) in tandem with intention (the mind and spirit) and an accompanying frequency of our choosing. (More on targeting specific body parts or emotions with specific frequencies later.) The aforementioned example is the agenda of this guide in a nutshell; an optimized you via the power of vibration.

With the correct knowledge, you will become empowered and inspired by the power within your body and its connection to the universe. Your journey to become a version of yourself that no longer clings to limiting beliefs of what is possible will take a stronger foothold once you befriend the power of sound within and all around you.

Through the pragmatic and straightforward exercises in this guide, you can reclaim the ancient wisdom of healing and health that was always your birthright. Solidify your understanding by reading and applying the knowledge provided until the practices become etched into the grey matter of your subconscious mind.

Challenge yourself to master vocal techniques via the thorough explanations provided and give yourself the gift of bathing your energy body in harmonic healing vibrations. Enjoy the calming and restoring benefits when you practice the step-by-step meditations provided at the end of this book. You can practice these in tandem with a sound-track infused with a specific frequency, binaural beats, or a natural soundscape.

This is a hands-on (or should we say note-on) handbook to redis-cover the power of sound as the ancient civilizations knew and used to the benefit of themselves and the planet. We can take back our power by harnessing sound the way it was intended to be used. We can heal ourselves and the earth before it's too late. No longer must humanity live in fear and anxiety of a diminishing body or planet when the only thing standing in our way to unlimited possibilities of healing and joy is knowledge. This knowledge is accessible to all, and so are the practices encouraged within these pages. I think you will find this guide quite straightforward and enjoyable.

All efforts have been made to provide you with the science, studies, and references to strengthen your belief and understanding of sound while making said information easily digestible for the budding sound practitioner. These studies and methodologies have been referenced in order for the analytical side of your brain to be satisfied so that the intuitive and creative part can flourish more easily. After all, scientists seem to be the high priests of our time, responsible for informing the everyday citizen on the street of the nature of our reality and what's possible. It seems that only in recent years has science been catching up with the wisdom our ancestors so passionately shared. Let's enjoy more evolution in this area.

I am delighted for you to join me in entering an exciting new chapter of healing, with sound and music in their rightful places as your unlimited tools in engendering a healthy and optimal life. A life that deserves to be lived with a much broader perception of what is possible via the nature of energy.

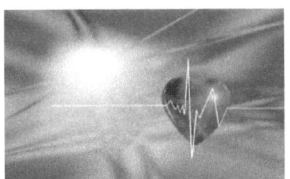

UNDERSTANDING SOUND CAN ALTER YOUR EXISTENCE PROFOUNDLY

The right frequency is life.

The Lost Chord (Music composed in 1877 by Arthur Sullivan, set to a poem by Adelaide Anne Procter) (Lin, n.d.).

> *"Seated one day at the organ*
> *I was weary and ill at ease.*
> *And my fingers wandered idly*
> *Over the noisy keys.*
> *I know not what I was playing*
> *Or what I was dreaming then;*
> *But I struck one chord of music*
> *Like the sound of a great Amen!*
> *Like the sound of a great Amen.*
> *It flooded the crimson twilight*
> *Like the close of an angel's psalm*
> *And it lay on my fevered spirit*
> *With a touch of infinite calm.*
> *It quieted pain and sorrow*
> *Like love overcoming strife;*

It seemed the harmonious echo
From our discordant life.
It linked all perplexéd meanings
Into one perfect peace
And trembled away into silence
As if it were loth to cease.
I have sought, but I seek it vainly
That one lost chord divine
Which came from the soul of the organ
And entered into mine.
It may be that death's bright angel
Will speak in that chord again.
It may be that only in Heav'n
I shall hear that grand Amen."

This poem may be old, but the fundamental truth about sound being a primal force in the universe remains true. Understanding sound and its role in life can make a profound difference to the rest of your existence, as well as to the health of our universe.

Sound has scientific, emotional, metaphysical, and therapeutic uses in our lives. Our modern lifestyles have mostly pushed the scientific side to the foreground while neglecting the rest, perhaps because the metaphysical benefits of sound don't seem to offer (at least overtly on the surface) economic and technological progress in our commercially oriented way of thinking.

Many of us are paying a steep price for neglecting the spiritual aspect of sound. Lifestyle diseases, such as diabetes and cardiovascular problems, and mental problems, such as depression, are at an all-time high worldwide. Stress has become the number one chronic problem, and we have not even comprehended the extent of how much damage it can do to our bodies and minds.

According to a recent report by the World Health Organization on non-communicable diseases, lifestyle diseases account for 71% of all global deaths each year. More than 15 million people die between the ages of 30 and 69. This is tragic, considering they would otherwise have had a productive life ahead of them. Cardiovascular diseases cause the most deaths, followed by various forms of cancer, respiratory diseases, and diabetes. Obesity due to chronic stress and harmful lifestyle habits contribute significantly to all these numbers (WHO, 2021).

Using sound to heal and comfort is one of the oldest forms of healing. It is believed to have originated in Ancient Greece, where healers tried to cure mental illness with music.

Music is used to stimulate mental and physical processes and speed up recovery from illnesses throughout the world. It is used to increase productivity in the workplace, boost the morale of military troops, and ward off evil spirits in some cultures (Santos-Longhurst, 2020).

A session of sound healing, whether experienced in a group or individually, provides endless benefits, a few being the unwinding of tense muscles and the cessation of anxious thoughts from spinning out of control.

The right vibrations will bring harmony back into your body and mind, clearing any blockages that prevent an optimum state of health and happiness. Sound can bring about deep healing from trauma and open up energy pathways and centers, known as meridians and chakras.

Sound healing's benefits even go so far as to lower blood pressure, make chronic pain more bearable, and aid in deep sleep.

WHAT IS SOUND?

To answer this question, we would have to first determine the nature and influence of vibration.

Have you ever been in your house when a big truck roared past, and you heard a faint, rattling hum in the window panes? Can you remember experiencing a vibration in your bones, corresponding to the deep rumble of the vehicle's engine? That is sound and vibration at work.

According to the scientific definition, sound is a pressure wave that is caused by a vibrating object. The vibration sets particles of air in motion, and our ears pick up the pressure wave (University of Toronto Computer Science, 2004).

Inside our ears, the vibration caused by the pressure wave is turned into electrical signals that our brains pick up through the auditory nerve and then interpret (National Institute on Deafness and Other Communication Disorders, Maryland, 2015).

The particles transporting the energy of the wave, which is usually air, move parallel to the pressure wave. Sound is, therefore, called a longitudinal wave.

The height and depth to which the particles oscillate before coming back to the middle are called the amplitude of sound. The number of complete back-and-forth movements of a particle in a second is measured in Hertz (Hz). This is known as the frequency of sound. The faster the movement is (the higher the frequency), the higher-pitched the sound is. The speed at which the sound wave travels is called the wavelength (University of Toronto Computer Science, 2004).

HOW DO WE HEAR?

The basic hearing mechanisms we are equipped with are our eardrums and a couple of tiny bones.

Sound waves enter our ears through the ear canal that leads to the eardrum. The eardrum is a thin, cone-shaped tissue membrane that is covered with skin on the outside and mucus on the inside of the ear. The membrane vibrates from the sound waves.

The vibrations travel to three small bones in the middle ear called the malleus, incus, and stapes. This amplifies the sound before it is passed on to the cochlea, which is a snail-shaped, fluid-filled structure in the inner ear.

The cochlea is divided into an upper and lower part by a partition called the basilar membrane, which is covered with sensory cells shaped like hairs.

The sound waves cause the fluid in the cochlea to ripple, and it creates a wave on top of the basilar membrane. The hair cells and the micro projections on top of them, called stereocilia, bump against the structure above them. As they bend during the bumping movement, small channels open up. Chemicals enter the channels, sending electrical signals to the brain through the auditory nerve.

The brain interprets the signals and turns them into sounds we can understand (National Institute on Deafness and Other Communication Disorders, Maryland, 2015).

How Do Sounds Influence Us?

You might ask how sound can affect our emotional and physical well-being.

Besides obvious things, such as acting as a warning in dangerous situations, sound can have a profound effect. It cannot be turned off like unwanted sights can be shut out by closing the eyes.

Just as the sound entering our awareness is a vibration of a certain frequency, our organs vibrate on their own specific frequencies. The frequency of an incoming sound may amplify our frequencies or oppose them.

It is widely believed that sound contains energy and information. This is told in stories of priests blessing bodies of water to cleanse them and scientists creating beautifully geometric crystals by saying loving and caring things to water. It is, therefore, safe to say that sound is a carrier of consciousness with far more power than it is often given credit for. It is not an overstatement to say we can make or break our world with sound.

Through sound healing techniques, we can benefit not only our physical bodies but access our spiritual and mental bodies to bring us back to a state of equilibrium and wellness.

Our being in a state of wellness extends to our environment and the rest of the cosmos. Remember the psychological concept known as the butterfly effect? According to the postulated theory, the mere sound of a butterfly's wings in one part of the world can cause a violent storm in another location.

We do not have to see something to feel its effect upon our consciousness, as demonstrated in many scientific experiments where unseen sounds brought visual signals into the participants' awareness (Aller et al., 2015).

THE BUILDING BLOCKS OF SOUND HEALING

There are a couple of mainstays that must be explained when discussing sound healing. One of the most important of these is resonance.

RESONANCE

Every object in the universe has a natural frequency at which it vibrates. If an external force, vibrating at a different frequency, touches the object, the contact will force the object to find and start vibrating at its natural frequency. That, in a nutshell, is how resonance works (The Physics Classroom, n.d.).

The external force does not necessarily have to be a physical object. It can be another sound, such as a note in a song, that sets the frequency of your body and its organs off to vibrate on their specific natural, healing frequencies. An example of this is when a note is sung in proximity to a musical instrument such as a violin, and the string corresponding with that pitch starts to sound.

Sound healers believe organs that do not vibrate at the frequencies they are supposed to cause illness and a feeling of unease, also known in the world of natural healing as dis-ease (Encyclopedia.com, 2014).

. . .

INTENT

According to experts in the field of sound healing, the right frequency alone is not enough to facilitate healing. The sound healer has to hold the intention of healing a person and/or organ in their heart and mind, too (Goldman, 2009a). This will be discussed later in greater detail.

TYPES OF SOUND THERAPY AND THE INSTRUMENTS USED

A sound healing session can take several different forms to effect healing and de-stressing. It may incorporate a variety of instruments and music, each type with specific benefits for specific scenarios.

TUNING FORKS

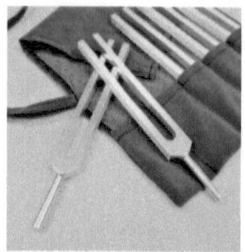

A tuning fork that is calibrated for a specific frequency to balance and heal organs is used by touching the part of the body that functions on that frequency. The vibrations can open up blocked energy channels and release tension stored in the muscles. It can also help to relieve pain.

A set of tuning forks.

GONGS

Gongs have been an integral part of sound healing for around 4,000 years (Bhaumik, 2019). The deep, rich sounds produced when a gong is hit create strong vibrations that can put the brain into a meditation pattern within a minute.

A set of gongs, with singing bowls in the foreground.

SINGING BOWLS

Metal singing bowls.

Singing bowls were first used in Tibetan culture as early as the 12th century (Bhaumik, 2019). They are usually made of metal and come in several sizes, each producing different vibrations that work to heal the mind and body. The bowls can be placed onto the body so that the water in the body's cells can convey the vibrations directly to the organ that is targeted.

WIND CHIMES

More than just a pretty window decoration, in Indian and Chinese civilizations, wind chimes date back several millennia. Wind chimes help to center and ground the mind and promote relaxation.

CRYSTALS

Singing bowls can also be made of crystal. The frequency that is released when a soft mallet is run around the edge of the bowl depends on the type of crystal the bowl is made of, as well as the size of the bowl. The vibrations of the bowls can be enhanced when rock crystals are placed nearby.

Crystal singing bowls.

Rock quartz crystals.

DIDGERIDOOS

The Australian didgeridoo is a type of flute created from bamboo or wood. It originated about 1,500 years ago to be used in spiritual ceremonies. It is believed to be highly effective in unblocking stagnant energy.

A modern street musician playing a large didgeridoo.

DJEMBES

A djembe is a Western African drum made of wood and covered with goat hide and rope. It is commonly used to start and enhance trance states, as well as give a boost to meditation. It is often used in drumming circles. This instrument has been reported to alleviate stress.

A traditional djembe.

KALIMBAS

Another instrument of African origin, the kalimba is also sometimes called a thumb piano. It consists of a small wooden platform with metal keys mounted on it. It is used for its calming effect.

Kalimbas range from very basic to fairly sophisticated instruments

HAMMERED DULCIMER

A hammered dulcimer.

A hammered dulcimer is a stringed instrument reminiscent of a zither (a wooden stringed instrument) that originated in medieval Europe. It has strings stretched over a wooden frame acting as a sound box, with two strings for every note. Instead of being plucked, the strings are hit with light hammers to produce the instrument's sound. It is commonly used to calm the mind and bring peace to upset emotions. The hammered dulcimer has been reported to be a powerful meditation aid.

MONOCHORDS

A monochord is a one-stringed instrument that is said to have been invented by the Greek philosopher and mathematician Pythagoras. The vibrations of the monochord's string are thought to bring renewed energy to the body and mind.

Several monochords sharing a single sound box to demonstrate harmonic intervals.

NATIVE AMERICAN FLUTES

A traditional musician holding a native American flute.

The soothing sounds emitted from these flutes are well-known and loved in sound healing. Native American flutes are used to reduce stress and anxiety. The use of these flutes in music is known as Ojibwe music, after the Ojibwe or Chippewa tribe, which was one of the most prominent tribes in North America.

RAIN STICKS

The origins of these shakers lie in the Aztec culture. In regards to materials used in creating these instruments, historians have revealed that the Aztecs used dried, hollow cacti that were filled with seeds or small stones. When shaken, the sticks make a sound resembling rain. Rain sticks are used to promote relaxation and decrease anxiety.

A rain stick.

HANGHANG

A hang handpan percussion instrument (the plural being "hanghang") is a Swedish creation dating back only a couple of years. They can vary greatly in size.

A hang handpan is somewhat similar to a singing bowl and produces deeply melodic sounds that are perfect for relaxation, while at the same time boosting focus and concentration that will increase the benefit of meditation.

SOLFEGGIO FREQUENCIES

The solfeggio frequencies consist of six tones that vibrate with specific organs and body parts. The tones are named according to the sol-fa designation, which consists of Ut-Re-Mi-Fa-Sol-La. Musicians may be familiar with the sol-fa designation. It is believed these six tones have been used since ancient times to promote healing and balance. See a more in-depth discussion of solfeggio tones in later chapters.

Listening to a solfeggio frequency through earphones can minimize distractions.

. . .

BINAURAL BEATS

This mode of sound healing is also known as brain entrainment. It uses pulsing, subtle beats that encourage the human brain to align to their frequencies and enter a specific wave state or even target a specific body part for healing . The beats are sometimes set to music. Binaural beats are a powerful meditation aid. The concept and theory will be discussed fully in a later chapter.

RHYTHM AND VOICE

Think sound healing tools and instruments need to be fancy devices? Think again! The human voice can even be used for sound healing by itself. In fact, some practitioners even swear by the fact that you have all the apparatus you need to heal just with your voice box alone. You don't even need background music, although some prefer to practice their vocal exercises with it. Using music as a healing tool will be discussed in greater detail in a later chapter. These healing methods can involve creating music, listening to it, singing, or even moving to the beat.

MEDITATION

Meditation, with or without chanting a mantra, is one of the first methods that comes to mind for most people when the topic sound healing is bought up. A mantra in conjunction with meditation helps prevent your mind from drifting, ensuring you get the full benefit from your practice. After all, meditation is the practice of getting past the thinking mind and focusing your attention in order to slow your brain waves down. What could help you focus more than chanting a mantra?

The sounds produced by the voice when chanting a mantra during meditation create vibrations in the body, which can aid healing. Some practitioners will target a specific frequency for a specific benefit. For example, one might align the frequency of their mantra with the frequency to target the root chakra, if this is the area they wish to focus on. In addition to a mantra aligned with a specific frequency for a chakra or body part, you can even couple the words of your mantra with affirmations that are associated with a particular chakra. For example, if you are working on your sacral chakra, in addition to aligning your mantra with the frequency of this energy center, an affirmation you might use for creativity (a trait associated with the energy center) could be something along the lines of "I am a divine and unique creator".

The same goes for a humming meditation, where the vibrations of the hum originate within the body and stimulate the vagus nerve for various benefits. See a later chapter for a more in-depth discussion of meditation and its benefits.

HARMONY

The harmonies that are created when different notes blend combine vibrations to form a powerful healing force. Administering healing through harmony requires a solid knowledge of the effects of various harmonies on the body and mind. Harmonic relationships will be thoroughly discussed later in the book.

HUMMING

The strong vibrations of humming pervade the whole body. Coupled with effective deep breathing, humming exercises can bring about powerful healing sessions.

NATURE SOUNDSCAPES

It is no coincidence that certain sounds of nature are soothing or inspiring. The frequencies of sounds, such as ocean waves or water running over pebbles, can influence us in powerful ways.

THE IMPORTANCE OF HOMEOSTASIS

In the end, all of these methods of healing aim to bring the mental, physical, and emotional body back into homeostasis. This state of equilibrium allows optimal functioning without any part of the body being in discomfort or disease due to an imbalance within the entire organism. Although we can see only the physical body, it does not exist in isolation from the mental and emotional (or energy) bodies—all are interdependent.

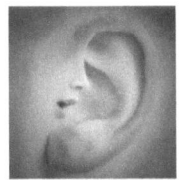

THE FORGOTTEN
SUPERPOWER: LISTENING

Hearing is automatic, but listening is not. Without listening, there can be no sound healing in its most effective form. Listening is a prerequisite for maximum healing to take place. The sounds and their vibrations must become a part of your body to reap the full benefit of treatment.

There are many different ways in which we listen, and not all of them involve the ears. There is a big difference between simply hearing and listening. When you listen, you move beyond the physical process of using your auditory organs to give meaning to the things you hear.

Listening is just as much about your inner voice as it is about what is going on externally. It is the art of tuning into vibrations and entering the sonic dimension, a type of meditation if you will.

OUTER LISTENING

To hear with the ears is an automatic activity that does not require any skills. Our ears are always on. Therefore, our brains must apply filters to determine which sounds register in our consciousness.

This filtering process, through which we make sense of the sounds our ears hear from outside our physical bodies, is called outer listening.

Sounds are always colored by our personal experiences and preferences.

INNER LISTENING

In contrast to listening to sounds from the outside, inner listening pertains to the voice inside our heads. Our feelings, preferences, and past experiences very much influence this voice.

An essential and influential point to realize regarding the inner voice is that it is not completely who we are. It is oftentimes the inner vocalization of our ego (who we think we are), and it will typically ruminate on our pains, embarrassments, and past disappointments. We must practice being the observer of this inner voice and not get dragged downstream by any negativity it presents us with. Being the observer of our egos is the gateway to spiritual connection.

Being the listener of our inner voice means we can discard any suggestions or information we do not consider helpful or accurate. This practice brings enormous personal power and peace. Practice this regularly for astronomical spiritual growth.

BECOMING AWARE OF FILTERS WHEN LISTENING

Our perceptions of who a person is or what they represent can color the way we listen to them. It is also common to apply a set of filters when listening to an individual, oftentimes remaining unaware that we are doing it. These filters can cause misunderstandings because our preconceived ideas of what a person is saying (or who we perceive them to be) might not be what they are actually trying to communicate. We must remain solid in our practice of mindfulness so as not to allow miscommunications to take place due to our unconscious filtering process.

DEEP LISTENING

The act of listening in order to learn with an open and receptive mind, whether from your inner voice or from someone else, is known as deep listening. The purpose of listening must be to understand, even if an agreement cannot be reached (Bakken Center for Spirituality and Healing, 2015). Deep listening also involves asking powerful questions. A powerful question draws one into the real meaning of the conversation and inspires one to reflect on it.

To practice this mode of listening, the listener has to empty their mind and open up to receive information. This is a powerful mindfulness practice.

In sound healing, this deep listening principle applies to one's ability to hear their own inner voice and allow it to say the things their core being knows deep down but is yet to utter.

- Become aware of the present moment first. Feel your body, clothes, and environment without thinking of any words. Try to become still and quiet within yourself. Experience your center of gravity and ground yourself.
- Now, become aware of and acknowledge anything that could be interfering with your quietness. Accept that you have feelings, judgments, fears, and sensations that move in your mind. These things are the triggers that can stop you from profoundly listening to yourself and allowing sound to heal you.
- Once you have identified your triggers, try to understand where they come from without judging or criticizing yourself. If you are stuck, you can simply ask the divine oneness within you to give you a clue as to what triggers or issues might be preventing you from receiving optimal healing through sound. Only when you identify and shine a light on what is keeping you stuck can you step into a deeper understanding of yourself.

Mindful and Conscious Listening

If we silence our inner voice, silence any outer noises, and become aware of our personal filters, we can listen with an open mind to another person or unfolding event. That is being fully conscious in the moment.

The increasingly noisy environment in which most of us constantly find ourselves is stumping our ability to listen with a conscious and active attitude. Our brains get overwhelmed by a bombardment of stimuli, and it is sometimes easier to simply shut down. By doing so, we enter into a prison of our own making, where we deny ourselves a rich life of healing and soothing sounds.

WHAT IS MINDFULNESS?

Many people equate mindfulness with meditation, but meditation is only one way of practicing mindfulness. Mindfulness practice, in conjunction with sound healing, can be used for dramatic results.

Mindfulness can be described as being fully aware of everything inside and outside of you without passing judgment on anything. It simply means noticing life unfolding without the need for an inner dialogue narrating every thought, either good or bad.

To remain a calm and still witness, the inner voice must be bypassed and not followed into a train of thought. Think of a thought as a cloud in the sky. One moment it's there; the next, it's not. Try to maintain this attitude of transience within your mind. It might seem challenging to do in the beginning, but it becomes easy when a couple of simple things are kept in mind.

- The first point, being present, seems self-explanatory, but it can seem tricky if you're not used to it. Presence helps to simplify all of your surroundings and not get distracted. Try switching off the television and cell phone and putting the computer away. Put a "do not disturb" sign on the door. Make sure anything on your desk that could distract your attention is also tidied up or put away in a drawer. Straighten your furniture and decor if you tend to get distracted by an untidy environment. Sometimes, something as simple as just putting all of your focus on a bare wall in a tidy environment can be a powerful access point to mindfulness.

- Sit quietly for a minute or two before starting a listening experience, whether it is a meeting with another person or a healing session. Prepare yourself mentally for what you are about to experience. Visualize emptying your head of all the thoughts that will interfere with your complete immersion in the material you will be listening to.
- Relax with a breathing exercise and muscle stress release. Focusing on your breathing to the exclusion of everything else is a form of meditation that can help muscles release the tension stored deep inside.

When you start paying attention to your breathing, you might find that your breath is shallow. In most people that have not practiced attentive breathing before, inhalations typically don't go deeper than the upper chest and often never reach the abdomen. This restrictive breathing limits the amount of oxygen that is beneficial to areas of the body that are hard to reach.

In contrast, diaphragmatic or belly breathing pulls the lungs downward and opens them up to receive much more oxygen. This reduces stress and has beneficial effects on blood pressure and heart rate.

When your breathing has deepened, you can combine your practice with contracting groups of muscles, one after the other, before releasing the tension. Move through the whole body and pay special attention to any muscles that store tension for you, such as the shoulders, neck, and abdomen.

- Centering is another excellent way to get into and remain in the present moment. While breathing deeply, become aware of your physical center of gravity. It is usually just below the waistline.
- Focus all your attention on your center while breathing deeply at least another five times. Be aware that you are in balance and have control of your body.

- Visualize all the negative energy collected in your body, concentrated in your center of gravity, where you control it. Move the ball of negative energy up toward your eyes and then visualize pushing it out and away from you. This can leave you calm, grounded, and happy in the present moment.
- Lastly, it is essential to become aware of the cues, or triggers, that launch the filters that color your listening. Perhaps a coworker has offended you in the past, and now the sound of their voice causes you great irritation. Once you can see and feel these triggers activating, you can sidestep them and remain open and mindfully listening. This is where sound meets mindfulness for true spiritual evolution.

NADA YOGA

The Vedic tradition known as nada yoga is a practice that can be described as sound yoga.

The word "nada" refers to the vibration of sound. In this form of yoga, sound is used not only to heal and balance body and mind but also to open the path to true spiritual awakening.

In nada yoga, a distinction is made between internal and external sounds.

External sounds, or ahata in Sanskrit, are paid attention to via listening. This practice can consist of something as simple as listening to calming non-vocal music and picking out the individual notes to focus on.

Nature also has sounds like birdsong, rain, or the wind rustling in the leaves. Chanting a mantra also represents ahata.

The point is to listen to external sounds in such a way that it opens up the door for you to travel inward within yourself.

Internal sounds are called anahata in Sanskrit. They are perceived through the anahata, or heart, chakra.

These sounds are the sacred inner music that is unique to each individual. When the breath is regulated and the sight is turned inward, these sounds can be perceived to balance the energy bodies and re-establish a connection with your true and divine self.

Some people can hear the cosmos itself hum after a time of rigorous practice.

MORE EXERCISES IN MINDFULNESS

To make the most of sound healing, you have to be able to listen effectively. In our modern, noisy world, it does not often come to us naturally.

SILENCE

A meaningful silence is more than a mere absence of sound. It has a voice of its own because vibrations never cease. It can be as therapeutic as music or the voice.

Many people have become afraid of silence because it is something strange in a world that never sleeps. In the task-centered Western world, being silent is often considered unproductive or lazy.

Eastern philosophies and most religions around the world make much of quiet contemplation, though. It brings an opportunity to reflect on what is really going on around and inside us, something that scares some people away. To someone who is used to being on the move, constantly producing results, being quiet can feel like a sort of death, which is scary for most of us.

There is, however, great healing in connecting with the self and hearing the inner voice again. In quiet times, the true vibration of our being can make itself heard.

Sound expert Julian Treasure calls the periodic immersion in total silence "recalibration" of our ears. It brings back awareness of subtle sounds while sensitizing us again to sounds that are loud enough to potentially damage our hearing (Treasure, 2017).

Try to experience silence for at least three minutes every day. Finding a quiet spot can be challenging, but choose somewhere that has as few sounds as possible. It can work well just after waking up or just before dozing off at night.

When you meditate, try to do it in silence, focusing on your breathing. While music and guided meditations can be beneficial, especially in the beginning, having music and the voice of a guide can potentially remove stillness as you progress. Some practitioners like to think of the voice of a guide and music as training wheels that eventually need to come off if they are to grow further. Others use music and guided meditations exclusively. We are all different. What suits you best?

ISOLATE SOUNDS

Another effective way to practice conscious listening is to isolate individual sounds in a noisy environment, such as a mall.

- Try to identify the different elements that make up the auditory "soup" that is known as mall mush. Zooming your focus like a spotlight forces the brain to concentrate on the immediate environment, helping to create a habit of being present and mindful.

NOTICING THE RAISIN

For this exercise, any other kind of food with an exciting texture will also work.

- Take the raisin in your hand and look at it really closely. Notice the feeling of it against your skin, as well as the weight. Look at the color and whether it is shiny or not.
- Smell the raisin and savor any aroma you pick up.
- Gently squeeze the fruit and notice how it changes shape.
- Don't judge anything you notice during this exercise. Just note it and let it pass.

This conscious listening exercise can supercharge your sound healing practice over time.

THE BODY SCAN

- Sit comfortably in a chair with your feet on the ground, or lie down on your back, feet slightly apart. Close your eyes and try to stay as still as possible for the whole duration of the exercise.
- Quiet your mind and start paying attention to all the sections of your body, starting at the top and moving down to your feet.
- Note to yourself which parts feel relaxed, tight, warm, cool, tired, or sore. Become aware of how the bed/chair and your clothes feel against each body part. Notice your breathing.
- Take your time to become fully present of every sensation in and against your body. This is equivalent to entering into a mindful conversation with your body, with you as a compassionate listener.
- Once you have finished the scan, open your eyes when you feel ready and sit up again.

A MIND SCAN

The same scanning principle described in the exercise above can be applied to your thoughts and feelings. This is a great way to learn to keep a quiet, open mind flowing like water.

- Take five minutes in which you imagine your feelings and thoughts as fish gliding through the water—you see them, but you don't try to catch them or pin them down for inspection. You just notice their existence.

- You also acknowledge the sensations these thoughts and feelings create in you without trying to evaluate or label them.

MINDFUL WATCHING

- Position yourself near a window where there is some scenery outside to observe. It can be nature or a busy city sidewalk, wherever you find yourself.
- Watch the scene with your mind as well as your eyes without cognitively naming any objects. Notice, for instance, the texture of the leaves on the tree and the way they move in the breeze without thinking "tree" to yourself. Just watch.
- Don't evaluate or pass judgment on anything.
- Notice if you get distracted and gently leave those thoughts to return to watching.

LET YOUR SENSES DO THE TALKING

This is an easy and fun exercise to do with children, especially, but adults benefit from it greatly, too.

- Make a mental list of five things you can see, four things you can touch and feel, three things you can hear, two things you can smell, and one thing you can taste.

The aforementioned conscious listening practices, in conjunction with sound healing, make for a potent recipe indeed.

PRIMORDIAL SOUND

The teachings pertaining to the primordial or primeval and basic sound of the universe originated centuries ago in India's Vedic system of wisdom.

The contemporary philosopher Deepak Chopra revived the tradition and developed meditations using a person's personal primordial sound at the time of their birth as the mantra. The personal mantra is calculated according to Vedic mathematics and astrology to determine which sound the universe made at the time of the individual's birth.

Incorporating this sound in the person's meditation mantra brings them back into contact with their innate wisdom and peaceful silence, what primordial meditation expert Julie Hunt calls "the space of infinite possibility between thoughts" (Hunt, 2020).

This is accomplished through chanting the mantra ohm (auhm) + personalized sound + m + namah. In between, four questions are asked of the self, in silence: Who am I, what do I want, what is my purpose, and what am I grateful for?

At the end of the meditation, four core intentions are left in the silence and sent into the universe. These are for having a joyful, energetic body, a compassionate and loving heart, an alert and reflective mind, and a lightness of being (Hunt, 2020).

BENEFITS OF PRIMORDIAL MEDITATION

Primordial sounds are considered to be the most basic sounds of nature and, as such, are believed to help us disconnect from everyday busyness. The basic vibrations that make up the universe can align our own vibrations with our true purpose and a deep sense of peace. It allows us to be fully aware without any intellectual questioning or evaluations and experience the innate stillness that is within all of us.

Several studies have shown meditation to have a beneficial effect on stress and emotion-related disorders (Goyal et al., 2014).

In another study, the participants also recorded higher subjective energy levels and an improvement in handling conflict (Walsh et al., 2019).

SOUND HEALING FOR TINNITUS

When the organs we use to hear healing sounds develop problems, it affects much more than hearing. Tinnitus, which causes a person to hear sounds such as ringing, hissing, buzzing, or whistling (sounds that don't exist externally to the sufferer), affects millions of people worldwide. Statistics from the American Tinnitus Association show that almost 20 million Americans alone suffer from the condition chronically (Clason, 2019).

In many cases, there is no cure for the condition (other than reports of people healing their tinnitus through meditation), but sound therapy is recognized as a successful treatment. It works by retraining the brain to stop noticing the sound, thereby eliminating the disturbance.

Audiologists use sounds we perceive as neutral, such as waves on the shore or falling rain. The sound is played continuously throughout the day, and gradually, the brain starts to equate the tinnitus sound with the neutral sound. The offending sound is, in effect, simply "relegated" to the subconscious. The important point to remember is that the background sound's volume should not be loud enough to drown out the tinnitus sound. It should co-exist with the tinnitus for the training to take place (Clason, 2019).

Recent scientific studies have shown this type of treatment to be effective for a broad range of tinnitus sufferers. It is an excellent example of how profoundly sound can affect our lives (Wang et al., 2020). In addition, there are many testimonials found online of individuals that have healed their tinnitus (among other hearing and health issues) through meditation and getting in touch with the divine oneness within us. After all, we are the most powerful healers, but many of us are in need of reconnecting with this powerful intelligence through spiritual practices.

❧ 14 ❧
CREATING MAGIC WITH
VOCAL TONING

T he experiments performed by Swiss medical doctor Hans Jenny in the 1960s to show how sound can change formless matter into intricate patterns are well-known. Jenny put powders, liquids, and pastes on steel plates and vibrated the plates on pure frequencies generated by a crystal oscillator. The photographs he took of the structured patterns that the substances formed can be found in the two volumes he wrote about the field of physics he called cymatics (Goldman & Sims, 2016).

You don't need plates and crystal oscillators to create with sound, though. Your voice is all you need.

Are you ready to experience the power of the musical instrument you were born with?

HOW DOES VOCAL TONING WORK?

Going back to the basic premise of sound healing, which is that every cell in the human body vibrates at its specific frequency and that the body functions as a harmonious unit when all the cells are at the correct frequency, it follows that the voice can correct imbalances easier than external instruments.

Goldman and Sims make the observation in their book *Sound Healing for Beginners* (2016) that not all the recordings that claim to be of specific frequencies are, in fact, on the same frequency. Even with the variety, people using the recordings report success. That creates the question of whether we all are vibrating at individual frequencies. If the answer to that is yes, it makes an even stronger case for the use of the voice in healing. There is yet no definitive conclusion regarding the question.

THE FOUNDATION

It has to be understood clearly that using the voice as a healing instrument is not simply just about singing. Healing with the voice can include speaking, humming, chanting, or simple sounds like breathing. Don't let the vocal part put you off from trying this amazing technique if you have any doubts about your singing ability.

One similarity vocal toning does have with singing is that it relies on conscious breathing. Breathing can change heart rate and brain states, altering consciousness (Goldman & Sims, 2016).

Every vocal toning session should start with attention to abdominal breathing, a technique that has been discussed in a previous chapter.

In addition to breathing in and releasing the breath immediately, the breath can also be held in for a couple of seconds before releasing it slowly.

Another excellent breathing exercise is the three-point-focused approach. Start the inhalation by focusing on the abdomen. While you feel it filling with air, shift to your ribs and fill that region with air. Next, direct your focus to your lungs. When you feel your lungs are about 90 percent filled with air, expand your awareness to the base of your throat and your collarbone and allow everything to expand—you should experience a pleasant sensation of relaxed openness at the base of the throat. Hold your breath for a second or two, savoring the feeling of being completely filled with air. Then gradually exhale by relaxing the diaphragm.

Exhaling entirely but in a controlled way is just as important as inhaling fully. Rather than forcing the air out in one go, try to let it out to a count of four. A controlled exhalation sustains vocal work. As you get more comfortable with the technique, you can extend the exhalation count to eight or even more. The key is to remain comfortable with how you are doing it.

ADDING SOUND

With the foundation of breathing under your belt, so to speak, it is time to add the first sound to the inhalations and exhalations.

Add any gentle sound that feels natural to you. An s-s-sound on inhaling and an ahh-sound on exhaling work for most people. Reverse the sounds after a couple of breaths and notice any subtle differences in energy you might feel. Even the smallest change in sound can have a big influence on energy fields and our experience of them.

THE IMPORTANCE OF SILENCE

Incorporating a short period of quiet contemplation after each vocal exercise is just as important as the sound itself. This gives you a chance to assimilate the shift that has just taken place and move it from your subconscious to your conscious experience to reap the full benefits.

EXERCISE 1: HUMMING

The humming sound is directed inwards, so it is easier for sound work beginners to focus on it. Choose any pitch that feels comfortable to you in the middle of your vocal range. Always remember vocal toning is not about performance, although regular vocal work can result in unexpected improvements to your singing and speaking voice.

- Ensure your facial muscles and tongue are relaxed when your mouth is closed. If you detect any tension, yawn and sigh a couple of times to loosen them up.
- Make a "hmmm" sound on your chosen pitch and sustain it for as long as it is comfortable in one breath. Note where you feel the resonance. It could be a ticklish sensation in your nose and head sinuses, as well as the back of the throat and the upper chest.
- Start another humming sound but imagine you are making an "ng" sound (as in the word sing) with your mouth still closed. Note where you feel the resonance now.
- For the next round, imagine you are humming on an "oh" sound, and again, be aware of where the resonance shifts.
- Now you can start playing with the pitch. Go up and down the musical scale as high and as low as you can. As the shape of your vocal cords change with the change in pitch, the resonance will shift throughout your body.

EXERCISE 2: FOCUSED HUMMING

Taking humming a step further, focus on any area in your body, such as the solar plexus or the base of the spine, before starting to hum.

- Start producing a humming sound and see if you feel any reaction in the targeted body part. If your first attempted sound has not elicited any sensation, change the pitch and see if your energy shifts and reaches the desired body part.
- Try to move through your whole body with this exercise, but in the beginning, try to keep the total session to five or ten minutes until you become accustomed and can keep your targeted concentration for longer periods.
- To enhance the strength of the humming even more, you can cover your ears lightly with your hands while humming and try to make the softest sound you can. Notice that while the sound may be barely detectable to outsiders, the resonance inside your body might be amplified.

EXERCISE 3: OPEN VOICE

A warm-up exercise that singers often use is the siren. It is not difficult to do and simply requires you to let go of your voice, like a child. Similar to how this exercise warms up a singer's voice getting ready to hit the stage, it will prepare your vocal cords for optimal healing potential in your vocal sessions.

- Start at the lowest pitch comfortable to you and, making any sound such as an "ah," glide your sound up to the highest pitch you can manage. It does not have to be loud, and no strain should be involved.
- Then reverse the sound, moving from the highest pitch down to the lowest.
- Keep to the counting pattern used in the breathing exercises, inhaling on a count of four and letting the sound

out on a count of four or eight, whatever you can manage comfortably.

THE POWER OF LAUGHTER

Of all the natural sounds we produce, laughter is one of the most healing vibrations. It is not only an emotional release but also brings about powerful shifts in energy vibrations. There is also scientific evidence of the beneficial physical changes that laughter can bring about.

A study done by researchers at the University of Maryland School of Medicine in Baltimore in 2005 found that a daily dose of laughter causes the inner lining of blood vessels, called the endothelium, to dilate, which increases the blood flow to all body systems. Increased blood flow means higher oxygen levels, which protect the heart, brain, and other organs, and strengthen the immune system.

A group of 20 healthy, non-smoking male and female individuals were shown 15 minutes of a movie that stimulated laughter. Their baseline blood vessel dilation was measured before they started and again after watching the scenes, and significant dilation was found.

Some hours later, the baseline measurements of the same group of volunteers were taken again. They were then shown a 15-minute segment of a movie that caused them mental agitation and stress. Their endothelium this time showed constriction, which is the first step toward hardening of the arteries and cardiovascular disease.

The endothelium also secretes chemicals that regulate blood flow and coagulation when injuries and infections are detected.

The leader of the study, Dr. Michael Miller, equated the benefits seen after the laughing session to the effects of aerobic exercise, but without the exertion and aches (University of Maryland Medical Center, 2005).

EXERCISE 4: LAUGHING

- Settle yourself where you won't have to worry about other people listening and thinking you've gone bananas. Start with a deep inhalation and breathe out with a sigh. Take another breath and expel it with a soft chuckle.

- Continue breathing and chuckling gently to yourself. Notice if you're starting to smile and spontaneously moving from chuckling to real laughter—it might feel silly at first, but that is fine.
- When you feel you have finished laughing, quiet down and take a few moments to reflect and tune in to whether you feel any different.
- Repeat the exercise and exhale on tones that might differ from your natural laughing sound. Try uttering "ha," "ho," and "he." Notice where in your body these sounds resonated. "Ho" is usually felt in the lower abdomen, "ha" more in the center, and "he" in the upper body and head.
- You can also vary the pitch for each sound.
- Finish by combining the sounds and moving the resonance up and down your body.

TONING SOUNDS FOR DIFFERENT PARTS OF THE BODY

Some sounds work specifically on targeted parts of the body, in contrast to the vowel sounds, which are non-specific to any anatomical area. However, chanting a vowel sound and mentally directing it to the area you want to target will work just as well, as there is great power in intention. This is because thought (intention) is also energy.

Here are a few examples of tones that work well for certain organs (Gabriel, 2015):

Mmmm	Sinus cavities
Mamm	Reproductive system
Wooo	Bladder and kidneys
Shhh	Small intestine and liver
Nnnn	Ears
Lemm	Nose
Maaa	Heart and surrounding muscles
Ssss	Large intestine and lungs
Paam	Stomach
Kaa-Gaa-Gha	Throat and larynx
Yaa-Yuu-Yii	Jaw and teeth
Haaa	Diaphragm muscle
Eemm	Eyes
Uu-Ah-Ee-Mm	Waking up and energizing
Mm-Ee-Ah-Uu	Relaxing, getting ready for bed

HEALING AND CLEARING THE CHAKRAS

Chakras are spinning energy centers situated at various areas throughout the body. There are seven of them, and each one is thought to correlate to specific organs and nerve bundles. It is important to keep them in balance for optimum emotional and physical health (Stelter, 2016).

The First Chakra: The Root
Located at the base of the spine, the root chakra is associated with grounding and physical identity. The color associated with this energy center is red.
Imbalances in this chakra can make one feel emotionally unstable and experience insecurities regarding their ability to meet their basic needs. On the physical level, a root imbalance is associated with issues such as constipation, urinary tract infections, and arthritis (Stelter, 2016).

The Second Chakra: The Sacral
The sacral energy center is located just below the belly button and above the pubic bone. It is associated with the color orange, as well as sexual health, creativity, and the capacity to experience pleasure in general.
Problems with lower back pain, infertility, and impotency can result from a sacral imbalance. On the emotional side, self-image and our feelings of self-worth, particularly in terms of experiencing pleasure on all levels, can suffer if this chakra is not balanced (Stelter, 2016).

The Third Chakra: The Solar Plexus
The third center is located in the area of the stomach, in the upper abdomen, and the associated color is yellow. It rules confidence and the experience of personal power.
If the solar plexus chakra is misaligned, it can cause feelings of help-lessness and a victim mentality. Physically speaking, ulcers, indigestion, and eating disorders can result (Stelter, 2016).

The Fourth Chakra: The Heart
The chakra associated with love and compassion is located in the middle of the chest, just above the heart. The color is green.
An imbalance in the heart chakra can manifest in people putting others' needs before their own to the extent that they harm them-selves. It also stands for connection to other people, with its location in the middle of the seven chakras. An imbalance could bring feelings

of isolation and insecurity. Physically, heart problems, asthma, and weight gain are associated with the heart chakra (Stelter, 2016).

The Fifth Chakra: The Throat
With its color of vibrant blue, the throat energy center represents verbal communication and the associated organs such as the mouth, teeth, gums, and vocal cords.
A blockage or problem with balance can manifest in physical problems in these areas, as well as hesitant or malicious communication (Stelter, 2016).

The Sixth Chakra: The Third Eye or Brow
This center is located between the eyes, and the associated color is indigo. It represents imagination, intuition, and physical conditions of the head.
A blockage can make itself known through headaches, eye, or ear problems. People who are out of touch with their intuition or who seem to live in their own world where they "know everything" can be suffering from a problem with the sixth chakra (Stelter, 2016).

The Seventh Chakra: The Crown
Spiritual awareness and intelligence are associated with this chakra, and its color is violet or white.
The crown chakra links the other chakras and is associated with the nervous system and brain.
People who stubbornly cling to narrow-minded views or drift aimlessly through life, always searching for their true purpose, might have an imbalance here (Stelter, 2016).

EXERCISE 5: THE ROLE OF SOUND

THERE ARE MANY WAYS OF HEALING CHAKRAS AND REMOVING blockages with sound. Two popular ways are by voice or with tuning forks.

A different vowel is associated with each chakra, and the voice can chant the specific vowel sound to balance or unblock a chakra.

To find the pitch for every chakra, use the same technique applied earlier in the resonance exercises. Choose a pitch and feel if it resonates in the targeted chakra region. If not, move your pitch up or down until you feel the energy moving in the right place. A rule of thumb is that the lower chakras vibrate to lower pitches. You can use videos and music online to help you match a specific pitch, but learning to do this instinctively by feeling your own inner vibrations will skyrocket your listening and sound-healing prowess.

There is no need to chant loudly.

Focus on your intention of balancing and clearing the specific chakra into your voice. Sit comfortably and keep your spine as straight as possible to allow energy to move freely.

Gently tone every sound seven times on your breath without forcing anything.

- The root: The associated sound is a deep, guttural "uuh," as in the word "duck."
- The sacral: The associated sound is "ooh," as in the word "do."
- The solar plexus: The associated sound is "ohh," as in the word "low."
- The heart: The associated sound is "aah," as in the word "ta."
- The throat: The associated sound is "eye," as in the word "rye."
- The third eye/brow: The associated sound is "ay," as in the word "bay."
- The crown: The associated sound is "eee," as in the word "bee."

Instead of using the balancing vowels, the chakra bija, or seed mantras can also be chanted. Every chakra has its own bija mantra that represents the primordial time of creation.

- The root: The associated sound is "lam."
- The sacral: The associated sound is "vam."

- The solar plexus: The associated sound is "ram."
- The heart: The associated sound is "yam."
- The throat: The associated sound is "ham."
- The third eye/brow: The associated sound is "aum."
- The crown: The associated sound is "om."

Afterward, sit quietly for at least 10 minutes to experience the flow of energy. If you feel lightheaded at all when getting up, make an "aah" sound to bring your energy down to the heart and then an "ooh" sound to ground yourself again properly (Wakeling, 2007).

Balancing the chakras using tuning forks requires more specialized knowledge and is usually done by practitioners qualified in sound healing. The chakras correspond to specific frequencies, and the tuning forks must be placed on the chakra area that is being treated in specific intervals and combinations. However, simply placing a tuning fork resonating in alignment with a specific chakra will also be packed with benefits.

This interacts with what has become known as the biofield of a person. The term biofield refers to the sum of the energetic body that surrounds every human being. The term was coined in 1992 by researchers and practitioners in the Office of Alternative Medicine at the US National Institutes of Health, which is now the National Center for Complementary and Alternative Medicine (Rubik et al., 2015).

When a person's body is in balance, all of its frequencies are in harmony. An organ or system that goes out of balance brings dissonance into this harmonic world. With the aid of tuning forks, the dissonant body part is gently brought back to the right frequency, and the sense of unease can disappear.

THE CHAKRAS CORRESPOND TO THE SAME SOLFEGGIO FREQUENCIES that were discussed in an earlier chapter (Weller, 2020).

- The root: 396 Hz.
- The sacral: 417 Hz.

- The solar plexus: 528 Hz.
- The heart: 639 Hz.
- The throat: 741 Hz.
- The third eye/brow: 852 Hz.
- The crown: 963 Hz.

SHAMAN SOUND HEALING WITH INSTRUMENTS

The rituals and sounds used by shamans worldwide bring another dimension to healing. A shamanic ceremony aims to alter consciousness, putting someone in a trance state where healing and balancing can take place, and an openness to receive wisdom and answers to specific questions a person might have is created. The shaman also enters into a trance and journeys to other worlds.

This is done by using various instruments such as drums, rattles, and Australian didgeridoos, as well as employing the voice of the shaman and sometimes the person being healed, depending on whether it is an active or passive session.

Shamanic drumming is perhaps the most well-known practice. Researchers have found rapid drumming of about 220 beats per minute to be a vehicle for putting a person in a trance. The frequency range correlates with theta brain waves at 3 to 8 Hz (Gingras et al., 2014).

Goldman and Sims explain the effect of drumming in terms of what is called auditory driving. Drumming stimulates the brain's reticular activating system (RAS). The primary function of the RAS is to regulate electrical activity in the brain. After a while of strong, repetitive drumming, the RAS gets overwhelmed, and all other stimuli are ignored. That frees the shaman's mind to travel to other worlds and communicate with spirit beings and animals (2016).

EXERCISE 6: USING YOUR VOICE AS A DRUM

It might not be possible to attend a session with a shaman, but you can create the same beneficial brain state for yourself by using your voice.

- To mimic the sound of a drum, you can start with a "kuh" sound, as in the word "cup." Inhale comfortably and exhale on the sound of "kuh." Keep the initial rhythm to one beat per second until you find your innate sense of rhythm. Gradually speed it up to a fast pace, keeping it going for about a minute. Notice any difference in energy you might feel.
- Slow right down again to about one beat every two to three seconds. Keep this up for a minute also, and be aware of your nervous system and heartbeat slowing down in time with the rhythm.
- You can repeat the exercise with a "boom" sound and notice if it makes you feel more grounded in contrast to the energizing effect of the "kuh" sound.

✻ 15 ✻

FROM POLLUTION TO
PANACEA

Cities are never quiet, not even at night.

Modern life offers very few opportunities for stillness and quality quiet time if we don't look for it on purpose. The everyday sounds we are constantly exposed to are often more damaging to our health than we might realize, both in their volume and their essence.

Blaring televisions, bleeping computers, and smartphones with a variety of ringtones all demand ongoing attention from our brains. This creates a stressful situation in the body.

NOISE POLLUTION

Noise pollution can be described as any noise we perceive as intruding on our thoughts and activities. It could be as loud as the club down the street or as soft as the audible conversation of the people sitting at the next table in the restaurant.

A couple of sounds have been identified as the main culprits that have a significant negative impact on people's health. They are airplanes, traffic, noisy workplaces, and incessant household sounds (Scott, 2020).

HEALTHY SOUND LEVELS

The human ear can get damaged by either one very loud sound or sounds over a period of time that are continuously higher than what scientists have determined to be a safe range to protect hearing.

Sound is measured in decibels (dB). For an introductory idea of decibel levels, breathing measures at about 10 dB, a whisper is about 30 dB, and normal conversation is between 55 and 60 dB.

When the sound level creeps up to 70 dB, such as in a washing machine or a dishwasher, slight annoyance might start to creep in. Traffic noise from inside a car can get up to 85 dB, which is significantly more annoying to the people in the vehicle.

Any sound louder than 70 dB that is sustained over a long time can potentially cause permanent damage to someone's hearing. (Permanent is a term used loosely here because, as mentioned earlier, many individuals claimed to have healed their hearing through methods such as meditation.)

Exposure to the sound of a motorcycle engine running at full speed and measuring at 95 dB can cause some hearing loss after only 50 minutes. Only 15 minutes of listening to a sound at 100 dB, such as an approaching subway train, has the potential to cause damage.

The sound levels in venues such as bars and nightclubs can get as high as 110 dB, and after only two minutes of exposure, a measure of hearing loss can occur.

Any sound louder than 120 dB will cause immediate pain and ear injury, possibly resulting in permanent hearing loss (National Center for Environmental Health, 2019).

THE EFFECTS OF NOISE POLLUTION

The World Health Organization (WHO) considers noise pollution to be the second most dangerous environmental threat to human health, behind air pollution. The European Environment Agency

(EEA) estimates that long-term exposure to high levels of environmental noise causes 12,000 premature deaths and 48,000 new cases of ischemic heart disease in Europe annually. They also point the finger to noise for more than 72,000 hospitalizations for a variety of causes every year in Europe alone (EEA, n.d.).

The negative impact of excessive noise lies in the fact that it raises our stress levels, even if it is only in the subconscious. This triggers the release of stress hormones such as cortisol. While cortisol is essential in body processes such as the metabolizing of glucose, secretion of insulin, and regulating of the immune response, sustained high levels of the hormone have been shown many times to be harmful to the human body.

Warning signs of harmful cortisol levels include blood sugar problems, elevated blood pressure, brain fog, increased abdominal fat, suppressed thyroid function, slow wound healing, and low immunity (Scott, 2021).

Under normal circumstances, the body's "off switch" kicks in after an acute stressor has passed, and cortisol production decreases again. When stress is chronic, as in the case of environmental noise, the de-stressing signal does not get a chance to activate.

AIRCRAFT

The engine sound of a modern passenger aircraft can reach up to 140 dB during takeoff.

A study undertaken by various European scientists found that aircraft noise can cause significant health problems. Besides disrupting sleep and hampering academic performance in children, people living close to airports were vulnerable to cardiac disease, elevated blood pressure, obesity due to increased stress hormones, and lower birth weight in newborns.

Psychologically, people complained of poor quality of life, anxiety, and depression (Basner et al., 2017).

An Australian study compared the effect of noise pollution caused by aircraft on memory and recall to the effects of drinking too much alcohol. After being exposed to simulated aircraft noise at 65 dB, their scores in an auditory recall exercise showed the same deterioration as they did after the participants were administered alcohol under monitored conditions until their blood alcohol concentration measured 0.10 (Molesworth et al., 2013). This level is double the legal limit imposed in many countries to drive a car.

Passengers inside airplane cabins are not safe from possible noise pollution, either. During an assessment of the noise levels within a number of modern passenger airplanes, the median level of sound was found to be 83.5 dB. The full range of sound measured was between 37.6 dB and 110 dB, and exposure varied with seating positions. Being closer to the engines, for example, in seats in line with the wings, aggravated the situation (Zevitas et al., 2018).

TRAFFIC

The WHO classifies road and railroad traffic as the second most harmful form of environmental pollution. Only air pollution is deemed to be worse (EEA, n.d.).

The stress responses provoked in the body by traffic noise do not even get turned off or lessened during sleep. Vehicle engines, tires, and road surfaces all combine to deliver a constant bombardment of sound levels above 55 dB. This has led one Danish technology company to describe traffic noise in one of their reports, quite aptly, as a slow death (Finne & Petersen, n.d.).

In another study conducted in Denmark, it was found that the risk of developing high blood pressure increased by 6% when noise levels experienced in the home increased by 10 dB. The risk of a stroke increased by 11% (Sørensen et al., 2013).

WORKPLACES

Besides the obvious pictures of construction sites and factories that come to mind, other work environments can be just as harmful in terms of the sound levels experienced.

Symptoms of noise-related problems can include frequent headaches, persistent irritability without an apparent cause, increasing

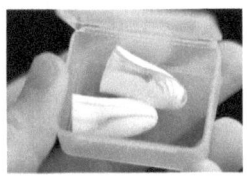

Earplugs are not always the best solution to cancel out the noise in an office.

stress, dizziness, unexplained increases in blood pressure and/or heart rate, frequent and uncharacteristic mistakes and work accidents, and trouble discerning someone's words when there are other sounds present. In addition, wearing earplugs to minimize distractions could lead to diminished productivity due to incidents such as missed phone calls.

Office workers who listen to their own music through earphones could damage their hearing even more if the volume is turned up too high for too long.

The open office model is very popular in large offices, but it could be detrimental to employees. A busy office can quickly reach a sound level of 50 dB. That is not only distracting but can also significantly increase stress levels and the accompanying health risks.

HOUSEHOLDS AND SHOPPING MALLS

Outdoor noise levels can also increase indoor levels. It becomes increasingly difficult to enjoy music or hear a phone conversation when traffic is roaring outside the window, for instance.

A French study done on the homes of 44 schoolchildren over eight months found them to be exposed to constant sounds such as television sets, music playing, cleaning equipment, cooking utensils and equipment, ventilation systems, freezers, and pets. The combined effect pushed the households' overall sound level several times during a 24-hour period higher than the level recommended by the European Environmental Agency (Pujol et al., 2014).

THE EFFECTS ON ANIMALS

The animal kingdom also suffers as a result of our noisy civilization. Many geographical surveys have shown a decline in births for many species in noisy environments.

Whales and dolphins are also significantly impacted by ocean noise caused by ship traffic, oil drills, sonar equipment, and seismic testing (National Geographic Society, 2019).

How to Turn the Noise Tide

It is impossible to avoid or stop all sounds that are too loud, so we have to learn to live with them and make them work in our favor whenever we can. The good news is we can use the sound healing practices outlined in this book to heal any ill effects we may encounter.

Limit the Noise

The first and probably most obvious solution would be to limit the amount of noise that reaches our living and working environment.

Physical (but admittedly arduous) steps to help you achieve this can include installing double window panes, applying weatherstripping to doors and windows, adding insulation to the ceilings, and installing soundproofing panels to your working and sleeping areas, if not the whole house or office. These methods are costly, however, and can be pretty invasive and disruptive for work and home routines during installation. A more realistic method would be to master sound healing methods to reverse any harm caused.

Start Over

Sometimes the only solution will be to move away from the job or area with unacceptable noise levels.

Although it is a drastic step, it is worth considering if it is possible for you. It could turn out to be the best gift you have given yourself in a long time.

Do Damage Control

We are not always able to control our environments and the amounts of noise we have to endure on a daily basis. Fortunately, there are ways to limit the damage and reverse the detrimental effects to recover your mental equilibrium and inner harmony.

Spend time in meditation and do some yoga stretches. Remember to breathe deeply and calmly—especially when you detect stress anywhere in your body. Taking a minute out to do a breathing exercise will bring amazing and quick changes.

Combine meditation with a mantra or chanting when you can to balance your vibrations and bring your body and mind back into harmony. Use good sounds to counteract bad sounds.

REPLACE THE NOISE

Fill your working and living space with soothing sounds to cancel out the noise. There are several online sources to find soundscapes from nature for free. Running rivers, booming ocean waves, rustling leaves, crackling fires—whatever combination of sounds resonates with you will be available to play, or sometimes to download, at only the cost of the data.

White, pink, brown, and blue noise can also be found in abundance online and in mobile applications.

The trusty pair of headphones to play your favorite music should not be forgotten either. Just remember to keep the volume low enough to protect your hearing.

IMPROVE CREATIVITY WITH VOLUME

In a 2012 experiment, a group of scientists found that people performing specific tasks with a soundtrack playing in the background at a consistent 70 dB performed better than those who worked in complete silence. That is the same sound level found in a typical busy coffee shop or restaurant (Mehta et al., 2012). Volumes lower or higher than 70 dB did not lead to good performance.

It seems sound levels have a sweet spot where creativity is concerned, and if we harness it, sounds that could have been deemed noise pollution can work to our benefit.

The science behind this insight started in the 1950s with a psychologist called J. P. Guilford. He distinguished between the processes of divergent and convergent thinking to arrive at a creative solution to a problem.

During the divergent phase, all possibilities are examined. When the best one is chosen, the convergent phase zooms in on it and makes it take shape.

Sometimes our creative processes seem to fail because we skip the divergent step or don't consider enough different options. That is where a sound environment of 70 dB comes in: That is just enough sound to keep us from concentrating so intently on a problem that we narrow the field before it has a chance to develop.

The type of sound is important, however. Only steady streams of jumbled familiar sounds will stimulate our creative cognitive processes, such as indistinct chatter or ocean waves. One-sided phone conversations and even white or pink noise won't do the trick.

These types of sounds are usually lower-pitched than isolated voices or phones, and we perceive the vibrations to be more relaxing, thereby stimulating our creativity.

USE SONIC TRANSMUTATION

The concept of transmuting something implies that a sound is being turned into something else—something that is useful instead of counterproductive.

The ancient Egyptians already understood this principle when they built the pyramids. These fascinating triangular shapes that have mesmerized people ever since seem to have been used for more than burial sites.

Besides being sites to send deceased kings into the afterlife with everything they needed, archaeologists believe the design of the pyramids was also used to benefit the living.

Scientific experiments conducted in the Great Pyramid of Giza, which was built as a tomb for the pharaoh Khufu, showed the design of the pyramid could collect electromagnetic waves and concentrate them in specific points. This fact, coupled with the highly resonant qualities of the walls because of the high quartz content in the limestone, has led some scientists to conclude the pyramids were also used as places of healing, maybe during worship rituals (Balezin et al., 2018).

The ancient Egyptians believed that seven of their vowel sounds were sacred. During rituals, the priests chanted these vowels in a convergent harmony that reverberated from the walls of structures such as pyramids.

Acoustic physics researcher John Stuart Reid conducted a cymatics experiment in the late 1990s to show the resonant power of the Great Pyramid by using an oscillator and a speaker arrangement that mimicked the vowel chant of the priests.

Many of the images he observed in the patterns formed by the quartz crystals he used in his experiment resembled Egyptian hieroglyphs. This led Reid to surmise that the ancient writing incorporated harmonies too.

Based on this experiment and others that followed, Egyptologists believe the measurements and angles on which the pyramids were built were designed to produce maximum resonance for the chanting sounds. The rituals were used to heal and, after death, to send the body of the king off to the stars to be reborn.

The patterns contained in the hieroglyphs were carried over through the years to come, but sadly, we lost the knowledge of the harmonies that accompanied them (Cymascope, n.d.).

CRYSTALS

Crystals can be a great aid in turning the noise tide. There are hundreds of different types available, each with its own vibration and area of benefit.

Gemstones have been used since ancient times to heal diseases and soothe troubled minds. When the power of the crystals is magnified with sound, they become even more effective.

Gemstones used in natural healing.

A Brief History

Crystals are first mentioned by the Sumerians. They were ancient Mesopotamian people who are credited with starting civil life in the way we modern humans understand a civilization to be. They included various crystals in their formulas for magic processes and potions.

The Egyptians put great stock in the power of stones such as lapis lazuli, turquoise, emerald, and carnelian. They used them as jewelry, as well as to treat the sick. Green stones were seen as symbols of a deceased heart and were used in burial rituals.

The ancient Greeks knew and used several gemstones, and many of the names for gemstones we know today are of Greek origin. They used stones for protection and healing.

Jade was valuable in old China, and emperors and other influential people were sometimes buried in suits of armor made from jade.

The tradition of green stones being seen as lucky continues to this day in some parts of the world, for instance, in New Zealand.

Most religions also use and value gemstones in some form. Their importance has waxed and waned with the trends in society and scientific developments.

In the 1980s, interest in New Age philosophies emerged, and gemstones and crystals were rediscovered as healing tools and emotional aids. They are still not accepted by mainstream medical science as valid healing tools, but crystal therapy is used by many people to enhance their lives and health.

How Do They Work?

Crystals, like any other part of the universe, vibrate at specific frequencies that give them their physical makeup and appearance. Some frequencies are the same as some of our organs and emotions, and by enhancing a positive vibration, it is believed that disease can be healed and emotions can be balanced and calmed.

Healers see themselves as mere conduits for healing vibrations, channeling them to the person receiving the therapy.

The roots of crystal healing therapy lie in Chinese and Indian culture, with the concepts of qi and the chakras.

CLEANSING AND RECHARGING YOUR CRYSTALS WITH SOUND

Most crystals are believed to absorb the negative energy they remove from the body and mind, as well as any energy around them when they are transported or stored. They have to be cleansed occasionally to continue to be of benefit in healing.

There are several ways to do this, but not all of them work for all crystals. Sound cleansing and charging is one method that will be effective on any type of crystal.

It is not difficult to do and cannot damage your crystals. Any resonating object that can hold the tone for ten minutes or more can be used, such as tuning forks and singing bowls.

Singing bowls are well suited to this because their high copper content ensures they keep their tone ringing for as long as they are in use. They are positioned on a cushion to prolong the bell-like sound even further.

Cleansing with singing bowls is a practical way to clean a whole array of crystals at once or to clean and charge big crystals that cannot be moved easily.

The size of the bowl does not matter that much. Smaller bowls emit a higher-pitched sound than larger ones, but both sides of the sound spectrum will do what is needed for your crystals.

Be sure to avoid buying decorated or painted bowls when you shop for new ones. The paint hides the copper and dulls, or even changes, the sound. It will also cause the sound to stop quickly instead of continuing its ringing for some time after being struck with its special wooden stick. If the bowl is made of the wrong metal or the wrong composition of metals, the ringing will also stop quickly, and the sound might be more similar to hitting a regular saucepan with a wooden spoon.

Arrange your crystals around the bowl, but never put them inside. The movements caused by the vibration of the bowl will make the stones hit against the metal insides of the bowl and each other. That can chip or otherwise damage your crystals, especially the softer or brittle ones.

CLEANSING SMALLER CRYSTALS WITH A SINGING BOWL

- Place the bowl on its cushion after making sure the cushion rests flat on a hard and stable surface.
- Arrange the crystals to be cleansed and recharged around the cushion. Make sure no stones touch the bowl.
- Strike the outside of the bowl gently with the wooden stick to start its ringing sound.
- Rub the outside of the bowl with the wooden stick in a clockwise direction to sustain the ringing. Apply some pressure to the rubbing, but keep it gentle.
- Hold your intention of purifying and recharging the crystals in mind while keeping up the rubbing.
- You can amplify the ringing sound by humming along with it.
- Keep rubbing until you feel your intention has been communicated.

CLEANSING LARGER STONES WITH A SINGING BOWL

- Stand as close to your crystals as you can.
- Hold the bowl on the flat palm of your non-dominant hand.
- If possible, hold your hand with the bowl over the crystals or right next to them.
- Take the wooden stick in your other hand and strike the side of the bowl gently to start the ringing.
- Follow the rest of the steps outlined in the section above.

RECHARGING AND RETUNING YOUR CRYSTALS WITH TUNING FORKS

The same sound effect can be created by using a good-sized tuning fork. The sound should be loud enough to penetrate the structure of the crystal to move its molecules and realign them to their own powerful vibrations.

The specific note struck does not matter as long as it is loud enough and can be sustained while sending your intention to the crystals.

- If you want to recharge your crystals with a specific frequency, you can consider using what is known as a crystal tuner. It is a tuning fork designed to resonate at 4,096 Hz. This is said to be the frequency of quartz as well as of the earth. Proponents of crystal tuners believe that pure frequency creates a bridge between the energies of heaven and earth when the ringing tuner is touched against a crystal.
- Tap the tuning fork gently in your hand, on a hard surface, or with a rubber mallet to start it ringing. Hold the vibrating tuning fork over the crystal you are retuning for as long as you feel it is needed while sending your clear intention to it.

RECHARGING CRYSTALS WITH TINGSHAS

Tibetan tingshas are sets of tiny copper cymbals joined by a leather thong. Buddhists have used them for centuries as traditional aids in prayers and ceremonies.

Tingshas emit a high-pitched sound that can be sustained for quite some time. The etymology of the name refers to its sustaining power— "ting" mimics the sound of the metal, while "sha" means "hanging" in the Tibetan language.

Traditional Buddhist Tingshas.

RETUNING YOUR CRYSTALS WITH VOCAL TONING

Vocal toning does not need a high note. You only need sustained sound at some degree of audible volume to move the molecules of the crystal. The louder your tone, the faster the molecules will vibrate to speed up the process.

Hold the crystal to be tuned in front of your mouth and take a deep, relaxed diaphragmatic breath. Imagine you are inhaling something with the power to purify and energize. Give a form and a color to this purifying energy.

Exhale the purifying energy slowly over the crystal, carrying it on your voice in any comfortable pitch. Don't think about the note before singing it. Allow the note that comes naturally at that moment and sustain it on your exhalation as long as you can.

Visualize your voice and the purifying sound wrapping around the crystal.

Keep toning until you feel you want to shift your pitch higher or lower. You will know the crystal is retuned and ready when that shift occurs.

THE POWER OF MUSIC AND THE VOICE

Never underestimate the powerful effect that your own voice and the vibrations it creates, which are like signatures of your true self, can have when used with pure intentions.

Whether you sing, speak, or chant, your intention of recharging and realigning the crystal to yourself and your needs makes all the difference.

Even just singing along to a favorite piece of music with a joyful and pure heart can accomplish everything your crystals need. Not all of us have the talents or available time of monks; use what you have and do it with enthusiasm and purity.

A REPROGRAMMING VISUALIZATION FOR CRYSTALS

In this visualization exercise, the spoken word is combined with an intention to create an effortless re-tuning of your crystals.

- Stand in natural light, outside, or at a window.
- Hold the crystal to be recharged in your left hand. Your left side is the receiving side of your body.
- If you want to, you can play music in the background at a frequency of your choice. If your purpose is to dedicate the stone for a specific use, you can choose the frequency that boosts that aspect of life.
- Breathe deeply and calmly for a couple of seconds to center yourself while being sensitive to the weight and the sensations of the crystal in your hand.
- While gazing with love and gratitude at the crystal, say aloud, "I dedicate this crystal to be used for my highest good and truest purposes. I welcome its energy into my life. I ask to receive its love and light."
- If you want the crystal's assistance with something specific, form that intention in your mind and speak it aloud toward the crystal. It could be anything from opening your heart up to finding a life partner to helping you heal from disease.

- Finish by saying aloud, "I now dedicate this crystal to... (your chosen purpose for the stone)".
- If it is practical to do, you can wear the reprogrammed crystal against your body for seven days to settle the new energy. Bigger crystals should be touched regularly in the week following the visualization.

A CLEANSING MEDITATION FOR CRYSTALS

For this meditation, you can either put your crystals in your lap or just visualize them in your mind's eye.

- Sit comfortably with your feet next to each other on the floor, ankles uncrossed, and arms and hands resting calmly in your lap.
- If you are holding crystals in your lap, you can rest your hands on them if you want.
- Play a soundscape of your choice in the background, or use music in the universal transformation frequency of 528 Hz.
- Close your eyes if you are comfortable doing so and breathe in deeply but comfortably, feeling your abdomen swelling with the air drawn deeply into your body.
- Breathe out until your stomach and rib cage are completely flat again.
- Experience the stillness and serenity in and around you, and bathe your spirit in it.
- Breathe in serenity... And breathe out inner chatter.
- And breathe in serenity... And breathe out inner chatter.
- Picture your crystals in your mind.
- Visualize a pure white light shining down to envelop you and the stones in energizing warmth.
- Savor the warmth for a while.
- Breathe in energy... And breathe out exhaustion.
- And breathe in energy... And breathe out exhaustion.
- [Pause for as long as you want in this feeling].

- Now see the white light gently washing every crystal, removing any negative energy and stagnant experience.
- See the brilliant colors of every gemstone reemerging to sparkle in the healing white light.
- Breathe in purity... And breathe out stagnant energy.
- And breathe in purity... And breathe out stagnant energy.
- Keep on doing the spiritual wash until you intuitively feel your crystals are cleansed and recharged.
- See the white light gently washing every crystal, removing any negative energy and stagnant experience.
- Enjoy the brilliant sparkle of the colors in every crystal, playing in the healing white light.
- Breathe in purity... And breathe out stagnant energy.
- And breathe in purity... And breathe out stagnant energy.
- When you are ready, become aware of your surroundings again and open your eyes.
- Hold the recharged crystals for a while and allow their vibrations to move you.

CHOOSING THE RIGHT CRYSTALS

You can be forgiven if you feel fairly bewildered by the wide variety of crystals and gemstones available to choose from. Each one has an area it specializes in, and the colors are also important.

It does not fall within the scope of this book to discuss all the criteria for choosing crystals. We are concerned with sound healing. However, it is good to know that some crystals will resonate more strongly than others.

To gather a beginner's set of stones, consider getting clear quartz, rose quartz, citrine, amethyst, black tourmaline, tiger's eye, aquamarine, green calcite, pyrite, and pink opal.

Clear Quartz

Clear quartz is known as the master healer. It is believed to balance mind, body, and soul. It also supercharges intentions, making it a great aid for beginners.

It not only amplifies its own energy but also boosts the energy of any crystals used alongside it.

Rose Quartz

This beautiful pink gemstone is known as the queen of self-love, relationships, and harmony.

It is credited with strengthening emotional and sexual bonds between partners, enhancing harmony, and neutralizing conflicts.

Citrine

The bright yellow of citrine awakens personal power. It also helps to get rid of negative energy and will boost confidence and conviction for people in stressful careers.

Amethyst

Amethyst is used to bring calm in a hectic schedule and relieve stress while enhancing spiritual connections, insights, and intuition, as well as opening the third eye.

Many healers use amethyst to get rid of addictions. Ancient Greeks carved their drinking vessels from amethyst in the belief that drinking from them would prevent intoxication.

Black Tourmaline

This stone is used as a powerful protector against negativity and people wanting to drain your personal energy.

It is also used to calm anxiety and balance the right and left sides of the brain.

Placing a black tourmaline crystal near electronic equipment can also mitigate the effect of electromagnetic waves on our energy levels and block some of the energy drain.

Tiger's Eye

Tiger's eye is used to ground a person. It can boost physical performance.

The stone also enhances focus and motivates you to take advantage of all the opportunities offered by the universe.

Aquamarine

This is the best stone to turn to when you find it difficult to speak your truth and stay true to yourself. It helps you to set boundaries without aggression or apology and guides you in tense conversations.

Aquamarine also boosts creativity.

Green Calcite

Green calcite helps us to get rid of blocks and obstacles to personal growth. It cleans our energy and amplifies the benefits.

Due to its green color, it is also strongly associated with prosperity and abundance.

Pyrite

Pyrite is used as a protector on all levels, from energetic to spiritual to physical. It is also said to boost one's effectiveness in manifesting when the crystal is used during meditation.

Pink Opal

Pink opal helps to release anger and tension, restoring calm and serenity. It also helps to relieve anxiety and insomnia.

It works on a subconscious level to heal old emotional wounds and release any lingering trauma and pain.

Does Size Matter?

The size of your crystal does not change the type of energy it can provide. A big chunk of the gemstone will pack a more powerful punch that may affect you more quickly, but the essential outcome will remain the same, whether the crystal is big or small.

How Do You Make a Choice?

It is often said that a person is chosen by a crystal and not the other way around.

Some crystals will "speak" to you if you need them at that point in your life. Touching various crystals for a few moments with your eyes closed may help you quickly detect a vibrational reaction.

✤ 16 ✤

UNLOCKING YOUR
MERIDIANS WITH SOUND

Meridians are concepts from traditional Chinese medicine (TCM). They are to chakras as railway lines are to stations—they form the channels along which energy travels through the body to arrive at the various centers where it is concentrated for specific purposes.

The physical existence of meridians has not been proved yet, but practitioners of the system firmly believe in them and use them to heal and restore.

TCM is an ancient medical system that has been around for almost 4,000 years.

KEY CONCEPTS IN TCM

The first concept to understand is qi. That refers to the invisible energy force that is life itself. In the literal sense, the Chinese word means "air."

TCM believes illness occurs whenever anything obstructs the free flow of qi through the body. The system of coordinated movements, breathing techniques, and meditation traditionally used to balance and maintain qi is called qigong.

The meridians through which the qi circulates are divided into two parts. The jingmai contains the main meridians, while the luomai contains the associated vessels, such as the arteries.

Every meridian exists as a part of a pair. One is yin in nature, and the other is yang. In TCM, yin corresponds to cold, darkness, and water. Yang corresponds to daylight, heat, and fire (Fellows, n.d.).

THE MERIDIANS

There are 12 main meridians. They run on each side of the body, and each meridian relates to an organ. The two sides mirror each other.

The meridian channels consist of the liver, gallbladder, heart, small intestine, spleen, stomach, lung, large intestine, kidney, urinary bladder, San Jiao, and Pericardium. The San Jiao meridian is also known as the triple burner and helps to regulate organs and energy in the same way that Western medicine understands metabolism. Its nature is yang. The pericardium meridian is the cardiovascular meridian, and it has a yin nature (Traditional Chinese Medicine World Foundation, 2019).

The Liver Meridian
The liver is essential for a healthy metabolism with its function of digesting nutrients. In TCM, it is associated with frustration, irritability, bitterness, depression, and sadness.
Physical symptoms that can manifest when this meridian is blocked include dizziness, dry eyes and other vision-related problems, dental issues, sinusitis, period pains, diseases of the reproductive system, and fatigue.

The Gallbladder Meridian
The gallbladder produces bile that helps with the detoxification of the body. In TCM, it is associated with rage.
Physical signs of a meridian problem include eye problems, hip, knee, and ankle joint problems, mouth ulcers, and pulmonary diseases.

The Heart Meridian

The heart is essential in providing life-giving oxygen to the body. It is seen as the seat of joy in TCM. Too little joy will result in depression, while too much joy may cause one to become manic.

Fearfulness, agitation, concentration difficulties, and resistance to forgiving people can manifest. Physical problems include heart palpitations and irregular heartbeat, as well as neuralgia of the arms and shoulders.

The Small Intestine Meridian

Magic happens inside the small intestine when food is converted into energy to fuel the body.

Psychologically, the small intestine meridian relates to the "digestion" of mental and emotional issues. Prolonged feelings of grief and sadness without an apparent cause can result from a blocked or imbalanced small intestine meridian.

Symptoms of problems with this meridian include food allergies, all types of frequent infections, a tendency to incur strain injuries, skin diseases, and rheumatism.

The Spleen Meridian

The spleen forms part of the body's filter system. It removes bacteria, dead blood cells, and any other impurities.

A tendency to worry in excess and dwell almost obsessively on one topic is an emotional sign of problems with this meridian.

Physically, loss of appetite, exhaustion, bloating, diarrhea, and blood disorders can point to spleen meridian dysfunction.

The Stomach Meridian

The stomach is not only the place where physical food is digested, but it also represents the digesting of ideas. Problems with the stomach meridian can show themselves as an inability to assimilate new ideas and incorporate them into your life.

The stomach meridian runs up to the top of the head and can also manifest in sinus irritations, tooth problems, facial palsy, thyroid issues, and lymph blockages.

Psychologically, depression, bitterness, and a constant, gnawing sense of hunger can be experienced.

The Lung Meridian
Without the lungs' ability to take in oxygen from the outside world and convert it into life-giving breath, we'd die. The lung meridian also represents communication with the outside world and our willingness to live life fully.

Allergies, skin problems, asthma, sweating, kidney problems, and digestive issues can indicate a blocked lung meridian.

Extreme worrying, feeling detached and overwhelmed, and having a scornful, intolerant disposition can indicate problems with the lung meridian.

The Large Intestine Meridian
The large intestine is situated at the end of the food's journey through our bodies. The associated meridian also represents our final evaluation of our life experiences.

Constant feelings of guilt and a lack of self-esteem, and a healthy self-image result when the large intestine meridian is blocked.

On a physical level, sinusitis, joint pain, rheumatic conditions, bronchitis, skin diseases, and stomach problems can be present.

The Kidney Meridian
In TCM, the kidneys relate to fear. A blockage in this meridian can show itself through fearfulness and anxiety, as well as aloofness which results from feeling insecure.

Possible diseases include chronic ear infections, non-age-related problems with eyesight, lower back problems, bone marrow and bone density issues, incontinence, prostate, and reproductive problems.

The Urinary Bladder Meridian
This is the longest meridian, running from the top of the head to the soles of the feet. In TCM, it has a close connection to the kidney meridian. Infections from sinusitis to chronic cystitis can therefore occur when this meridian is blocked.

In addition, eye and ear diseases, sciatica, and issues with the reproductive system can be experienced.

The emotions expressed can include acute restlessness, frustration, and impatience.

The San Jiao/Triple Burner Meridian

All hormonal glands are included in this meridian. It represents our inspiration to act powerfully and energetically.

Fever or shivers, headaches, and a sore throat can result from an imbalance or blockage in this meridian.

Feelings of despair, hopelessness, loneliness, and isolation can be experienced.

The Pericardium Meridian

A person's zest for life and his/her level of motivation are closely connected to this meridian in TCM. The libido is also linked.

Possible diseases include heart and angina problems, feelings of pressure in the heart area, pain in the lung area, spasms, bad blood circulation, hernias, and gastritis.

On the psychological level, a blockage here can result in manic emotional episodes, delirium, and experiencing a lack of joy in life in general.

OPENING THE FLOW OF QI WITH SOUND

THE CHINESE DEVELOPED A SYSTEM CALLED QIGONG TO CLEAR blockages and balance meridians to ensure qi flows freely through the body.

A BRIEF HISTORY

Qigong dates back more than 4,000 years. It has roots in Chinese culture, philosophy, medicine, and martial arts. It involves slow, coordinated movements, sounds, and meditation.

Liu Guizhen is the man credited with giving the system its name. In 1947, at 27 years of age, Guizhen was sent home to his village from his job as a clerk for the Communist Party due to his critical health. He suffered from tuberculosis and nervous system problems, as well as severe gastric ulcers. He weighed less than 80 pounds.

His uncle claimed to know the secrets of a Buddhist tradition called Neiyang gong and decided to teach his nephew how to practice it to save his life.

The next 100 days under the guidance of his uncle were grueling. Guizhen was not allowed to speak, wash, or receive visitors. He had to practice a series of movements every other waking hour and had to drink four to five thermos bottles of water per day, two of which had to be boiled water.

The exercises involved a lot of breathwork and mantras.

At the end of this period, Guizhen had gained 30 pounds and was a healthy man. He returned to work, much to the amazement of the Communist officials. They were eager to learn Guizhen's secret because China's people were suffering after the war, and there were very few doctors.

He returned to his uncle and learned everything he could. His uncle told him the real secret was this: Chanting a silent mantra while focusing all the attention on a point below the navel slows down brain activity. That allows the organs to strengthen and heal on their own accord.

The communist party instructed Guizhen to standardize and simplify all the elements of the system and remove any religious and feudal connotations. They also changed the name to the more neutral word qigong, which has no roots in Buddhism.

In 1964, the official party line changed, and the political leaders tried to eradicate the practice of qigong. Guizhen was imprisoned, and the institutions where it was practiced were closed.

Its popularity was revived in 1978 and has endured to this day (Voigt, 2013).

QIGONG TODAY

In qigong, the emphasis has shifted from spiritual enlightenment to health and fitness. In China, it has been recognized as standard medical practice since 1989. In the Western tradition, it is still regarded as an alternative therapy to mainstream medicine.

THE FIVE ELEMENTS

The original masters of qigong studied nature closely and concluded that the human body functions in synchronization with the elements and seasons found in nature.

The movements and the associated healing sounds were developed to bring the body gently back into the same rhythm as the earth's cycles to achieve balance.

They identified five elements, and each one is associated with a season, color, sound, and system of organs (Flood, 2016).

Element	Organ	Color	Season	Sound
Wood	Liver	Green	Spring	Shoo
Fire	Heart	Red	Summer	Haaw
Earth	Spleen	Yellow	Late summer	Whoo
Metal	Lungs	White	Fall	Tzzz
Water	Kidneys	Blue	Winter	Ch-way
Triple Burner	Harmonizer			S-Hee (done silently)

AN EXERCISE TO STRENGTHEN THE WOOD ELEMENT

The wood element represents energy for life, freedom, and high spirits. A strong presence of this element reflects creativity and flexibility.

- Stand in the basic qigong stance, which is feet apart shoulder-width, knees slightly bent, and hands hanging loosely by the sides. The mouth should be closed with the tongue against the upper palate, and the gaze should be fixed on the far horizon.
- Put one foot forward and turn your body 90 degrees to the other side while swinging your arms along. Breathe in while

you twist and exhale as you come back to the starting position (Isahak, 2005).

AN EXERCISE TO STRENGTHEN THE FIRE ELEMENT

Our connection to ourselves and to everything else in the universe is influenced by the strength of the fire element. It brings a calm and controlled life filled with compassion for all beings.

- This exercise starts with a meditative posture—lotus if you can. Otherwise, just sit comfortably in a chair. Keep your hands resting comfortably on your knees with your palms facing upward.
- Bring your heels together and fold your hands in front of your chest in the Eastern greeting posture. Breathe in, then bend forward slightly while exhaling and contemplating compassion.
- After four to six repeats of the movement, fold your arms and bend down fully while exhaling. Hold the position for a couple of moments while resolving to be more loving and tolerant (Isahak, 2005).

AN EXERCISE TO STRENGTHEN THE EARTH ELEMENT

The earth element is interpreted as being about caring for oneself, others, and the environment.

- Start with the basic stance. Bend one leg up behind you and grab that foot with both hands. Stretch the leg gently while breathing in. Exhale while relaxing and letting go of the foot, taking care to keep your balance (Isahak, 2005).

AN EXERCISE TO STRENGTHEN THE METAL ELEMENT

A harmonious metal element brings with it clarity of mind and freedom from prejudices and the ability to let go of emotions that no longer serve you.

- Stand in the basic stance and lift your outstretched arms toward the sky, palms facing upward while breathing in. Lower your arms with the palms facing downward while exhaling.
- Do four to six repetitions. On the last one, bend down completely as far as you can go while stretching your arms backward and locking your thumbs with the index fingers pointing up. Do three to six cycles of breathing in and out in this position.
- Straighten up on the next inhalation with your arms pointing skyward again. Breathe out and bring your arms down the last time (Isahak, 2005).

AN EXERCISE TO STRENGTHEN THE WATER ELEMENT

This element is about the self—who you are and where you are going.

- Stand in the basic stance and raise your arms no higher than your waist with your palms turned outward. Keep your posture right, with the lower spine as straight as possible and the upper spine relaxed without hunching over.
- Visualize qi entering your body through the top of your head and flowing down your spine in a river of white light. Imagine the qi energizing your brain, spine, and all of the organs and body systems.
- Next, sit down on the floor with your legs outstretched. Bend forward slightly while stretching your arms out with your palms facing upward. Breathe in and slowly swing your arms to the side as if you are swimming, and straighten your back again. Breathe out and bring your arms back to your chest.
- Repeat the whole cycle four to six times (Isahak, 2005).

USING THE ASSOCIATED ELEMENTAL SOUNDS

The sounds associated with each element, as shown in the table earlier in this section, can be incorporated with the exercises or used on their own.

There is a sound for each element and a sixth sound to harmonize them all.

The tones should be made in a steady voice except for the sixth sound, which will be made silently and in the middle range of the voice where it is comfortable for you. Each sound should be repeated at least five times, with the sixth one always last.

The order in which you voice them is not important. You can also hone in on the specific tone that is associated with an organ or system you are concerned about.

The sounds create vibrations that act like a massage for the organs, thereby healing and stabilizing them.

There are no standardized movements with the sounds, and many variations exist. The basic premise from which all of them start is that wood (trees) grow upward, fire moves in all directions, earth expands horizontally, metal contracts and holds, and water flows downward. You can improvise your own movements along these lines (Voigt, 2012).

The following section contains guidelines for visualizations that accompany each sound to make full use of its qualities. Remember that organs don't correspond strictly with only the anatomical pinpoints we give them. The following visualizations target entire organ systems.

In every instance, inhale as deeply as is comfortable through the nose and exhale while silently making the sound.

- Liver: While making the sound, use your imagination to guide the qi (white light) up from the inner sides of your big toes. Let it move up along the insides of the thighs, through the abdomen, and up to the throat. Allow the qi to move to the eyes, forehead, and right up to the crown of the head. Turn it back to move down into the lungs, flow down the inner sides of the arms, and end at the outer tips of the thumbs before inhaling.

- Heart: Imagine the qi starting on the outer sides of the big toes this time and moving up along the inner legs to enter the abdomen. From there, let it move to the upper chest and armpits and flow along the inner arms, ending at the inside tips of the little fingers.
- Spleen: Start once again on the outer sides of the big toes and allow the qi to move up the inner sides of the legs into the abdomen. From there, guide the light to the stomach and then into the upper chest. Upon reaching the chest, imagine the qi dividing into two streams. The first stream brings the qi to the throat and lets it flow under the tongue. At the same time, the second stream moves the qi into the inner arms and allows it to flow down to the inside tips of the little fingers.
- Lungs: Starting the flow of the brilliant white light that is qi at the inner sides of the big toes, imagine it traveling up the inner legs and entering the abdomen. From there, let it move up into the lungs. The qi ends its round by flowing down the inner sides of the arms, ending at the inner tips of both thumbs.
- Kidney: From the balls of the feet, visualize the qi moving up through the inner thighs. Let it flow along the spine and enter the kidneys. Imagine it moving into the chest before going down the inner arms and ending in the tips of the middle fingers.
- Triple burner: To harmonize and unite all the other sounds, visualize the qi starting at the outer tips of the fourth toes. See it moving up the outer legs into the sides of the torso. From there, allow the white light to flow to the sides of the neck and enter the head. Let it move back down again along the sides of the head, through the neck, over the shoulders, and along the backs of the arms, to end at the outside tips of the ring fingers (Voigt, 2012).
- When you've done one set of exercises, you can repeat them while gently shaking your body. This is a natural way of getting rid of all trapped stress and concerns.

❧ 17 ❧

EMOTIONAL SOUND HEALING
SECRETS

W e all go through an emotional dip at times. Some bouts of the blues occur after a traumatic or sad event, but sometimes we are simply caught off guard by it.

In times like these, it would be nice to have a magic solution, but that's just wishful thinking. Or is it?

Sound healing and balancing can make such a profound difference to your emotional and mental state that it can seem like magic.

Suppose you think back to the introduction of this book for a moment. You might remember us talking about all particles of the universe, including those that make up our bodies, being in constant movement and vibration.

When something upsets this vibrational pattern, the cells retain a memory of the event, and the energy becomes stagnant. That can cause long-term emotional problems.

Tuning in to the right sounds and music can erase the memory and restore the proper balance needed for a happy, relaxed life.

THE RELATIONSHIP BETWEEN SOUND HEALING AND INTUITION

Intuition refers to our innate ability to perceive things directly from the universe. We are all born with it, but as life progresses, we often choose to ignore intuitive messages to the point where it feels as though we have lost the capability.

We never lose it, however, and with the right stimulation and intention to allow intuition back into our lives, it can open up again and become our greatest ally in sound healing.

WHAT IS INTUITION?

One of the most concise explanations of the nature of intuition can be found in the Japanese word for the concept. It consists of three written characters that represent directness, perception, and power.

When we allow our direct perception to be active, we once again become capable of discerning the truth in all matters, including the real roots of ailments and emotional upsets.

Intuition awakens our consciousness of being a part of the one source of creation that unites us all. There is one common thread flowing through all of creation: vibration.

Synchronicities and flashes of insight become commonplace, and it gets much easier to reach the heart of any disease—whether in ourselves or others.

An active intuitive life raises our vibration, and it becomes easier to be in tune with positive emotions. This also makes it easier for a healer to distinguish between lighter, higher vibrations and the heavier, denser ones that are present in someone in need of healing.

INTUITION AND MUSIC

The legendary Albert Einstein said that great scientists are artists too. True knowledge cannot exist without true, intuitive beauty.

The same is true about our health, and music is one of the best ways to awaken our intuitive road to complete wellness.

To Einstein, the only difference between science, including formal music, and intuition was the language in which the subject matter was presented. If it was expressed in terms of logic and formally accepted scientific concepts, it qualified as science. If it dealt with what he called "forms whose constructions are not accessible to the conscious mind but are recognized intuitively," Einstein grouped a project with intuition (Root-Bernstein & Root-Bernstein, 2010).

It is clear that music can access our essence at the base level and bring about positive changes if we allow it to.

THE ROLE OF INTENTION

Healing with sound is one of the most powerful healing modalities available to us, but without the intention to heal, sound remains just another tool. A healing intention lifts the process to magical heights.

Sound healing expert Jonathan Goldman explains this in terms of a formula: Frequency + intent = healing (Goldman, 2009c).

While frequency represents the actual sound, Goldman describes intent as the energy behind the music or sound that gives it its power.

He relates a confusing experience in his authoring life when he was writing a book on the different mantras and sounds used in healing and their results. He noticed that many of the gurus had different takes on which sound and mantra worked for which organ and where each sound resonated. That did not make sense to Goldman because he was trying to compile a system for sound healing.

He then experienced an "aha" moment when he realized that many of the experts get positive results because of their intentions. The sound and mantra are not the essential ingredients—the intention with which they are used is. All the healers intended to help their clients and facilitate their road back to optimum wellness, and those are the results they produced, regardless of where they felt resonance or which sound they used for an organ.

It is easy to prove this to yourself from everyday experiences. Have you ever met someone you haven't seen in a while and felt, after their enthusiastic greeting, that they would have preferred not to run into you?

We perceive the intention behind sounds on a subconscious level, and we also respond to the intention on a subconscious level.

Goodman uses the example of a kinesiology experiment in which people's muscle strength was tested after listening to ocean sounds infused with good wishes from others. Another group was also tested after listening to wave sounds infused with anger and bad feelings. While listening to the sounds infused with love, light, and happiness, the test participants' muscles stayed strong. When tested while listening to the "bad-vibe" ocean sounds, this group's muscles became weak. Their physical structure and responses were influenced by the intentions captured within the sounds they were listening to.

When working with vibrations, you can visualize the sound coming to you like a current. If you are the healer, your current has to be positive—but so, too, if you are the receiver of a treatment. Energy follows intention because intention vibrates molecules.

BRAIN WAVE STATES

Our brains function through ongoing electrical impulses that measure only a few millionths of a volt. These waves vary with the different states our brains are in and the activities we are occupied with.

Five frequencies are widely used in scientific literature and can be measured on an EEG scan, as shown in the table below (Abhang et al., 2016).

Frequency	Brain State	Associated Activities
0.5–4 Hz	Delta	Sleeping; being in a deep trance
4–8 Hz	Theta	Deeply relaxed; focused; meditative; "in the zone"
8–12 Hz	Alpha	Passively attentive and very relaxed; observant
12–35 Hz	Beta	Alert but still relaxed, paying active attention to outside stimuli; anxiety-prone
35-80 Hz	Gamma	Deep concentration and hyper-focus; consciously paying attention and recalling memories

Brain wave patterns are as unique as fingerprints and can vary in different parts of the brain at the same time.

Low-frequency brain waves are activated when we listen to music, and our brains and bodies synchronize themselves to it.

This makes music one of the most powerful tools in a sound healing arsenal. It calms down the nervous system so that intuition can come through.

To prove this, Goldman explains his experience with shamans and other healers who are in deep trances, and their brain waves are measured at the delta frequency, during which they, theoretically, should have been asleep. They are, however, alert and talking, often channeling higher guidance in the trance state (2009c).

A MEDITATION TO SLOW DOWN

While listening to some calming music (that can be found anywhere online) through earphones for the best effect, close your eyes and try the following short meditation to experience the calming effect of music while still concentrating and raising your vibration.

- Sit comfortably, or lie down, with the music swirling around you. Feel the music going through you.

- Breathe in deeply and imagine taking the sound with your breath into your heart.
- Exhale completely and visualize the music moving through your heart and out again, taking restlessness and frustration with it.
- Try that a couple of times and feel your heart slowing down any knots in your stomach loosening.
- Now, think of anyone or anything you are grateful for. It could be a pet, a sibling, a partner, or something material such as your home.
- Visualize the person, object, or place while breathing in the music... and out again.
- Next, imagine a beautiful rose-gold cloud starting to form around you. See the cloud moving up and connecting to a huge rose-gold cloud from the universe.
- See your cloud being carried on the sound of the music and merging with the universe's loving rose-gold cloud. Feel the peace of coming home and being loved and well.
- Hold this oneness inside your mind for as long as the music is playing.
- Open your eyes and carry the calm, loving, peaceful feeling with you as you go about the rest of your day.

OUR OWN MUSIC

All of us have music inside us. We can call upon our personal sounds in times of emotional turmoil if we would only realize they are there.

Heartbeats, sighs, and breathing are all forms of sound therapy that are freely available to us. If you know how to utilize them, they are powerful aids in mobilizing every human being's innate ability to heal and balance themselves.

THE HEARTBEAT

It is no coincidence that your heart races when you are upset and slows down when you feel calm. Besides the physical requirements of getting more blood to the vital organs more quickly, the sound and feel of a heart beating fast speeds up our reactions and helps to create a sense of urgency.

A racing heart in favorable situations, such as being in love, also prepares us for action.

Musicians have known and used this fact through the ages to create specific emotions and experiences with their music. Even without a melody, the varying tempi in a shaman's drumming are crucial to the start, development, and call-back from a shamanic journey.

It is not only events but also decision-making that can lead to much stress and upset. Sometimes, the importance of a decision gets so overwhelming that we can't think straight anymore, and feelings of depression are not uncommon.

Allow your heart to take the lead. Open your mind to its guidance; invite it to soothe your emotions and give you a clear mind.

Let's do an easy meditation exercise together to help you get more in touch with your heart.

- Sit or lie down in a comfortable place where you'll be undisturbed for about 20 minutes.
- Close your eyes if you feel comfortable doing so, or fix a soft, unfocused gaze somewhere ahead.
- Breathe in deeply from your stomach without lifting your shoulders, hold your breath for a moment or two, and exhale fully. Visualize blowing out all the feelings of stress on your breath and see them leave you.
- Try to keep your mind neutral, but don't force anything—you do not have to stop thinking. See the thoughts coming and going like fish swimming past in an aquarium.
- Breathe in again and visualize the breath going into your heart, opening it up. Breathe out again.
- Put one hand over your heart now and breathe into it again. Hold the thought in your mind that you are touching something sacred given to you by the universe. Hold the breath in your heart for a moment before releasing it fully.

- Still holding your hand gently over your heart, breathe in again and send the gentlest of hugs to your heart on your breath. Feel warm gratitude for the power of your heart flooding your being. Breathe out again.
- Keep breathing in... Caressing and thanking your heart... And breathing out again for as long as you want.
- When you feel ready, open your eyes and move your body.
- Keep that open, loving feeling in and around you when you go on with your day. Give your brain a break if it has been doing a lot of hard work lately. Leave the doubts, second-guessing, and limiting beliefs behind and move to the song of your heart.

BREATHING AND SIGHING

Every inhalation brings life force to our existence. With every sigh and exhalation, we have the opportunity to get rid of everything that opposes our life force and makes our existence difficult.

Since ancient times, people have viewed breathing as an equivalent to life. One of the best examples of this is the Egyptian Books of Breathing, dating back to about 350 BCE. They were texts intended to teach people how to continue living in the afterlife. The first chapter starts with these words: "Do not show this script to anybody. It may benefit only the shades who, confined to the Underworld, are reborn endlessly in the breath of truth" (Balsamo & Dagnese, 2012).

A scientific study conducted in Australia to assess the physiological impact of slow, deep breathing found that feeling better when breathing consciously is not all in the mind. The scientists found that controlled slow breathing changes the parameters of bodily systems that significantly influence health and longevity. The systems include heart rate, the strength of respiratory muscles, and the efficiency of oxygen exchange. They also found slow breathing toned the vagus nerve. The vagus nerve stimulates the parasympathetic nervous system, which in turn, sends signals to the body to relax and calm down (Russo et al., 2017).

In our hectic modern lifestyles, we have forgotten how powerful breathing can be. Taking deep, controlled breaths is the last thing on our minds when we have to take care of a stressful job, family responsibilities, and health and environmental challenges.

Take a moment to become aware of your breathing and use your sighs as vehicles to get rid of the tension stored in your body.

Incorporate sound in your deep breathing by doing an exercise that is called the lion's breath (simhasana) in Sanskrit.

- Sit comfortably and lean forward slightly, supporting your hands on your knees.
- Keep your fingers spread as widely as possible without putting stress on your fingers or hands.
- Inhale deeply through your nose.
- Now open your mouth widely and stick your tongue out, stretching it down toward your chin.
- Exhale forcefully, feeling the breath move over the back of your tongue and make a deep "haaa" sound.
- Be aware of the vibrations the sound sends through your body and welcome them.
- Breathe normally a couple of times.
- Repeat the lion's breath six or seven times.
- A quieter breath-sound exercise that will also allow you to experience powerful calming vibrations is known as the humming bee breath.
- Sit comfortably with your eyes closed or your unfocused gaze fixed somewhere ahead.
- Keep your back straight.
- Close your ears with your index or middle fingers.
- Keep your mouth closed but leave a slight opening between your upper and lower teeth.
- Breathe deeply through your nose without moving your shoulders, allowing your abdomen to expand.
- Exhale while making a smooth, humming sound like a bee. The sound need not be loud.
- Continue breathing this way for about five minutes, keeping full awareness of the vibrations throughout your body.

If any thoughts pop up during this time, put them aside gently for later. Try to remember them after the exercise—they might be answers you've been seeking for a long time.

A MEDITATION TO UNIFY THE HEART AND THE BREATH

Try this effective but straightforward meditation to combine your heart and breathing into a powerful inner symphony to calm and heal you. Do it once a day for a month and see if you experience any benefits from it.

It involves three deep breaths.

- Stand comfortably with your feet spread slightly wider than your shoulders, as if your body is in the form of a pyramid.
- Place your hands gently over your heart.
- Inhale deeply and calmly while visualizing the breath coming in through your feet, moving up through your legs, hips, abdomen, and chest, and reaching your heart.
- Exhale with a forceful sigh. Imagine expelling the breath from your heart, taking with it all the stagnant energy that was trapped in your lower body.
- Visualize your feet safely and firmly connected to the earth.
- For the second breath, extend your arms fully above your head. Imagine your body forming an upside-down pyramid that points at your heart.
- Breathe in again, and while you listen to the sound of your breath, visualize it coming in through the top of your head, moving down through your brain, face, neck, shoulders, upper back, and chest, and reaching your heart.
- Exhale again forcefully while imagining expelling stagnant energy on the breath from your upper body as well as your mind.
- Visualize an open communication channel to the divine energy of the cosmos, stretching through your arms upward.
- The third breath will balance the earth and sky energies in the heart.

- Lower your arms and place your hands again over your heart.
- Inhale audibly and deeply through your nose, and visualize the breath entering your heart.
- Exhale forcefully and visualize the breath going out from your heart again.
- Stand quietly for a moment and savor the quiet, calm feeling of connectedness.
- Take this feeling with you wherever you go for the rest of the day.

EARTH'S OWN MUSIC

Did you know the earth has a song vibrating at its own frequency? It is known as the Schumann resonances. You can tap into it, too, and use its healing properties to enhance your life.

In 1952, the German scientist Winfried Otto Schumann, who was a professor at the Technische Hochschule in Munich, suggested the existence of low-frequency resonances in the cavity formed between the earth's surface and the ionosphere. The ionosphere is the very top part of the earth's atmosphere that borders space, stretching from 50 to 400 miles above the earth (Besser, 2007).

The Schumann resonances are electromagnetic frequencies in the extremely low range of 7 to 8 Hz. The electromagnetic waves are put into motion by lightning strikes all over the planet that happen many times per second.

These frequencies also resonate with 432 Hz.

MUSIC THERAPY

We are more than physical bodies. We have mental, spiritual, and emotional bodies too. All these facets that make up a human being have to synchronize in tempo and musical key. Otherwise, the music that emanates from us is fragmented and dissonant.

Emotions act as the conductor of the orchestra, and when they are upset, everything tends to get into a shambles.

When our emotions are positive, on the other hand, scientific research has proven all our systems run smoothly (McCraty et al., 1995).

This dynamic interaction is known in biology as coherence.

The right music can play an essential role in obtaining coherence in the body when we allow ourselves to adapt to its constant rhythm. This is called entrainment.

An article published in the Journal of Music Therapy noted that even the sound of a metronome at a steady, relaxing 66 beats per minute reduced anxiety more effectively than sitting in silence (Gadberry, 2011).

Our emotions also vibrate. Negative emotions such as anger and resentment vibrate at a lower frequency than positive feelings. Listening to the right music can lift the vibration of negative emotions and thereby influence our emotional well-being.

ANXIETY AND DEPRESSION

Music therapy and other forms of sound healing have been effective in helping sufferers of anxiety, panic attacks, and depression. Even when only used in conjunction with conventional forms of therapy, studies have found higher success rates with those who received a musical component in tandem (Erkkilä et al., 2011).

The brain processes the rhythm, tempo, and pitch in separate locations, and when all of these combine in a calming experience, it can change a person's life for the better.

Music therapy is so effective because it targets a part of our emotional and mental makeup that has existed even before speech. Linear, logical cognitive reasoning is less likely to interfere with calming anxiety and lifting depression on a subconscious level when one is engrossed in music therapy.

On a physiological level, partaking in an enjoyable activity (such as becoming engrossed in the bliss of music) causes the brain to release the hormone dopamine, which is known as the "pleasure hormone," as well as endorphins, also known as "feel-good hormones," which are chemical components capable of reducing stress.

Anxious reactions to outside stimuli occur when our fight-or-flight response gets activated. While the ancient human had to contend with real tigers and lions chasing them, our modern society has symbolic wild animals baying for our blood, such as hectic work schedules, deadlines, and a never-ending stream of text and email messages. We rarely become mindful enough to turn off the adrenaline and cortisol rush of fight-or-flight, and it has negative consequences for our emotions and bodies.

Calming down the nervous inner chatter helps us to settle the stress responses, too. Music works on the body's parasympathetic nervous system, which is the network that allows us to feel safe, settled, and supported.

When the parasympathetic system is activated, the sympathetic network stops producing the inflammation-inducing hormone cortisol, and adrenaline production decreases rapidly.

If music vibrates at a frequency that is especially beneficial to our emotions, a quiet and calm sympathetic nervous network opens the way for our bodies to take on these healing frequencies and find their own inner harmony again.

A HEALING MEDITATION FOR DEPRESSION

Play your choice of soothing music or soundscape in the background while doing this guided meditation. (If you want to listen to solfeggio frequencies, 741 Hz facilitates change and helps us find our inner, true voice again. An alternative is the universal frequency of 528 Hz.)

- Settle down in a comfortable position and close your eyes if you are comfortable doing so. If not, you can direct an unfocused, soft gaze to the floor.
- Be gentle with yourself and listen to the needs of your body. If it needs to lie down, do so. If your body wants you to sit, perhaps in a favorite armchair, honor its request.
- Become aware of the feeling of your feet on the floor or your legs touching the fabric of the chair. Allow this

sensation to assure you that you are grounded and safe on a solid surface.

- Place one of your hands over your heart and position the other one over your lower belly.
- Inhale deeply through your nose, feeling your belly rising as you pull the life-giving breath entering and filling you.
- Slowly exhale completely, feeling your belly flatten again.
- And breathe in again deeply into your belly... And out completely.
- Be conscious of the air nourishing every muscle and cell in your body, moving through you and bringing new life.
- And breathe in again deeply into your belly... And out completely. Imagine the exhaled breath carrying away any heaviness and sadness from every corner of your being.
- Become aware of a sensation of lightness in your body.
- Continue breathing this way for a minute or two, focusing on the rhythm of your breathing and your feeling of freedom and lightness only.
- [Pause]
- Getting distracted is also okay, be gentle with yourself. Just return your attention to your breathing.
- Feel yourself opening up to make space for gratitude and feeling at ease after the heaviness has left.
- [Pause]
- Look at yourself with compassion and recognize the heavy burden you have been carrying, living with depression. Assure yourself that you understand why you feel depleted and used up, and hug yourself mentally for staying strong for so long.
- Give yourself the time and kindness that your struggle with depression deserves.
- If your inner voice comes up with judgment and accusations, breathe compassion and love into it and see it dissolve on your exhaled breath.
- Become aware of the easy stillness that has come into the core of your being and savor its presence.

- Allow yourself to hope again for a better today, a better tomorrow, and a better life.
- Breathe in again deeply into your belly... And out completely.
- Feel the breath moving through your body and fill you from your toes up to the crown of your head.
- Remembering the easy stillness, open your eyes when you are ready.

BINAURAL BEATS

Another popular concept in New Age terminology is binaural beats. Some people believe in their effectiveness firmly, while others reject the claims as hype over nothing.

They can be a great aid in sound healing, however. Let's look at what binaural beats really are and how they work.

WHAT ARE BINAURAL BEATS, AND HOW DO THEY WORK?

One way to describe this phenomenon would be to think of binaural beats as an auditory brain illusion with real effects. A binaural beat can be described as a beat (rhythm) created entirely by the brain.

Binaural beats only work when listening through stereo head-phones. A tone at one frequency is played in one ear, and a tone with a slightly different frequency is played in the other ear at the same time. The sounds arrive independently at the inferior colliculus in the midbrain, which is where auditory input is processed. The brain combines the two different tones into a new frequency that creates a pulsing effect, which is perceived as one incoming sound. The sound that is heard does not actually exist.

It is easy to test whether you are hearing binaural beats or regular, acoustic beats. If you lift one stereo headphone from your ear, you will hear only one tone playing in the other ear. The same is true for the other side if you reverse the process. If you replace both earphones, the pulsing beat will be back. That is proof that the frequencies are "mixed" by your brain and not by the speakers before the sounds reach your ears.

The frequencies are chosen to align with the frequencies of the five states of brain waves. The brain aligns itself with the combined frequency it hears in what is known as the frequency-following effect.

It is, therefore, possible to induce a specific brain wave frequency by listening to binaural beats of the right frequency. This is what is meant by brain entrainment—you align your brain to a desired and chosen mental state.

Brain entrainment can work negatively, for example, in people with epilepsy. Seizures can be triggered by flashing lights or certain rhythms in music that entrain the brain to a frequency where it malfunctions. This is usually due to the specific person's physical makeup.

The brain waves involved are the five main states discussed earlier in this chapter. Just to recap, they are, from slowest to fastest:

- Delta: Deep sleep, healing, intense meditation, and accessing the subconscious.
- Theta: Meditation, relaxation, and creative activities.
- Alpha: Focus, learning activities, positive thoughts, and relaxation.
- Beta: Sharply focused, solving problems, analytical thinking, and energetic.
- Gamma: Advanced cognitive action, great attention to detail, and unorthodox creativity.

Medical opinions regarding the effectiveness of binaural beats are divided, but research is ongoing.

Sound therapists and healers have been using them successfully for many years to alleviate anxiety and combat depression. They have even been used by out-of-body practitioners to achieve their transcendent states.

It is worth noting that some studies found binaural beats in the lower frequencies (theta and delta) increased depression, while those in the higher frequencies, such as beta, consistently lowered anxiety levels and decreased depression.

The same holds true for memory enhancement or hindering. Higher frequencies produced better memory recall, while slower frequencies interfered with it (Chaieb et al., 2015).

It is important to remember that humans are very different from each other, despite our similarities. Experiment with binaural beats (taking full responsibility for your own well-being) until you find a frequency that suits your desired effect.

Important Things to Remember

When starting out with binaural beats, it can be tempting to overdo it to speed up results. It will, however, not work that way.

- Start with slower frequencies rather than quick ones to give your brain a chance to adapt to the new pattern.
- Listen through the whole track from start to finish. Don't jump to the middle, thinking you'll get to the powerful stuff more quickly. The tracks are designed to work up to a climax and back down again. It is a bit like warming up first in the gym before starting your exercise routine.
- Limit listening time to 90 minutes daily for the first two weeks. Just like your muscles in the gym, the brain also needs time to rest between entrainment exercises.
- Don't turn the volume up too high. The brain focuses better on the sound if the volume is low. You should just be able to hear the wobbling sound of the beat.
- In the beginning, some people might experience side effects from binaural beats, such as slight nausea, headaches, and old memories and emotions resurfacing. This is natural because you are building new neural pathways in your brain and rearranging some neural elements, so to speak. The side effects will pass after a few days. Once the new pathway is formed, it will be there for you to access when you need it to change your brain wave state.

There are many binaural beat soundtracks available for free download if you want to experiment first before spending money to purchase tracks.

Keep the above guidelines in mind and start using them to your advantage.

ASMR

Another useful technique is autonomous sensory meridian response (ASMR).

The sensation of ASMR can be described as a pleasant tingling. Sensations are produced by auditory stimuli and are often felt on the scalp, neck, upper spine, and sometimes the legs. It helps people to feel more alert while remaining relaxed and deeply calm.

The stimuli can include anything from whispers, light tapping, brush strokes, and towels being folded, to loud chewing, light patterns, and playing with artificial slime.

The name autonomous sensory meridian response was coined in 2010 by Jennifer Allen. Discussions about the phenomenon started in 2007 on a Facebook group, but at that point, no one knew what to call the feelings or what caused them. Some people gave sexual content to the sensations, likening the brain tingles to an orgasm, although most people seem to agree that it has nothing to do with sexual arousal.

Allen proposed the now-accepted name to standardize the terminology and keep it neutral.

The Effects of ASMR

According to neuroscientific investigations, there are definite physiological responses when listening to these auditory inputs.

In an online interview, psychologist and neuroscientist Nick Davis explained that during an ASMR listening session, the heart rate slows, and the hairs on the skin stand on end. This is induced by the associated psychological state that the sounds trigger for the listener. Davis proposes that the sounds bring up sensations of being safe, warm, and comforted because the sounds are soft enough that you would normally only hear them if you were very close to someone (Wired, 2019).

In a study where participants watched ASMR videos in an fMRI scanner, their brains showed activity in the areas where emotions, behaviors associated with pleasing people, and empathy were located. The activities in these brain regions were previously observed by scientists when study participants listened to exceptionally moving music that caused the phenomenon known as frisson, as well as during social bonding experiences (Lochte et al., 2018).

The question can be asked whether the noisy and intimidating environment of an fMRI machine could have been inhibiting to the participants. If yes, it implies that even more brain regions could be involved that we don't know of yet.

How Is ASMR Relevant to Sound Healing?

One of the emotional symptoms commonly experienced by patients of sound healers is a feeling of isolation, often accompanied by anxiety and depression. Our modern lifestyles and the abundance of online communication are not conducive to the same degree of social contact and bonding earlier generations knew.

If the theory that one of the possible roots of ASMR lies in the grooming behavior of animals is accepted, it is easy to see how ASMR sounds that stimulate a feeling of closeness can help someone overcome thoughts of loneliness and anxiousness.

The detailed nature of some ASMR videos also points to viewers experiencing a feeling of being paid attention to by someone close to them.

Psychologist Nick Davis has suggested the possibility of an affinity for ASMR stimulation being a genetic trait. Depression and other mental conditions can also have a genetic component—maybe that is not coincidental (Wired, 2019).

The same sounds that bring comfort to lovers of ASMR can bring immense irritation and an intense aversion to others. This condition is known as misophonia and is also often genetic.

Many ASMR aficionados have a caring, emotionally vulnerable, and empathetic disposition in common, according to some scientists. They might be more open to allowing responses to external stimuli to come through in their conscious world than those with a different emotional framework (Wired, 2019).

If you look at the comments on ASMR videos posted online, it becomes clear that people experience real relief from conditions such as insomnia, mood swings, and loneliness.

ISOCHRONIC TONES

Another tool at the disposal of brain entrainment creators is the technique of using isochronic tones.

Isochronic tones are short, singular tones that come and go at regular intervals and can be used alongside binaural and monaural beats. They create sharp, distinctive sounds and are often mixed with nature sounds or soothing music.

Isochronic tones are used, together with the other types of brain entrainment techniques, to treat insomnia, anxiety, pain management, mood regulation, and attention deficit hyperactivity disorder (ADHD).

SUBLIMINAL MESSAGE-INFUSED PASSIVE HEALING

Subliminal messages can be described as information given to the brain in such a short time frame that it is not registered consciously. It falls below what is known as the absolute threshold level of our conscious awareness. Even if we focus and listen out for these messages, we would not be able to detect them. This includes auditory, sensory, and visible stimuli.

Supraliminal messages, in contrast, can be detected; we just don't necessarily notice them.

The popular story about the origins of subliminal messaging started in 1957 with a marketing researcher named James Vicary. He claimed to have boosted the sales of soda and popcorn during the screening of the Academy Award-winning film Picnic by flashing very short ads for the two products on the screen every five seconds. The ads were only 1/3,000th of a second long.

In a follow-up experiment, Vicary could not replicate these results and later admitted to lying about the whole thing.

Subsequent research found that subliminal messages can work, but they cannot force anyone to do or buy something against their will. They only work when there is an existing desire.

When used in healing techniques, subliminal messaging can strengthen the patient's intention to get better because the desire is already there—the person wants to feel better.

In a study done in England, psychologists proved that depressed people are tuned to subconscious signals and information that will reinforce their negative mental state. These individuals are unconscious of this fact and cannot consciously stop it or change their behavior (Mogg et al., 1993).

A sound healer can tap into this subconscious behavior and counter negative messages with positive statements and encouragement, coaxing the person's subconscious to start looking for positive reinforcement rather than depressing statements and information.

HOW TO MAKE YOUR OWN SUBLIMINAL MESSAGES

Hearing subliminal messages tailored to your needs and delivered in your own voice can be much more powerful than purchasing something made by a stranger.

You don't need complicated computer software or engineering-level skills to do it, either.

Download any of the free audio editors available, such as Audacity, which is simple to use and user-friendly to learn. Make sure you have a working microphone that plugs directly into your computer to get clear recordings, such as the microphones that form part of a headset.

Make a list of exactly what you want to say. Formulate your subliminal messages to the last word, so you can just read and put your emotion into it when it's time to record without having to think about the content.

Be specific. "I want to be depression-free in 90 days" is more focused on the present and precisely what you want to achieve than a blanket statement such as "I want to be happy."

Keep your messages positive. Don't concentrate on what you don't want, but rather on what you do want as a replacement for an undesired situation. "I don't want to be depressed anymore" puts the focus on the negative side of your life. Rather, use "I am not depressed anymore"—start from a perspective as if you have achieved your goal already.

Use present tense and write from your heart. You know your true desires better than anyone else.

Record your messages with your chosen music and export the file to a format that can play on your phone or computer, such as mp3. Enjoy absorbing the subliminal messages that have the power to alter your subconscious for the better.

18

TUNE YOUR BODY, MIND, AND SOUL INTO AN UPGRADED PARADIGM

Listening to a musical instrument that is out of tune grates on the mind and feelings. It just doesn't sit right, even if you're not a musical guru and can't pinpoint the problem. You just know you are uneasy, and something has to change.

The same situation happens in our bodies, minds, and souls when our inner melodies go out of tune. We get distressed and uneasy, often without knowing why. The distress can show itself in disease in the body and mind.

Sound healing can retune our inner harmonies to function together again into the glorious symphony we were created to be.

RECOVERY AND TOTAL WELLNESS THROUGH SOUND

Great progress has been made in the fields of vibrational and regenerative medicine over the last decades. This proves, even to the skeptics, that our bodies are composed of vibrations and energy. Sound waves are an integral part of manipulating and resetting our vibrations to obtain optimum wellness.

The scientist Nikola Tesla said all the secrets of the universe could be found if you think in terms of energy, frequency, and vibration.

Health is mainly about the degree of homeostasis we can achieve among all these factors. A healthy person vibrates, as a whole, at a constant tempo, and all the cells and organs are in tune with each other.

Any upset with this homeostasis can cause disease and discomfort. Bringing our energy and vibrations back to where they should be through the use of tools such as tuning forks and singing bowls is an excellent and non-invasive way to regain total wellness.

VIBRATIONAL MOVEMENT

While some vibrations consist of big waves we can see, such as ocean tides and changing seasons, there are vibrations on every scale happening in and around us all the time.

Under powerful atomic microscopes, scientists have detected nano vibrations even smaller than 1/1,000th of the diameter of a human hair. Every nano-vibration generates an electromagnetic field that influences the chemical composition responsible for the functioning of our cells. The same type of energy has been detected emitting from the hands of Reiki and Qigong practitioners (Kučera & Havelka, 2012).

Different molecules vibrate at different rates, and when there is a change in the vibrational environment, it will influence all the molecules. The influence can sometimes be for the worse.

Our behavior, thoughts, ambient temperature, and environment are some of the factors that can change the vibrational tempo in cells and molecules down to the nano level. Music can do the same thing, as shown in previous chapters.

A healthy vibrational energy system is vital for physical, mental, and spiritual health.

The right sounds at the right frequencies, combined with breathing exercises, meditation, yoga, a responsible physical exercise program, a healthy diet, and healing touch modalities such as Reiki, will be a winning formula to get yourself back on track to attain total health in all aspects.

Later in this chapter, we'll look in more detail than previously discussed at some of the tools available to practice sound healing.

ENERGY MEDICINE

One of the more recent appearances in the field of therapy is called energy medicine. While it includes some touch therapies, energy medicine is a wide concept that touches on regenerative medicine as well. Regenerative medicine is concerned with techniques to repair and replace diseased and dysfunctional tissues, cells, and organs.

The basis for energy medicine lies in quantum physics and Einstein's demonstration that energy and matter are interchangeable. No matter exists with complete certainty, but rather only with the possibility to exist. That means we can change the condition of matter by adding specific types and amounts of energy.

This principle has been in use in orthopedics to heal bone breaks where the bone failed to heal through conventional methods. This is known as a chronic nonunion fracture. Through the use of a pulsed electromagnetic field induced by specialized equipment, the same type of current is induced in a broken bone that mechanical manipulation would have produced. That helps the fracture to heal (Prestwood, 2003).

ESSENCE AND ENERGETIC RE-CREATION

We are constantly bombarded with discordant, disharmonious frequencies. Anxious or angry interactions with people, stress, noisy or polluted environments, feelings of guilt, and sadness are only a few of the sound challenges we face every day.

All of these things pull our systems out of tune, and when the disrupted condition continues long enough, we can start suffering from illness in mind and body. Practitioners of energy medicine believe the changes in our cells caused by disharmony open the gates for bacteria and viruses to enter and flourish.

Human beings consist of much more than only the sum of our physical components—we are not just biological machines like scientists once thought. We are made up of several subtle energy bodies, too, that form the whole of our being. The interaction between our energy bodies and our physical form creates our existence here on earth.

These energies can be knocked out of balance easily, and rebalancing is essential to stay true to our essence.

There are seven energy bodies, also called biofields, that have been recognized in several cultures since ancient times, although they have been referred to by many different names. They are the etheric, emotional, lower mental, higher mental, causal, soul, and integrated spiritual bodies.

- The etheric body is the closest to the physical body. It is denser than any of the other bodies. It contains the energy "master plan" of the physical body and vibrates at a slightly higher frequency than the physical.
- The emotional body is the home of our feelings and emotions.
- The lower mental body accommodates our mental processes and rational thoughts. Thoughts driven by a specific emotion can take on a material form.
- The higher mental body receives insights from the spiritual realm.
- The causal body is the doorway to the collective consciousness of all humankind.
- The soul body is pure spirit. Inspiration and information needed by the lower bodies are obtained here and filtered through to where they are needed.
- The integrated spiritual body merges all the other subtle bodies.

The lines of energy that run through all of our bodies are known by different names. The Indian Ayurvedic literature talks about nadis, while TCM calls them meridians.

The channels run through seven energy vortices that connect them, known as chakras. Chakras are depicted as spinning wheels of energy that can be thrown off balance or blocked, resulting in off-kilter energy running at the wrong vibrational tempo.

Although some ancient literature speaks of 112 chakras, there are seven that are generally recognized. It is worth outlining the chakras once again, as they are of significant importance.

The chakras are arranged through the body from low to high.

- The root chakra: Located at the base of the spine, the root chakra is the seat of our physical connection to the earth, feelings of mental stability, self-confidence, and the degree to which we feel safe and secure. It is associated with the legs and feet.
- The sacral chakra: Just above the root chakra, in the middle of the lower abdomen, and about four fingers below the navel, is the second chakra. It is connected to reproductive health, as well as the emotional side of relationships.
- The solar plexus chakra: It is situated in the area of the navel and is believed to be a meeting point for all the nadis, or energy channels, that run through the body. It is associated with self-image and digestive issues.
- The heart chakra: It is found where the physical heart is and relates to all things regarding love for the self and others.
- The throat chakra: It is at the base of the throat and rules all types of communication, the confidence to speak out for the truth, as well as the head, neck, shoulders, and mouth.
- The third eye chakra: This is located between the eyebrows and in the center of the head. It relates to the connection of the self to the spiritual world and enhances intuition.
- The crown chakra: The seventh chakra is located outside the body, at the crown of the head. It is described as a bridge between heaven and earth. Physically, the crown chakra is associated with coordination and the neurological system.

DEEP RELAXATION AND WHOLENESS

The best reset switch for our bodies and minds is deep relaxation. It turns off harmful chemical reactions, strengthens the immune system, and brings peace to our hearts.

Sound is one of the most effective ways to relax fully. A sound bath can cleanse you down to a cellular level, the way a physical soak in the tub can do for your body. The harmonic vibrations stimulate alpha and theta brain waves that make deep healing possible. The heart rate and respiratory system slow down, the blood pressure drops to relaxed levels, and stress can be released completely.

People with chronic illnesses and pain can benefit greatly from regular sound baths.

The sound is less structured than conventional music, allowing the mind to roam free of preoccupations with rhythms and melody.

Singing bowls, chimes, and gongs are some of the instruments commonly used. They are discussed in more detail throughout this book.

The effects of a sound bath are similar to those experienced with regular deep meditation.

A study undertaken by German and Austrian scientists on the effectiveness of music added to a relaxation program found definite superior results among a group who listened to music in tandem with other relaxation practices (Kappert et al., 2019).

A NEW PARADIGM OF HOLISTIC MEDICINE

The Western scientific and medical approach has always been reductionist, in contrast to the Eastern model of a holistic paradigm.

According to reductionist principles, a whole is broken down into its constituent parts to understand how it all works together. It is accepted that the whole cannot be more than the sum of its parts.

Nerves, blood cells, bones, and muscles must provide all the answers to medical questions and facilitate all treatments.

A patient is often looked at in isolation from their history and environment. This is because these factors are often viewed as irrelevant and are not taken into account regarding the patient's overall condition.

A procedure performed in a certain way and within certain parameters is expected to deliver the same results every time. Any deviations are viewed unfavorably.

Practitioners' worldview is often one of a chaotic universe that can only be managed through dissection and control.

In contrast, a holistic attitude starts from the belief that the whole can never be understood by looking at its parts only because it is much bigger than its visible parts.

Memories of the past, together with the present environment, are seen as interacting partners regarding the patient's health.

The practitioner's senses are just as much a part of the diagnosing procedure as any medical equipment.

Opposite outcomes in procedures are taken in stride because it is accepted that humans differ greatly, especially when viewed within the framework of their past.

Remedies are used just as nature created them.

To holistic health practitioners, the universe is an ordered, organic, and meaningful place to be studied and enjoyed.

Sound healing strives to be fully holistic to heal the entire person, not just one organ or one health issue.

EXPLORING THE INNER-DIMENSIONAL SOUND CHAMBER

It has been said that the cells in the body were made to regenerate themselves according to complex geometric patterns.

Assisting with this is a device created by acupressurist and Reiki master Tom Hunt, which he calls the inner-dimensional sound chamber. According to online resources, only a few of the chambers are in operation across America, but those who have been treated in them, have found the experience to be remarkably relaxing and balancing (Sound Coherence, n.d.).

The structure has a hollow framework built in a sacred geometrical pattern that is said to resemble the gridlike frame around the cosmos. Specialized music is played through the structure, creating vibrational patterns that move molecules on their most basic level to heal and relax the body.

Hunt believes an hour of sound meditation in his chamber is equivalent to a year's worth of deep meditation (Sound Coherence, n.d.).

SOUND SYNTHESIS

Sound synthesis is the process of creating a sound signal electronically without the presence of any type of acoustic source.

This has given rise to what has become known as electronic meditation. Sounds produced by a synthesizer can be played through speakers that can be embedded in recliners or massage tables to provide an immersion in vibration and sound. Techniques such as binaural beats all make use of this technology.

Another type of electronic sound healing is called bioacoustics therapy. It involves analyzing someone's voice for so-called missing frequencies. Proponents of the therapy say the missing frequencies are related to illnesses in the body and mind. They produce a recording of those frequencies, and the patient listens to the recording regularly until the vocal profile is complete.

In cymatic therapy, organs are exposed to specific frequencies and combinations of frequencies that have been carefully selected to balance and heal a particular organ (Snow, 2011).

Some people do not agree that electronic signals can deliver the same effective healing as acoustic sounds, while others believe using more electronic equipment will make the therapies more agreeable to the mainstream medical community.

SOUND BALANCING WITH TUNING FORKS

When disease alerts you to the fact that your body has gone out of rhythm, a tuning session with tuning forks could be all you need. The tuning forks stimulate the body to start its natural healing process and strengthen the immune system to assist with this.

Water, which makes up the most significant part of our bodies, carries vibrations throughout the body when tuning forks are used.

They open the energy pathways, help to remove blockages, relieve pain, and release tension.

WHAT ARE TUNING FORKS?

Tuning forks are resonating devices, meaning they can produce a sound, and they are usually made of aluminum. In earlier times, steel was used. They consist of two prongs, or tines, in a U-shape that sit on top of a handle or stem.

Tuning forks were invented in 1711 by a British musician called John Shore to tune musical instruments.

The pitch of the musical note they emit when the prongs are hit against the heel of the palm or an object is determined by the length and mass of the prongs. The device is held by the stem because the two prongs of the fork shape vibrate in opposite directions, and touching the stem does not affect its movement at all.

Tuning forks produce a pure tone. The harmonic overtone that is automatically created when the prongs are struck to start the fundamental tone dies out quickly because of the forked design, and the fundamental tone is sustained on its own for quite a while. That makes it an effective tool for sound healers.

They are manufactured to deliver frequencies from 64 Hz to 4,096 Hz and are usually sold in sets covering all the frequencies. They don't need attention too often to stay on pitch.

Some tuning forks have a round weight at the tops of each prong. The weights can slide up and down. They are called weighted tuning forks or Otto tuners. The word "Otto" is short for "osteophonic." "Osteo" relates to bones, and "phonic" to sound.

The weights can strengthen the vibration delivered, so it can reach the bones to ease joint pain.

WHAT ARE TUNING FORKS USED FOR?

Sound healing practitioners use tuning forks to relieve tension, ease muscle and joint pain, reduce inflammation by stimulating the release of nitric oxide into the bloodstream, ease muscle spasms, calm anxiety, center, ground, rebalance body systems to bring homeostasis, boost digestion, and promote deep sleep.

The vibrations work on energy channels and points in a somewhat similar way to acupuncture, only using sound instead of needles to stimulate the body.

Important Points When Shopping for Tuning Forks

There are many different types of forks available, and choosing an individual fork or set can be difficult. Which metal should it be made from, weighted or unweighted, and which frequencies are the best for my needs?

The first question to answer is what you want to use the tuning forks for. What are your intentions and needs? Do you want to use them in a healing practice with others or just on yourself? Are you still experimenting with their effects, or are you experienced in their use? What types of ailments and problems will you be treating?

It is also important to approach your choice with a gut feeling, too, not only with left-brained, logical reasoning. Some tuning forks will resonate with your soul without making a sound, and others will not. Ultimately, your decision should be based on who you are as well as on what you want to achieve.

Some sets are based on solfeggio frequencies with their roots in numerology and the digits three, six, and nine. Solar harmonic sets are based on the five elements of water, fire, earth, ether, and air. Which set are you drawn to?

Close your eyes and think of each of the sets you are considering. Do you feel any unease when thinking about one of them? If so, then another set is perhaps the one you should choose.

SOLFEGGIO TUNING FORKS

The solfeggio musical scale is part of a system believed to be old, even older than the well-known Gregorian chants that utilize them. They are also reputed to have been used in ancient Indian Sanskrit teachings and ceremonies.

Each tone comprises frequencies that are believed to impart blessings and spiritual balance to anyone listening to them.

The name solfeggio comes from the use of sol-fa syllables to denote the tones—a musical system known as solmization. Originally there were six frequencies. Three more were added later. The syllables for the first six are ut, re, mi, fa, sol, and la.

- Ut queant laxis: Liberating guilt and fear
- Resonare fibris: Undoing situations and facilitating change
- Mira gestorum: Transformation and miracles
- Famuli tuorum: Connecting/relationships
- Solve polluti: Awakening intuition
- Labii reatum: Returning to spiritual order

The six phrases now associated with the solfeggio tones formed most of the first verse of a hymn in honor of John the Baptist, written by Guido of Arezzo. Guido used the well-known hymn to teach his music students the sounds and notes of the scale—a scale that was already in existence. The hymn has led many to believe, mistakenly, that Guido was the originator of the solfeggio tones.

The knowledge of solfeggio tones was brought into modern awareness in the 1970s by the researcher and physicist Dr. Joseph Puleo. He used numerological principles to identify the first six frequencies.

They have been called the only pure tones because they are in harmony with the structure of the universe. They are also closely aligned with the Schumann resonances' frequency of 8 Hz (see the discussion of these resonances in Chapter 6).

The original frequencies are 396 Hz, 417 Hz, 528 Hz, 639 Hz, 741 Hz, and 852 Hz. The three that were added later are 174 Hz, 285 Hz, and 963 Hz. Solfeggio tuning fork sets usually include all nine frequencies.

174 Hz

This frequency is used to relieve pain and stress. Some healers describe it as a natural anesthetic that brings a sense of safety and security to all organs in the body. It has a low, soothing quality to the sound that is a good start to any grounding and centering session.

285 Hz

This is the frequency commonly used to encourage physical rejuvenation to repair damage to cells and tissues. It also targets the energetic field to repair holes in the aura, clear blockages, and align all the chakras.

396 Hz

This frequency is credited with being able to penetrate deep into our subconscious to bring freedom from fear and guilt and is also known to alleviate grief. This will remove any blocks to reaching your full potential.

It is associated with the first, or root chakra, and the color red.

417 Hz

This frequency brings about positive change and stimulates creativity, helping us find solutions to problems. It removes negative energy from a person as well as from the environment. It can assist in laying down new, healthier habits.

It can assist in loosening stiff muscles and tight joints to improve mobility.

The frequency is associated with the second or sacral chakra and the color orange.

528 Hz

This frequency is often called the universal frequency of miracles. It is believed to be capable of repairing DNA, transforming relationships, boosting spirituality, and helping a person regain their emotional equilibrium.

It is often used to relieve pain and alleviate anxiety. Many healers use it to help with weight loss because it can form new neural pathways in the brain, leading to healthier eating and lifestyle habits.

It is associated with the third or solar plexus chakra and the color yellow.

639 Hz

This is the frequency of connections. It can help to repair and strengthen relationships between people and with the self, bringing harmony if there is discord. It is also associated with making people brave enough to be emotionally vulnerable and to make intimate connections.

It is associated with the fourth or heart chakra and the color pink.

741 Hz

Also known as the detoxification frequency, 741 Hz helps to purify the body, heart, and mind of harmful intentions and residues. It awakens intuition and boosts mental clarity. It also brings the courage to speak out for one's truth.

It is associated with the fifth or throat chakra and the color blue.

852 Hz

This is the frequency that helps us to align with spiritual truths and regain our awareness of the spiritual order of all things.

It helps us to recognize illusions and see through them. It can bring about deep and meaningful dreams.

The frequency is associated with the sixth or third eye chakra and the color violet/purple.

936 Hz

The highest tone of them all brings us closer to a perfect state of unity with the spirit of the universe.

It can assist with spiritual channeling and contacting ascended masters and higher dimensions.

It is associated with the seventh or crown chakra and the colors white and gold.

SOLAR HARMONIC TUNING FORKS

A set of solar harmonic tuning forks consist of a full octave of music notes, starting at a C note and ending at the next, higher C note. Each note has a specific frequency. They are used together to utilize the intervals (distance) between the notes.

The C-note (256 Hz) and G-note (384 Hz) together are specifically effective. The interval between them is known as a perfect fifth. They vibrate together at a ratio of 2:3. That means the C-tuning fork vibrates twice as fast as an unstruck C-fork of 128 cycles per second, while the G-tuning fork vibrates three times as fast as that unstruck C.

It is a ratio that is considered sacred in many traditions and is associated with the relationship between mathematics and the universe.

According to some legends, the Greek mathematician Pythagoras considered this interval to be extremely therapeutic and capable of transformation. A set consisting of these two tuning forks only is also known as a Pythagorean set.

The frequencies are, in Hertz:

- 256 (C)
- 288 (D)
- 320 (E)
- 341.3 (F)
- 384 (G)
- 426.7 (A)
- 480 (B)
- 512 (C)

Harmonic tuning forks also work with the five elements of the universe, as explained in Ayurvedic teachings. These are space/ether, air, fire, water, and earth.

A person's health and personality depend on the mix of these five elements contained within them. When one element goes out of balance, the person will not be completely well.

Space/Ether

This is the element of emptiness. It is specifically associated with the mouth, ears, and hearing—cavities that are to be filled by other elements.

Air

Air represents movement, lightness, breathing, and oxygen in Ayurveda (a system of natural medicine thousands of years old, with its origins in India). In excess, it can cause hyperactivity. Deficiency in the air element can bring fatigue. Digestive, heart and joint health are associated with this element.

Fire

Linked to the mind, thoughts, emotions, and obsessions, fire is a powerful Ayurvedic element. Physically, it is linked to the eyes and body temperature.

Water

The element of water is associated with the nervous system, blood supply, joints, saliva, and respiratory system.

Earth

The last to note is the grounding element, representing our bones, teeth, nails, and sense of smell. An overall and inexplicable feeling of weakness in the whole body is also associated with an earth element that is not in harmony with the others.

FIBONACCI TUNING FORKS

Another way to use intervals (the distance between two notes that can harness healing vibrations) is by working with tuning forks created according to a Fibonacci number sequence.

A spiraling sound effect is created when two forks are used together that can be used to balance the nervous system, increase creativity, heal trauma, and break addictions.

These forks are sold in sets of eight. If you already have a harmonic set, it is only necessary to purchase four Fibonacci tuners to have a complete set; the two notes of C, the note of G, and the note of A are already part of a harmonic set.

- The interval 1/1 is used to symbolize the beginning of all things, to which everything will return again.
- The interval 1/2 is associated with space. It balances the element of space/ether and helps to cope with loss and grief.
- The interval 2/3 represents balance and works with the nervous system and pituitary gland. It is a good interval to center yourself.

- The interval 3/5 is associated with dreams. In music, it is a sixth interval that is also sometimes called the mystic fire. It helps with the visualization and creation of new ideas.
- The interval 5/8 works with the inner voice. It helps you to access your inner wisdom and peace.
- The interval 8/13 represents the mystical pathway for clean and pure alignment with the source of the universe.
- The interval 13/21 is associated with the great divide between spiritual truths and earthly reality. It assists in establishing communication with higher beings such as angels.
- The interval 21/34 represents the eye of God/god. It relates to the pineal gland and helps us to understand higher realms and see eternal truths in ourselves.

HOW TO USE TUNING FORKS TO RELIEVE PAIN

Now it is time to get practical. Let's look at three different ways to treat joint and muscle pain, as explained by Jane Satchwell, the Vice-Principal of the Sound Healing Academy in Cornwall in the United Kingdom (2019).

USING A 174 Hz UNWEIGHTED TUNING FORK

In this technique, the tuning fork is not used directly on the body but just slightly away from it.

- Activate the tuning fork by tapping it lightly on a rubber puck or striking it gently with a mallet. The sound will ring clearly and cleanly.
- Hold the ringing tuning fork close to the painful area of the body without actually touching it.
- Reactivate the tuning fork when the sound dies down.
- Keep this up for five to 10 minutes.

Using Either a 128 Hz Tuning Fork or a 136.1 Hz Weighted Tuning Fork

Weighted tuning forks are used directly on painful or afflicted areas of the body. Their sound is somewhat muted when compared with unweighted tuners.

- Activate the tuning fork.
- Place the lower end of the tuning fork (the stem) on the muscle or joint that is causing pain. Feel the vibrations of the ringing sound going into your body.
- Reactivate the sound before it dies down completely.
- Keep this up for as long as needed to reduce the discomfort and pain.

Using a Weighted 128 Hz Tuning Fork and a 136.1 Hz Tuning Fork Together

The dissonance created by the pitches of these two tuning forks, when close together, causes strong vibrations that make it easier to dislodge any stuck energy.

- Activate one tuning fork and then the other in close succession so that they ring together.
- Place both on the part of the body to be treated. They should be held close together, but make sure they are not touching.
- Reactivate the vibrations before the sound dies down.
- Keep this up for as long as needed to reduce the discomfort and pain.
- Return to using the first technique for a while longer (using the unweighted 174 Hz tuning fork a little way away from the body) if necessary.

USEFUL TIPS

Some painful areas are tender to the touch. Reduce the hardness of the tuning fork by putting a rubber ball on the end of the stem.

You can amplify the vibrations of the tuning fork by placing a crystal at the end of the stem, such as clear quartz, which is known as the master healer. Rose quartz is good for emotional release and healing.

USING THE PYTHAGOREAN TUNING FORKS IN CROSS-Lateralization

The purpose of the process called cross-lateralization is to balance the left and right hemispheres of the brain, using the two tuning forks in the sacred ratio of the fifth interval (a C-note and a G-note together).

- Activate the two tuning forks either simultaneously or in quick succession.
- Holding them by their stems, one in each hand, bring them up to your ears and hold them about two inches away.
- After a few seconds, cross your hands so that the tuning forks have switched ears.
- Hold that position for a few seconds and change back to the original position.

HOW TO USE AN OTTO-WEIGHTED TUNING FORK TO TREAT the Skull

Treating and retuning your skull and brain with a tuning fork will enable you to release tension and heal old emotional wounds.

The Otto 128 Hz weighted tuning fork is specifically designed for use directly on the bone, and the vibrations will be felt through your head and brain.

The skull has two sutures joining different parts. Treatment works best if the tuning fork is placed along the main suture line, called the parietal or sagittal suture, and then on both sides of the line.

- Strike the fork and place it on the front hairline, right in the center of the skull.
- Hold it there during its full cycle (a cycle being the length of the vibration before it dies out).
- When the sound of the tuning fork dies down, strike it again and move your placement point about an inch back from the first hairline point.
- Breathe deeply and calmly, and hold the fork still until the vibrations die down.
- Repeat the process twice more, every time moving back about an inch.
- Next, repeat the sequence on four points to the right and then to the left of the center suture line.
- Pay attention to any feelings that arise. Be alert to changes in your breathing—do some points you've placed your tuning fork against make you breathe faster or slower? There might be some sensations manifesting that you can explore further and heal.
- In the next section, move around both ears in four points, keeping about an inch from the base of each ear.
- Next, move around to the back of the head. Place the tuning fork on points in a triangular shape that has its apex at the top of the head.

A Buyer's Guide

Although tuning forks are generally durable, low-quality alloys can wear out with constant use.

Many of the cheaper versions are molded, and their sound quality can be tinny and feeble. Their therapeutic value is not of the highest caliber because of the diminished quality of vibration.

There are good quality tuning forks made in America that cost a bit more, but they are made of a really good alloy that lasts and produces a strong, clear sound.

Look for a supplier that sells good quality hockey pucks to strike them against as a part of the tuning fork set rather than lightweight wooden sticks that cannot produce a strong sound and will not last long.

SOUND HEALING WITH SINGING BOWLS AND CRYSTAL BOWLS

The rich tones of singing bowls have been part of healing rituals since ancient times. They are gaining in popularity today, but just as with tuning forks, the choices available can be bewildering.

Some are made of metal, others of crystal; some are decorated, and some are plain. There are big bowls, small bowls, deep bowls, and shallow bowls. Each type has its uses, and together we'll explore all of them in this section.

HOW AND WHY DO SINGING BOWLS WORK?

Singing bowls are also sometimes called Tibetan or Himalayan singing bowls. They have been a part of Tibetan Buddhist rituals for centuries. They started gaining popularity in the Western world with New Age philosophies, and many modern yogis and energy medicine practitioners have unwavering faith in their effectiveness.

Traditionally, the bowls were made from different metal alloys, including copper, silver, tin, lead, iron, and gold. By the end of the 20th century, crystal bowls became more popular.

When struck gently with a felt or suede-covered striker or mallet, the bowls produce a beautifully clear, ringing sound that is sustained for some time.

When the rim of the bowl is lightly rubbed with the mallet, the friction causes the bowls to produce a high, prolonged whistling sound that is known as their "singing." The effect is similar to what you will hear when you rub a wet finger on the edge of a wine glass filled with water. This is called resonance, and it is sustained for some time, even after the friction stops. When the bowl is touched with the fingertips, the singing stops.

The volume of the singing is controlled by the tempo at which the edge of the bowl is circled with the mallet.

The ringing sound produces vibrations at the pitch and frequency that largely relate to the size of the singing bowl, although other factors, such as the material of which both the bowl and the mallet are made and the surface on which the bowl rests, also play a role.

When the bowl is placed on someone's body or held close to them, the vibrations enter their body and help them to heal, relax, and balance themselves according to the frequency of the sound.

The scientific community is divided in opinion about sound healers' claims regarding the therapeutic effects of singing bowls, but anecdotal evidence of their healing and relaxing role abounds.

Some of their reported healing properties include stress relief, deep relaxation, pain relief, muscle regeneration, immune strengthening, blood pressure regulation, relief from depression, and balancing of all the body's energy systems for optimum functioning (Shanti Bowl, n.d.).

In an observational study done by researchers from the University of California to observe the effects of singing bowls on mood, pain relief, and tension release, significant differences were found after the participants completed a meditation with singing bowls. The age group between 40 and 59 seemed to benefit more than the others, especially those people who did not have previous experience with bowls. Their tension levels, as well as physical pain, were much lower, while their spiritual feelings of well-being were measurably higher on a scale of 1 to 5 (Goldsby et al., 2016).

SINGING BOWL FREQUENCIES

Assigning a completely accurate frequency reading to a specific bowl can be tricky because many things can influence the pitch. Striking the sides of the bowl with the mallet will produce a different sound from rubbing the top edge. Striking high on the sidewall will also sound different from a strike low on the side. Rubbing the sidewall also produces a different pitch than rubbing the top.

Singing bowl frequencies can range between 110 Hz and 800 or even 900 Hz. Bowls with bigger diameters generally produce lower frequencies. Thicker walls will bring higher frequencies forth.

The bowls cannot produce chords, only single notes. They can, however, be tuned to a chord, such as a fifth interval. Crystal bowls, in contrast to other types of bowls, generally produce a third interval harmonic pattern.

The sounds from metal bowls have three-tone colors, so to speak, although it is technically only one note.

- The fundamental tone is heard when the outside of the sidewall is rubbed with a mallet. It is a slightly lower pitch than the others.
- The highest tone a singing bowl can produce is called its female overtone. That can be heard when the top edge is rubbed with the mallet.
- The third tone color is only present in large to mid-sized bowls. They have a mid-tone that starts once the bowl is warmed up and the female overtone has been played.

The bowls can be tuned to produce specific notes, such as the notes in the harmonic octave or the solfeggio tones. They can also be made to produce specific octaves.

DIFFERENCES BETWEEN METAL AND CRYSTAL SINGING BOWLS

The sound of crystal bowls is clearer and smoother than that of metal bowls. Crystal bowls don't have the overtones of the fundamental, female overtone, and mid-tone. Instead, they produce only one clear, ringing note.

Crystal bowls are not manufactured to specific frequencies like metal bowls. Their size, thickness, and whether they are frosted or not will determine the pitch of their singing. The fast vibration produced by the thick walls of frosted bowls will create a loud sound with a high pitch. A clear bowl of the same size will sound lower and softer.

ADDING A WATER DIMENSION

Adding water to your singing bowl meditation can add a great visual and auditory enhancing effect to your relaxation.

The vibrations created in the bowl to produce the sound get transferred to the water inside the bowl. That sets the water in motion, and soon it almost looks as if the water is lightly boiling. In scientific terms, it is known as the Faraday instability of fluids.

The constraints of the bowl change the typical pattern of the Faraday instability enough, however, to cause droplets to start leaping into the air and bouncing on the surface of the water.

The accompanying sound is like light rain falling, which can be very soothing during a meditation. The patterns on the water and any light it might reflect are also mesmerizing.

The general rule is to fill the bowl no more than halfway with water, to prevent the instability from becoming so great that everything just splashes out.

If you use less than that, there will hardly be anything to see.

It is important to empty the bowl after use and dry it thoroughly to prevent rust and any moldy buildup from forming.

Some people take it a step further and water their plants with the water that was agitated in the singing bowl. Many believe that the healing properties of the bowl are transferred to the water and will benefit their plants.

USING SINGING BOWLS IN YOUR YOGA PRACTICE

The restful tones of a singing bowl can bring new depth to your yoga practice. When used at the beginning of a session, it can set the scene for deep relaxation in the body and mind.

It can also be used during or between positions to promote stillness and mindfulness.

During breathing exercises, a singing bowl can also help to keep one's attention focused.

Ending a good yoga session with a singing bowl meditation will settle the harmonic pattern between body and mind and promote deep tranquility.

TYPES OF SINGING BOWLS

About 50 different styles and types of bowls have been identified, but there are only a few general styles that you will find in most stores. Most of the styles can be traced back to Tibet, India, Nepal, and Mongolia.

Thadobati
Thadobati is the oldest bowl form, and some of the ancient bowls still around date back as far as the 15th century. They are characterized by high walls, flat bottoms, straight sides, and undecorated lips.
When played with a mallet, they can produce up to five octaves.
They are usually small to medium-sized and are popular acquisitions.

Jambati
Flat bottoms but curved sidewalls, an inward-facing lip, and hammer marks on the outside are distinguishing features of jambati bowls.
They can play up to four different octaves when a mallet is used.
Jambati is the heaviest and largest style, and several craftsmen usually work together to produce one jambati bowl.
There are many antique examples still around. Their size made them great grain storage containers, which preserved them.
You will also need to purchase a cushion or mat to place the bowl on while playing it due to its weight.

Naga
These small to medium-sized pedestal bowls are considered quite rare. Antique examples are usually found in great condition, which has led specialist collectors to suspect the naga bowls had ceremonial usage, such as holding offerings.
Due to the pedestal, the sound of a naga bowl can, unfortunately, sometimes be distorted. If you can find one to buy, it would be wise to test it first.

Mani

Mani bowls, also known as mudra bowls, have flat bottoms, but their lips face inward. They are short and fairly thick and can be small to medium-sized.

Their range is three octaves, and their tone is considerably higher than other bowls.

It is believed mani bowls also had significance in rituals and ceremonies.

Ultabati

They are also big and heavy bowls like jambati and produce sounds in the two low octaves. They can also provide the "om" sound.

The outer walls are dark to black, and the lips curve outward.

Manipuri

Manipuri bowls can be small to medium-sized. They are shallow with splayed rims.

Most beginners find them easy to play, and they can produce a wide range of primary tones.

Lingam

Lingam, or lingham bowls, are rare. They are shallow bowls like the manipuri, but they have a protrusion in the center that gives them a unique sound. They are not so easy to play.

Remuna

Remuna bowls have thin, straight walls and can have beautiful artwork on the outside.

They are generally medium-sized and easy to play.

HOW TO USE YOUR SINGING BOWL FOR A SOUND BATH MEDITATION

ENJOYING A NEXT-LEVEL MEDITATION EXPERIENCE WITH A SINGING bowl need not be an expensive exercise; in fact, you don't even need to leave your home if you own a bowl.

Decide how long you want to spend on your sound bath before you start (it can be as short as five minutes and still be effective), set your alarm, and relax!

- Find a quiet, comfortable spot where you can relax without disturbances. Silence your phone and turn off any nearby computers.
- Take three deep, slow breaths: In through your nose and out through your mouth.
- And in... and out.
- And in... and out.
- Set the intention for your sound bath meditation. Possible intentions could be relaxing fully, grounding yourself, releasing anxiety, releasing anger toward someone specific, cultivating patience, strengthening compassion, or managing chronic pain.
- Put the bowl flat on your open palm without your fingertips touching it while holding the mallet in the other hand.
- Activate the bowl by tapping it lightly on the side with the mallet. Be firm but gentle, even with a metal bowl. There is no need for a hard whack. Keep all your movements restful.
- Hold your intention in your mind while you listen to the first chime of the bowl ringing out.
- Start circling the outside of the bowl with the mallet to create a sustained singing sound, or keep chiming it softly—do whatever feels right for you at that moment.
- Keep the mallet in contact with the bowl, and don't worry if the singing doesn't start immediately. It takes a while for the vibration to build.
- Keep breathing deeply and calmly... in through your nose... out through your mouth.
- Hold your intention in your mind.
- Let the ringing flow over you and through you, freeing your energy to move through your body and mind as it should.
- Do a mental scan of your body and notice any sensations there might be. Just notice them and let them go.
- If any thoughts or mental pictures come to you while you're listening to the sound, allow them and let them go again. Gently bring your attention back to the sound and your breathing.

- Breathe deeply and calmly... in through your nose... out through your mouth.
- Keep doing this until the end of your sound bath session.
- Before you still the bowl, express your gratitude for the experience to any spiritual figure or source that resonates with you. You can also thank the bowl for its service if that feels right for you.
- Notice any mental or physical shifts that might have occurred during this time.
- Still the bowl by touching it gently with your fingers, and slowly return to your normal activities.

New or Old?

Antique bowls can be expensive, but their sound quality is often superior to that of modern, machine-made bowls.

Older bowls were generally made with thinner bottoms than modern versions. Thinner bottoms, in tandem with the wear and tear that 100 years or more of use brings, will make their warm, rich singing stand out among new bowls that tend to have sharper sounds.

If you want to buy old bowls, make sure their age and quality are authenticated by a reputable dealer.

Making the Decision to Buy

Ultimately, the only real deciding factor should be whether the sound of the singing bowl speaks to you. Does it touch your heart and soul and move you?

Before buying, you should play the bowl or listen to a good-quality sound clip of it being played.

A good quality bowl will produce a strong, sustained sound with several harmonics and overtones. If the sound appears to flutter away, the quality of the bowl is not of a high caliber.

The time it takes to get the bowl singing is not an indication of quality.

It also helps to consider the size and weight of the bowl you want to buy. Is it a good fit for you physically? You might want to play it for long sessions, and if you have to hold something that is too heavy, it will be detrimental to the healing and de-stressing effect. Holding any object heavier than three pounds for long periods of time will get too uncomfortable.

You also have to be clear on your purpose. Are you going to use the singing bowl for yoga classes, healing, meditation, grounding, or chakra balancing? Some bowls will be better than others for specific setups and uses. Low tones work better for grounding and meditation, for instance, but meditating in a small room will make it uncomfortable to work with a large bowl.

Similarly, take into account if you have to move meditation or yoga locations frequently. Lugging huge bowls around might just make you decide to give up on the exercise altogether.

If you plan to use the bowl/s for healing and chakra balancing, remember that huge bowls cannot be used near the head and ears. They have to be placed at the feet, and you need smaller, lighter bowls to hold near the head and upper body. A crystal bowl with a handle is easier to move over the whole body.

THE POWER OF HARMONIC HEALING

We are sound—pure, vibrating sound. We are not only individual tones but also harmonic combinations of sound. Some harmonic resonant relationships sustain us, while others relax and balance us.

Harmonic healing explores the power of harmonics and their effects on us.

WHAT IS HARMONIC RESONANCE?

Scientifically spoken, any sound consists of a fundamental (main) tone and overtones. An overtone is any frequency higher than the fundamental tone.

Getting technical, if the value of an overtone is an integer multiple of the fundamental (main) tone, the overtone is called a harmonic (integer multiple means "can be multiplied into").

If that hurts your brain, don't worry; these technical aspects are out of the scope of a beginner's book and are absolutely not necessary to memorize in order for you to benefit from the healing power of harmonics (overtones).

To put it simply, just imagine that a pitch (note or sound) contains another "hidden" note (or the same note in a different octave) resonating within it.

The frequencies at which certain harmonic combinations vibrate have the power to heal the human body and mind.

We'll explore harmonic combinations and how to use them in more detail later in this section.

THE HISTORY OF HARMONIC HEALING

Ancient civilizations understood this basic concept about the power of sound, and many old structures still preserved reflect this.

Have you ever walked into a historic cathedral and felt the lofty silence lifting your soul without a sound? That is the power of a space built to harmonic proportions at work.

Many cultures and religions talk about the universe being created through a sound or spoken word. The ancient mystery schools of Greece, Rome, Egypt, India, and Tibet all based their teachings on the belief that vibration is the primary cause of the existence of the universe.

Priests were often musicians, too; scientists were equally well versed in esoteric knowledge and music as they were in scientific principles. They had temples dedicated solely to the purpose of healing.

Fundamental to this belief were the teachings of Hermes Trismegistus. The spiritual and philosophical movement called Hermeticism dates back as far as the 1st century CE.

Hermes was believed to be a combination between the Greek god Hermes and the Egyptian god Thoth. His writings can be found in what is known as The Hermetica, a huge body of works spanning from about 300 BCE to 1,200 CE.

Hermes laid down seven main principles of the universe:

- The principle of Mentalism, according to which all is mind.
- The principle of Correspondence, according to which everything in heaven and on earth corresponds to each other.
- The principle of Vibration, according to which all is vibration.
- The principle of Polarity, according to which everything has a dual nature.
- The principle of Rhythm, according to which everything is in a constant state of flow.
- The principle of Cause and Effect, according to which everything happens to a law.
- The principle of Gender, according to which everything has both male and female sides and energies.

Both the principles of vibration and rhythm involve sound. According to Jonathan Goldman in his book *Healing Sounds: The Power of Harmonics* (1996), the principle of correspondence is also relevant to sound healing. Goldman explains that the rotation of planets can be calculated mathematically into frequencies that the human ear can hear. These calculations mean we have the potential to emulate the frequencies of the planets rotating, hence the law of correspondence (heaven and earth corresponding with one another) being relevant to sound healing.

Healing temples utilized mathematically calculated intervals (the space between notes). These calculations were pioneered by the Greek mathematician Pythagoras, who is known today as the father of modern geometry.

Using a monochord, he discovered whole-number ratios between the notes.

Pythagoras believed the whole universe was one big monochord, with a string stretched between heaven and earth. The upper end was anchored in what he called absolute spirit. The lower end went down to, in Pythagoras' terminology, absolute matter.

Therefore, he postulated that everything in the universe can be explained in terms of harmonic ratios. He demonstrated harmonic relationships in nature, the planets, and the heavenly constellations.

Pythagoras was rumored to have been able to hear the vibrations of the planets. In modern astronomy, scientists have equated sounds to different planets, and they appear to be in harmonic relationships with each other. Maybe Pythagoras could hear what no other human being has since heard without aid!

His teachings were passed on to his students at his monastery-like school in Crotona, in what is now the Italian region of Calabria. The school later burned down, and many of his teachings were lost. Scientists have been searching through the years to understand his principles based on what was preserved.

Notable among these scientists is the Swiss researcher Dr. Hans Jenny. He devoted his life to studying the effects of different frequencies on inorganic matter and called his work cymatics.

He clearly demonstrated that specific harmonies could rearrange inorganic matter into recognizable forms.

HARMONICS IN SHAMANISM

Shamanism is thought to be the oldest form of healing known to man, and sound has always been an integral part of a shaman's work. For a discussion on the musical instruments favored by shamans, see the section earlier in the book about shamanic healing and journeying through the use of instruments.

Shamans communicate with the spirit world to do their work and to obtain knowledge. The voice is the most commonly used medium to achieve this.

Overtone chanting, or hoomi/xoomij/choomig, is a form of throat singing from the Tuvic region in Mongolia. It involves the singing of one note with two different and distinct pitches that are audible at the same time.

A bass-like, nasally droning sound forms the fundamental tone, while the overtone is a piercingly high sound that forms a melody above the droning.

The effect of this ghostly-sounding melody strengthened the ancient people's belief that shamans were in direct contact with super-natural powers.

Hoomi singing has since spread to many other cultures. The didgeridoo used by Australian aborigines produces the same type of sound.

Tibetan monks use it, too, in a form known as tantric harmonics. Chanting in their "one voice chords," they manage to produce three different notes at the same time.

It is said that their chanting style started with a dream experienced by the Tibetan lama of 1433, in which he received this tantric voice. He was told in his dream that the voice is meant to unite the male and female sides of the divine energy to bring about a universal conscious-ness. It had to be used to show life in its fullness, with all the overtones that are normally only felt and not seen.

He taught the other monks to do it, and they started a tantric monastery in Gyume. In the same century, at another monastery in Lhasa, the Gyuto Tantric College was founded.

Until China's 1950 invasion of Tibet, knowledge of this technique and the rituals of the monks were unknown to the outside world. Some monks escaped the invasion by fleeing to India, where they continued their practices.

Goldman talks about the effects of hearing these monks chant as "one of the most powerful sonic experiences imaginable" (1996). Musi-cologists have measured one instance of them singing and found the bass note to be two octaves below middle C. The frequency is 75.5 Hz. The deepest note reachable for any known professional opera singer is 150 Hz.

HARMONICS IN MEDITATION

Once you've attuned your ears and senses to the subtleties of over-tones, a new listening experience opens up for you. It is suddenly possible to tune in to surrounding sounds in fine detail.

Consciousness seems to expand into a more profound and different awareness of the world, which includes actively and intuitively listening to other people.

This new way of listening also includes tuning in to your inner voice with new attention. Meditation gets new meaning as you open up to receive messages from your higher self and the creating spirit that pervades all things.

If you regularly listen to sounds that charge your brain positively, you will start to hear more of them. You will start hearing overtones in everyday sounds, opening up the path to a new level of awareness. Your imagination will get a new life, too, building a richness into your experience you never thought possible.

Most of the cranial nerves, including the vital vagus nerve, are linked to the ear. The vagus nerve affects the heart, the bronchi of the lungs, the gastrointestinal tract, and the larynx. Listening to harmonics will, therefore, influence our voices, breathing, heart rate, and digestion positively.

Creating overtones yourself and actively engaging in the process will trigger the relaxation response just like toning elongated vowels in a mantra does. The relaxation response was described by Dr. Herbert Benson as a marked decrease in respiration, oxygen consumption, heart rate, and metabolism. Alpha waves in the brain also increased. Alpha-state brain waves are found in expert meditators who are proficient at slowing their brain waves down from the usual thinking state of beta.

One of the first Sufi leaders in the Western tradition, Pir Vilayat Khan, said overtones are like a Jacob's ladder in that the conscious mind can climb to the metaphysical realm to understand higher truths.

Opening up to other levels of consciousness is an excellent way to practice deep meditation. It can make it possible to become one with sound, which is a cherished tool in meditation. Sound becomes something that is alive with an energy of its own. Once you stop trying to control the sound and just allow it to be, you can travel to other planes of consciousness.

We can find answers that may have been eluding us and experience true oneness with others and the universe.

HARMONICS IN HEALING

One can't help but ask the question of whether the future of healing lies in sound and, specifically, in harmonics. The American clairvoyant Edgar Cayce (1877-1945) predicted that sound would become the mainstream medicine of the future. That future might be closer than we think.

True healing means becoming whole in body and mind. Our minds and bodies are inextricably linked to each other. A healthy body with a fragmented mind will never lead to optimum fulfillment and vice versa. It is important to realize that the concept of a whole body does not refer to physical impairments; a paraplegic person can be as healthy as possible in the circumstances and still have a whole body from an energetic perspective.

It's worth remembering: the intention of the healer, as discussed earlier in the book, is always crucial when healing with sound, whether using the voice, an instrument, or an electronic device.

THE CYMASCOPE

At the forefront of scientific developments in harmonic healing is an electronic instrument that uses harmonic relationships to treat cancer patients. It is called a cymascope and has evolved thanks to the work of Dr. Jenny in cymatics (see the discussion about his work earlier on).

Physics and acoustics researcher John Stuart Reid developed the instrument to assist surgeons during cancer surgery. It can be difficult for surgeons to distinguish between cancerous and non-cancerous cells, and the cymascope clears up the confusion by creating cymatic images of cells.

The cymascope also rests on a 2002 discovery by Dr. James Gimzewski that states that all cells have their own sound (Price, 2021). The sound emitted by a healthy cell differs from that emitted by a cancer cell.

The cymascope makes the cells' "songs" visible. Reid found that cancer cells have chaotic sounds without any pattern to them. In contrast, healthy cells emitted harmonious sounds. When injected into the cymascope, two radically different pictures emerge. The cancer cells have none of the beautiful, symmetric patterns that form healthy cells. Instead, they depict skewed lines and a chaotic jumble of patterns.

The cymascope works through a light that is shone on the surface of water that is added inside the machine. The images are captured digitally. In a surgical environment, the camera feed will be sent directly to the surgeon's eyewear.

Reid envisages a device on the surgical spectacles that will be linked to a laser scanner, which the surgeon will move over the patient's body. The visual feed will go directly to the cymascope, and when the surgeon looks down at the patient, the images created of the "cell songs" will be superimposed on the body. That will make it easier for the surgeon to decide where to cut.

The aforementioned breakthroughs and ingenuity demonstrated in recent years prove that even the fields of science, medicine, and technology acknowledge the healing power of sound.

CHAKRA BALANCING

Author Dr. Randall McClellan developed a system to balance the chakras using the human voice. The series of fundamental notes range over two full octaves and are harmonically related.

McClellan associated the root chakra with a C-note, the sacral with a G, the solar plexus with the next C, the heart with an E, the throat with a G, the third eye with a B-flat, and the crown with a high C.

If you're not a musician that has developed perfect pitch, then why not play these notes on a keyboard or listen to them online? This way, you can match your vocal toning exercises to your chosen pitch for accurate chakra targeting.

MOBILIZING CEREBROSPINAL FLUID

The free movement and flow of cerebrospinal fluid is essential for overall health. It is a clear liquid that cushions the brain and spine, delivers nutrients, and removes waste.

The interaction between the fluid and the brain has to go on unhindered; otherwise, it could result in illness, brain damage, and ultimately death. Some people associate cerebral fluid with the eastern concept of kundalini energy.

Goldman recounts a demonstration of the effects of harmonics on skull bones and cerebrospinal fluid during a meeting of his Sound Healers Association in Boston in 1986. During his presentation, a guest speaker, chiropractor Dr. Harlan Sparer, checked the cranium bones of a person to whom Goldman was administering toning harmonics.

The bones of the skull not only moved during the toning, but the fluid moved more easily while the respiratory rate slowed (1996).

DIFFERENT STYLES OF HARMONIC OVERTONE SINGING

Similar techniques to Mongolian throat singing and Western overtone singing are practiced in several other parts of the world. Not all singers create melodies; some only use intonation and resonance to achieve the results they aim for.

It is important to distinguish between overtone singing and real throat singing, although throat singing has become interchangeable with overtone singing since the 1990s. Genuine throat singing is done by narrowing the larynx, and there are no overtones involved.

UMNGQOKOLO: XHOSA OVERTONE SINGING

The music found among the Xhosa tribe in the eastern part of South Africa is one example where both types of singing, throat and overtone, can be found.

Male diviners practice throat singing, which is a coarse, rough sound made in the throat, and often performed as a kind of percussion. The women practice a type of overtone singing that is also known as umngqokolo.

They make the sounds to imitate their bow musical instruments, such as the "umrhube" and "uhadi," believing it will help them to make contact with their ancestors to receive healing and spiritual guidance.

Songs of the Dani of Papua-New Guinea

The Dani, also spelled Ndani, live in the western part of New Guinea. They use overtone singing to contact the ancestors and obtain spiritual knowledge.

Cuncordu a Tenore From Sardinia

The "tenore" singing is a specific style of folk music from the Barbagia region of the island of Sardinia. Cuncordu is Sardinian sacred music used since ancient times to heal and teach.

It is performed by four men standing close together in a circle. The leader, or "voche," sings the solo melody in a regular voice. The second voice is called the "mesuvoche," and he also uses his regular voice. The third and fourth voices, called the "contra" and "bassu," respectively, utilize overtone singing.

THE RATIOS OF HARMONIC INTERVALS

1:1	Fundamental	55 Hz	A
2:1	Octave	110 Hz	A
3:2	Fifth	165 Hz	E
4:3	Fourth	220 Hz	A
5:4	Major third	275 Hz	C#
6:5	Minor third	330 Hz	E
7:6	Minor third	385 Hz	G
8:7	Major second	440 Hz	A

There are basic ratios that make up the main intervals.

LEARNING TO PRACTICE OVERTONE SINGING YOURSELF

Our voices are the cheapest and most accessible instruments we have if we want to work and heal with sound. While not everyone can chant like a Tibetan monk, overtone singing is accessible to anyone who can speak.

Overtone singer Jill Purce said that the concentration demanded by and the mechanism of practicing overtone singing are, in her experience, the best way to utilize parts of the brain that never get used. That makes it possible to enter into the presence of pure spirit (Goldman, 1996).

A quick recap of a couple of the important concepts might be helpful.

FREQUENCY

The number of cycles per second in the vibrational movement of a sound; the tempo at which the sound wave oscillates (moves back and forth).

THE ROLE OF FREQUENCY IN TUNING

Musical instruments are tuned to specific frequencies. The standard tone, known as concert pitch, varies in different parts of the world and for different instruments and has changed through the years.

The most commonly used modern standard that came into use in 1939 is 440 Hz, corresponding to the A-note above middle C. The pitch was affirmed by the International Organization for Standardization in 1975 as the ISO 16 standard.

Since the beginning of the 21st century, many people have started advocating the use of 432 Hz instead of 440 Hz. No official changes have been made to the standard pitch yet.

FUNDAMENTAL TONE

If you play a C-note on a piano, the first sound you hear is the actual pitch of the C. This is called the fundamental tone.

OVERTONES

The overtones mean the other sounds that are also present besides the C. They are usually not audible to the average human ear.

INTERVALS

Overtones are mathematically related to each other, and the difference between them is called an interval. An interval is also the distance between a fundamental note - or any other note, for that matter.

TONING THE VOWELS

The sounds of the vowels "aa," "ee," "ii," "oo," and "uu," and the musical crossings from one to another (the sound of switching between them), when toning them, contain harmonics within. Sounding "aaa" offers a different quality to sounding "eee" as in "me," for instance. The way every vowel is formed brings specific harmonics to the forefront in every respective sound.

Try to sing "uuh," "ooo," "ohh," "aaa," "eye," "aye," and "eee" in one breath at a pitch that is comfortable for you, and listen to the harmonics already contained within your voice without you even really trying.

Your pronunciation of each vowel and your mouth position when singing the crossings between the vowels will determine the exact intervals of the overtones produced. Generally, according to Goldman, the "ooo" sound helps to create the overtones of the octave and the fifth interval for the fundamental tone. The "ohh" sound will create overtones of the major third and the fifth intervals of the next octave. The "ahh" or "aye" sound will help with the overtones of the seventh interval. Moving from "ooo" to "eee" will produce higher overtones with every new vowel (1996).

Contrary to what may feel right for you, you will be more

successful with creating harmonic overtones if you pronounce them less rigorously. Keep the sound in your throat, and do not try to speak the vowels. Shape your mouth as if you are going to speak the vowel, but do not actually enunciate it. The sound should be formed by changing the position of your jaw, tongue, and cheeks.

Cupping one ear with your hand, in the beginning, will allow you to hear the sounds more clearly. If you hold the other hand with the palm facing you about two to three inches from your mouth, it will reflect the sound to your cupped ear, making it even easier to hear the different tones emerging.

Don't try to sing the initial, fundamental tone loudly. Keep it to the level of your regular speaking voice. The volume of the overtones is in inverse proportion to the fundamental tone in the beginning. Focus the energy of the sound in your throat rather than outside your mouth, and use all your vocal resonating cavities to amplify the harmonics. Creating harmonics is not about giving a performance in the regular sense; it is more about facilitating the production of the right sound that will allow the overtones to come into their own.

Sit comfortably before you start. With experience, it will become possible to sing harmonics while standing or even lying down. Still, in the beginning, you need the physical support to your diaphragm and breathing that sitting provides. Standing can also add an unnecessary layer of concentration to keep the proper posture.

You might struggle a bit to distinguish the overtones in the beginning. The Western ear is not generally trained to focus on individual tones, except if you are a musician or sound engineer. With practice, it will become second nature to you, however.

- Begin by humming an "mmm" sound on a pitch that comes naturally and comfortably for you. Keep the volume low. Concentrate the sound energy on your lips to create a strong vibrating sensation. You can test this by touching one finger to your lips—you should be able to feel them vibrating.
- Move from "mmm" to "uuu" (as in "moo") without breaking off the sound. Just move your lips. Then move on to "ooo"

(as in "go"), to "aaa," to "iii" (as in "my"), to "aye" (as in "may"), to "eee".

- Open your lips just wide enough to allow the vowel to be audible after the "mmm," and keep the vibration up.
- Next, round your lips as if you want to start whistling. Imagine making a face like a fish when you open your lips.
- Change your sound to "mmmooorrrreee" (as in "more") in one breath and draw it out as long as you can.

Take a nice deep breath and turn your attention to your nasal cavity next. It is important to project sound into the nasal cavity to produce overtones. It is not something that comes naturally to Westerners, and you will have to practice it.

- One way of learning nasal projection is to put two fingers on either side of your nose while making a "neeee" (as in "knee") sound. You should be able to feel a vibration in your fingers. It is completely normal to experience a draining of your sinuses while doing this—you might want to keep a tissue handy!
- Another good sound to practice next is "nnnuuurrrr" (as in "her"). First, get your nasal cavity vibrating on the "nnnn" sound. Then add the "uuurr" part to "nnnn." The sound of the "nnnn" will still be vibrating in the nose while the rest of the sound is added in the back of the throat.
- The "rrrr" part of the sound is produced by the tongue that has moved forward to vibrate close to the roof of the mouth. That is a particularly important placement to remember, as it helps to control the higher harmonic tones. Take note of the fact that the tongue is not actually touching the roof of the mouth but vibrating on saliva. If there is contact between the tongue and the mouth, the sound will be muffled, and the vibrating of the tongue will be impeded.
- Move your tongue back and forth in a straight line and listen to the changes in the sound. Find the one spot where

the high tone, sounding like a small whistle, is the loudest. Once you're on that spot, change the shape of your mouth and enjoy the different harmonics you will be producing.

Another useful sound to practice is the "nnnguuunnng" sound. It works with the muscle at the back of the throat that is called the glottis. You can teach it to produce harmonics.

- Start with "nnnn" in the nasal cavity, and then say the word "gung" (as in "tongue"). Go back to "nnnn" and say the word "gong." Nasalize another "nnnn" and say the word "gang." Do another nasal "nnnn" and say the word "ging" (as in "sing").
- Do the whole sequence now in one breath. Go from "nnnngung" to "nnngong," to "nnnngang," to "nnnging." You are essentially keeping the nasal "nnnn" sound going while intoning the other words. Become aware of the different harmonics that are produced from the back of your throat.
- The next step is to try a combination of "mmmooorrr," "nnnuuurrr," and "nnngong." Do the whole sequence in one breath and listen to the changes in harmonics flowing from you.
- Reverse the sequence to start with "nnnngong" and end with "mmmooorrr" next. You can also mix them up further and start with "nnnuuurrr."

According to Goldman, these three phonemes (sounds in any language that distinguish the separation of words) are the most useful for producing overtones. There are other combinations you can move on to, such as "wwwooowww," "hhhuuurrreee" (like "nnnnuuurrr" but with an added "eee"), and "oooeee." The last one works best on a high pitch or in your falsetto voice.

Moving from "uhhh" to "eee" covers the whole spectrum of overtones (1996).

Your natural vocal range seems to influence the production of harmonics. If you are still struggling to produce them after practicing for a while, try to shift your starting pitch a bit higher or lower and see if it makes a change. Harmonics are as individual as the singing voice itself.

You will probably hit on a specific phoneme that becomes your favorite. Focus your attention on it and work to make it louder. When you have succeeded in one harmonic line, it will be easier to practice all the others to perfection.

Try to practice in a quiet environment to make it easier to hear the overtones. Your brain and ears are not used to the sounds, and you might take a while to pick them up when other sounds are present.

The resonance formed in your head by the sound of your voice (in the fundamental tone) also has to be mentally tuned out by your brain before you will be able to discern the overtones easily.

It can be helpful to record yourself during practice. We do not always hear ourselves as someone else does because some sounds get muffled to our own ears while traveling through bone. We can also forget to listen when we are concentrating so hard on producing the sounds.

Listening to a recording of yourself can also be a tremendous boost to your confidence because it might be difficult at first to believe that you really succeeded in making the sounds.

The key component is practice. Don't get disheartened if you don't get it right in a few days. It is not a process that happens without thinking and working on it because most of us have not been taught since childhood to experiment with sound. It is as much a brain shift as a physical sound-producing shift that you have to make. Be kind and gentle with yourself, and remind yourself constantly that you can do it. It cannot harm you; in fact, it can only benefit you.

You have to have a positive attitude toward harmonics when practicing, even if you are unsure if you will be able to master the technique. Set aside a minimum of 15 minutes every day at a time and place where you can be calm and focused on your practice. Switch off any distractions, such as a computer, and put your phone on airplane mode if you're keeping it on to record yourself.

Don't rush through the phonemes (sounds). Tone them deliberately and mindfully. Take some time between exercises to reflect on what you have achieved and any sensations you might feel in your body. Your heart rate, blood pressure, respiration, and skin temperature might change.

If toning brings up any mental images or memories, take a moment to notice them too. Don't dwell on any emotions. Just acknowledge them and let them go. You are healing.

Keeping a journal can be helpful in tracking your restorative journey. Once you put a sensation, thought, memory, or emotion into words on paper, it is out of your mental way, and you can move on.

Many traditions view harmonics as sacred sounds. You now have the ability to create them in your own life and body. Accept them with joy and respect for the immensely wonderful way the universe works. Enjoy their rejuvenating and balancing power!

A SLIGHTLY MORE SIMPLIFIED APPROACH

A more condensed approach from a slightly different angle is also practical, but it might take a while longer to fully master harmonics this way. Make sure your trachea and vocal cords are well hydrated because a dry mouth and throat will make it difficult to sing.

- Relax your lips and jaw. If you find that difficult, choose any note at a pitch that is in a comfortable range for you and drone on it. Choose a vowel sound such as "aa" or "oo," inhale, and drone the vowel sound on a full, slow exhale.
- Do this as many times as you need to feel fully relaxed. You should be able to hang your jaw without any sensation of tension or tightness in your neck and throat muscles.
- Open your mouth and hold your tongue just under the roof of your mouth. Make an "rrr" or "lll" sound without touching your tongue anywhere against your mouth. If it brushes against the roof of your mouth occasionally, that is fine; just lower it slightly again so as not to dampen the sound.

- Holding your tongue in this position, change your sound to "oo." Try to sing it in your chest voice as deeply as you can. It's like saying the word 'cool' to someone in a bass voice.
- Now move the body of your tongue backward and forward (or up and down, if that feels more intuitive to you) without changing the position of the tip of your tongue. Think of it as alternating between an "r" and an "l" sound without moving your whole tongue. It will take some time to get used to doing this—be patient and take it slow.
- Slowly change the position of your lips to an "ee" sound while still keeping your tongue in the same spot.
- Move your lips again to form a "uu" sound (as if saying "see you" without the "s").
- Do it slowly and listen to the changes in resonance in your mouth.
- You are now ready to put it all together: Place your tongue near the roof of your mouth as if you are going to say an "rrr"; move the position of your lips slowly between the "ee" and "uu" sounds.
- Now curl your tongue up, move it backward, and away from your lips.
- When you hear the overtones emerging, stop moving your mouth and hold the position.

Make sure you sing from your chest and not your head. A head voice is higher in pitch, and you don't feel the resonance as clearly in your body as with a chest voice.

When you have the basics going smoothly, you can create melodies by changing your fundamental tone and moving your lips.

Listening to recordings and watching videos of overtone singers can also help you. Practice your mouth positions in front of a mirror to make sure you imitate the videos correctly.

⚜ 19 ⚜

MANTRA MAGIC

Mantras are words or phrases that are repeated during meditation to aid concentration. They originated in the Indian tradition, where it was viewed as a sacred utterance.

Instructors in Hinduism and Buddhism gave personal mantras to their students when they were initiated.

The use of mantras has become much more popular around the world in recent decades. The great efficacy with which mantas can focus the mind makes them a powerful tool in a sound healer's arsenal. Mantras are not always meant to silence all thoughts completely but rather to expand the mind and increase awareness of outside stimuli and emotional sensations without getting thought involved.

THE ANATOMY OF A MANTRA

Although many people understand a mantra as an intention or an affirmation, it is much more than that. The word is made up of two parts "man" and "tra."

"Man" comes from the Sanskrit word "manas," which refers to the linear thinking mind, while "tra" means "crossing over." A mantra is a way to help the mind cross over into a state of deep relaxation, meditation, and awareness.

Mantras can consist of any sound that does not include distracting content, but they often don't mean anything. The mantras without meaning are merely aids to reach a heightened level of awareness about the self and our responses to our sensations and surroundings (Thorp, 2021).

Other mantras refer to deities and petition them for certain tasks and outcomes (Atkins, 2015).

THE HISTORY

The earliest mantras date back at least 3,500 years. They were composed in Vedic Sanskrit, which was an Indo-European language that existed in India long before the advent of writing.

The Veda refers to a collection of hymns and verses that were regarded as sacred. People believed the words were given to the seers by the gods themselves (Feuerstein, 2011).

In early Hinduism, mantras were used to solemnize rituals. Each mantra was associated with a specific ritual. The purposes of the rituals were to solve concrete, everyday problems, such as finding missing cattle.

Over time, the concepts of abstract virtues and intentions developed.

The first known mantra was om/ohm/aum—there are several different spellings of the mantra. This mantra refers to the origins of everything and the creator and is prefixed to all Hindu prayers (Feuerstein, 2011).

THE SCIENCE

A study conducted by scientists in Israel confirmed what yogis have been saying for years: Repeating a word or phrase slows down a part of the brain that deals with, among other things, our response to stressors.

Activity in the brain quiets down, eliminating any processes that compete with the repetition of the mantra. What the researchers call "high-level cortical responses" are reduced, producing a pervading calming effect (Berkovich-Ohana et al., 2015).

In relation to healing, this means that external stimuli that compete with the mind's focus on the healing activity are muted, so to speak. Physical processes also calm down enough that they don't interfere with the mind's healing work.

The sound of the mantra, whether spoken audibly or silently, creates vibrations that aid in healing.

The healing effect of meditation was proven in a study in which eight people older than 60 with memory loss were asked to perform a Kirtan Kriya meditation for 12 minutes every day, keeping it up for eight weeks. After eight weeks, key points in their brains and cognitive performance were assessed and compared to the beginning of the study.

Significant improvements in memory and mood, among other benefits, were found (Moss et al., 2012).

TYPES OF MANTRAS

There are three main types of mantras.

- A bija (pronounced "beej") is a Vedic seed mantra. Bija mantras are seen as the core sounds that are associated with deities. It is believed they are endowed with spiritual powers to grant wishes. They are often incorporated into other mantras to boost their effectiveness. Bija mantras are used to open and balance the chakras (Yogapedia, 2017).
- Saguna mantras are believed to have the power to give rise to the form of deities. The Sanskrit word "saguna" means

having qualities associated. Saguna mantras are used to invoke specific deities to obtain something from them, such as their protection (Yogapedia, 2017).

- Nirguna mantras are abstract philosophical statements. The Sanskrit word "nirguna" means being without form. The mantra that is seen as the original creation sound, "aum," is a nirguna. Nirguna mantras are the oldest and originate from Vedic texts (Yogapedia, 2017).

SOME WELL-KNOWN MANTRAS

If you've ever wondered what words like "om" and "padme" mean and what they are used for, this section is for you.

OM MANI PADME HUM

This is one of the best-known mantras in the world. Its origins are in India and Tibet.

Many Tibetan monks chant the words thousands of times every day as part of their rituals. The Dalai Lama translated the words as "the jewel is in the lotus" (Atkins, 2015).

In the yogic tradition, the lotus symbolizes the power of transformation out of the mud into a magnificent flower. Chanting the mantra means affirming the power to do what is necessary to transform one's life out of darkness and ignorance into wisdom, grace, and beauty.

Part of the appeal of this mantra lies in the universal aspect. At any given time, many people all over the world are chanting these words at the same time. This creates a link to all who have strived in the past to move on from ignorance to wisdom and to all those who, in the future, will keep on doing the same.

OM NAMAH SHIVAYA

This mantra is a salutation to the god Shiva, who is associated with transformation through destruction. It speaks of finding peace and solace despite knowing that destruction is unavoidable.

It is often referred to as the five-syllable mantra, evoking the five elements of existence according to the Hindu and Vedic traditions: Fire, air, water, earth, and space.

So Hum

This is considered to be what is known as a breath mantra. The philosophical meaning of the words is considered to be "I am that," but the mantra can also be paired with inhalations and exhalations without contemplating any deeper meaning.

In the yogic tradition, it is believed that So Hum vibrates at the same frequency as Om, the sound of creation. It is said to bring expansion to one's consciousness, symbolizing the constant state of change that we and creation are forever a part of.

When used as an aid to breathing, inhalation is done on "hum" and exhalation on "sa" (Atkins, 2015).

Aham Prema

Loosely translated from Sanskrit, this mantra means "I am divine love." When chanting the words, the person affirms that he/she is aligning him/herself with the purity of divine love (Yogapedia, 2017).

Transcendental Meditation

Transcendental meditation falls into the category of no-concentration meditation. It is a way of allowing the mind to move freely within the stillness which is already there without focusing on anything specific.

Proponents of the technique believe it is, among other things, better at reducing anxiety and drug-dependent behaviors and decreasing blood pressure (The Meditation Trust, n.d.).

It differs from many mindfulness meditation techniques in that there is no effort involved to focus the mind on the breath or any other element.

By allowing the mind to roam while chanting a mantra, brain waves change to an alpha pattern. Alpha waves are associated with deep relaxation and restful alertness (The Meditation Trust, n.d.).

ORIGINS

Transcendental meditation comes from the Vedic tradition. The Indian sages practiced meditation for years, but the techniques and knowledge were not accessible to the general population.

In 1953, a famous guru named Brahmananda Saraswati, called Guru Dev by his followers, set his student by the name of Maharishi Mahesh Yogi, to the task of spreading the knowledge of meditation all over the world.

In 1958, Maharishi Mahesh Yogi traveled to the USA and Europe with his message. He was so successful that meditation became a well-known and often-practiced activity in the West. The pop group, The Beatles even went to India in 1968 to study with him.

By the time of his death in 2008, Maharishi Mahesh Yogi had certified more than 40,000 meditation teachers and established numerous transcendental meditation centers all over the world (TMHome, n.d.).

WHAT'S IN THE NAME?

Maharishi Mahesh Yogi coined the term "transcendental" to distinguish the meditation technique he was teaching from other types of meditation.

He wanted to emphasize the process of transcending the ordinary thought patterns of the mind to reach perfect stillness.

TRANSCENDENTAL MEDITATION MANTRAS

The mantras that are silently repeated during transcendental meditation are personalized and given to a student by an instructor. The instructor follows the guidelines laid down by Maharishi Mahesh Yogi.

During this type of meditation, the mantra and its sound are not used as a focal point but rather as a vehicle to transport the mind effortlessly into deeper realms.

To be considered a transcendental meditation mantra, it must consist of a meaningless sound to bypass the cognitive mind. It also must resonate with the sound of creation, "om," to attract the mind into seeking greater happiness and harmony (TMHome, n.d.).

The mantras are Sanskrit sounds that are believed to produce healing for the whole body and mind.

Students of the technique are required to keep their mantra secret to preserve its power for them when used correctly.

The mantra is always used silently to allow both the body and mind to sink into a deep state of rest. Speaking the mantra aloud engages muscles and occupies the mind, which will prevent one from reaching natural silence.

❧ 20 ❧

SOUND-POWERED GUIDED
MEDITATIONS

The relationship between sound and meditation is a powerful one. Both of these healing giants do a sterling job on their own, but together, their effects are amplified.

Many experts have created sounds and music specifically for meditation, and a lot of it is available for free on an array of websites. There are also numerous free apps for mobile devices.

Any sound can, however, be used for a sound meditation if you are in the right frame of mind.

In this chapter, we'll first explore why sound and meditation are such good partners before moving on to some guided meditations you can try. The scripts of the meditations are fully written out, so you can easily read and record the lines for yourself on your cell phone. If you add your own music or downloaded sounds, you can sit or lie back and enjoy the benefits of the meditations whenever you feel drawn to do so.

Sound and Meditation: Perfect Partners

Just like meditation alters some aspects of brain function, sound does, too. Does that sound far-fetched to you? We'll explore both statements in more depth before we get to the meditation scripts.

Sound

The world of sound, and its effect on us, is so profound that scientists discover new facets all the time.

Whether you listen to sounds of nature, music, your own voice, or even sounds that are normally perceived as intrusive noise, your brain responds to both the sounds and your intentions while listening (Mac-Millan, 2017).

Scientists from the Brighton and Sussex Medical School in England conducted functional magnetic resonance image (fMRI) scans on the brains of 17 young adults while they listened to nature sounds. The participants were between 17 and 34 years of age, with no prolonged medication use or history of significant physical or mental illness.

Their brains were monitored through four separate sets of soundscapes lasting a little more than five minutes each. While listening, they had to perform a monitoring task on a computer screen that required a low level of attention.

Besides the scans, the participants also reported on their subjective experiences of the soundscapes and the monitoring task.

The scientists found a remarkable difference between the attention spans and heart rates of those who listened to nature sounds as compared to the participants who did not have nature sounds to listen to.

Regarding brain activity, the fMRI scans showed a shift in the region of the brain where the activity of performing the monitoring task took place after listening to nature sounds. These scans were compared to the participants who did not listen to the soundscapes before completing the same monitoring task. The main brain activity in the soundscape listeners moved from the anterior (front part of the brain) to the posterior (back part of the brain)(Gould van Praag et al., 2017).

Put simplistically; this implies that cognitive actions moved from being purely rational to becoming more visually guided. Expressed differently, the focus of those who listened to the sounds of nature was turned outward, while the focus of the other group was turned inward —a brain pattern that is associated with stress.

That implies further that listening to certain sounds can alter the way we see and interpret the world.

MEDITATION

Meditation has been practiced for centuries, and many people swear by its effectiveness. In addition to this praise, the medical community has found scientific proof of the changes brought about by the practice.

Through the use of fMRI scans, brain activity could be mapped and studied, providing visuals of how we respond to meditation.

A study in Italy found that meditation leads to neurobiological modifications in people's self-awareness, attention, and memory, as well as the regulation of their emotions and responses to stimuli. After as little as 20 minutes of meditation, alpha and beta waves, which indicate rational reasoning decreased, and theta waves, associated with deep relaxation, increased. This pattern persisted for a significant time after the meditation session was over. According to the scientists conducting the study, meditation engenders a neurobiological effect similar to regular exercise (Boccia et al., 2015).

There is no right or wrong way to meditate. It is something you can practice in a fashion that suits you best. Guided meditations, scripts, and other informational materials are simply opening the way for your own experimentation.

Meditation can be focused on relaxation and calming, solving a specific issue, or gaining insight into a situation or problem. Your meditation can also incorporate all these elements in one session.

There are various styles of meditation, incorporating different types of sounds or silence.

If you choose sound, you can use soundscapes of nature, a voice, mantras, music such as solfeggio frequencies and binaural beats, or ambient sounds. You can even use everyday noises—one of the scripts later in this chapter deals with noise.

Humming is another powerful type of meditation.

To help focus the mind, meditations can start with a mental body scan. It is like doing an awareness inventory of your body, from head to toe. This brings all sensations, tensions, or aches to your attention. You can then relax and send healing energy to every part of the body that needs it.

Don't forget to pair your intention with meditation should the purpose of your session be solving a problem or manifesting a certain event or outcome in your life. If you are focusing on pure presence, then your intention will be a silent intention for stillness.

Let's put your newfound knowledge into practice now.

SCRIPTS FOR GUIDED MEDITATIONS

Below are some scripts for meditations designed to help you cultivate mindfulness and address common problems in need of healing.

These meditations will work best if you record the scripts via voice and play them back to yourself. A couple of tips for successful meditation script recording are:

- Don't read too fast. What feels like slow reading sounds different when you listen to it. Allow at least two to three breaths between every line.
- Many people don't like listening to their own voices. Don't let that put you off, though. Subconsciously, we often listen better to suggestions given by ourselves than by others. That way, the suggestions don't feel like orders.
- Read in a calm voice, pausing in the middle of phrases whenever it feels comfortable to do so.
- Say the words clearly without over pronouncing anything.
- Play the audio back at a low enough volume to be calming but loud enough that you can listen to it without straining.
- Try adding background music of a frequency of your choosing. Perhaps you are working on creativity and want to

target the sacral chakra. Or perhaps you want to target the solar-plexus chakra in preparation for a difficult conversation with a business partner. (Don't forget about the chakra frequencies outlined earlier in the book.)

TURNING NOISE INTO HEALING SOUNDS

Would you believe that everyday noises that are usually perceived as annoying can be used in meditation to bring about healing and balance?

It is not the sound itself that is bad; it is our perception of the sound that gives it a "bad" quality. If we change our attitude toward the sound from aversion to curiosity, the sound is just as effective in meditation as a soothing nature soundscape.

- Find a comfortable place to sit or lie down.
- Don't cross your ankles, and stretch your legs out straight if you're lying down. If you're sitting, keep your feet flat on the floor next to each other.
- Relax your arms and hands, either in your lap or next to you on the bed.
- Close your eyes if you feel comfortable doing so, or direct a soft gaze toward the horizon or a point ahead.
- Breathe in deeply to the count of four... Hold it for two... And exhale to the count of four.
- Become aware of all the sounds you can hear. The sounds are outside but also inside your body.
- Hear your breathing.
- Hear your heartbeat.
- Hear your blood rushing.
- Hear any sounds your stomach might be making.
- And breathe in.
- 1... 2... 3... 4.
- Hold your breath.
- 1... 2.
- Let it out through your mouth.

- 1... 2... 3... 4.
- And again... Breathe in.
- 1... 2... 3... 4.
- Hold your breath.
- 1... 2.
- Let it out through your mouth.
- 1... 2... 3... 4.
- ow become aware of sounds outside. Do you hear car horns blaring? Do you hear people talking? Do you hear traffic roaring? Do you perhaps hear a lawnmower or a leaf blower somewhere? Do you hear children playing or a baby crying? Is there a plane flying over?
- Turn your attention to your house. Is there a television playing? Are there cell phones ringing? Is someone cleaning the house or doing something in the kitchen? Is there a microwave beeping? Are there dogs barking or parrots whistling?
- Notice all these sounds without emotion. Don't resent them, and don't try to block them. Open your mind to them and follow them. Be curious about them. Let them be. Listen.
- [Pause]
- Feel your whole being becoming light, and allow your awareness to be carried on the waves of the sounds. Feel all the tension stored in your body drop away and stay behind while you drift on the currents of sound.
- Don't think about anything. Just drift and observe and relax.
- And breathe in... Hold for a moment... And breathe out.
- Feel the warmth and incredible lightness of being at peace with yourself and your surroundings.
- Gradually return your attention from the outside to the inside of your mind and body again.
- Allow the sound waves to float into your body and remove all discomfort and tension. Feel the restful peace and gently push all doubts and worries out of your mind until you're completely quiet inside.

- Stay in this stillness for as long as you like.
- [Pause]
- Turn your awareness slowly back to the outside world when you are ready.
- Move your limbs and open your eyes.

RELIEVING PHYSICAL PAIN

People who experience deep relaxation as in a state of meditation stand the best chance to manage chronic pain. Much of the success of a pain relief meditation depends on whether you accept or fight your pain.

Pain is the body's way of telling you there is an imbalance somewhere that needs to be addressed. You need to fully accept and recognize this as your body's loving way of guiding you and then work with it. Then will you be able to transform the pain and find relief.

For this meditation, you can choose any nature sounds that you find soothing and relaxing. Sounds such as surf breaking, water flowing over stones, or soft rain falling can all work well, depending on your preference. Using earphones will make it easier to focus on the sounds and avoid distractions.

- Sit or lie in a comfortable position in which you experience the least pain and discomfort.
- Focus on the sounds of nature you hear and try to exclude other sounds for now.
- Next, focus on your breathing. Without forcing anything, start breathing from your abdomen instead of your chest.
- Now stand back mentally and observe your physical sensations. Where are you feeling pain? How intense is it? Does it bring color, taste, form, or smell to your mind?
- Locate your tension. Take note of where it is stored and how it makes that part of your body feel. Does the tension's color, taste, form, or smell differ from the pain?
- Continue breathing smoothly and deeply, exhaling fully.

- Hold the picture of your pain and tension before you. Don't judge or try to change or fight anything. Simply observe. It is what it is at this moment.
- As each moment passes, observe how subtle changes take place. No moment is exactly the same as the previous one.
- Now, try to look at your pain and tension with acceptance. If you have a personal soothing color, try to mentally change the colors of the discomforts to that shade in your mind.
- If you feel yourself tensing up with the effort, ease up and breathe first. Then try again. This is not a race or a test.
- Repeat some affirmations for pain management. Try these in any order:

1. I accept myself
2. I accept my pain
3. I accept my tension

- Relax for a moment and just observe again. Breathe in deeply and exhale fully.
- Turn your mind's eye back to your pain and tension. Did anything change? Did you manage to change anything, even if ever so slightly?
- Now picture your pain again and imagine it is a cold patch instead of a painful one. Breathe in deeply and breathe cool air out into the pain, borne on the waves or wind you are listening to.
- Visualize the cooling sensation moving in under the pain and replacing discomfort with a pleasant tingle.
- Experience the pleasant sensation growing, taking over the painful area and allowing you to relax your tired muscles that were clenched to fight the pain.
- Take a deep breath in... And let it out.
- And in... and out.
- And in... and out.
- Choose a focus word to repeat while you keep on breathing calmly, such as restful.

- Breathe in and exhale on "restful" in your mind. Allow yourself to drift away to your focus word peacefully. When other thoughts try to intrude, gently bring your focus back to "restful."
- In... restful... out.
- In... restful... out.
- In... restful... out.
- Keep this up for as long as you like. You don't have to make anything happen, and you are under no pressure to produce anything. Just relax into your restfulness.
- When you are ready to return to your regular activities, take a moment to become aware of the sensations in your body again. Take note of how relaxed your muscles are and how still everything inside you is.
- Memorize this feeling and take it with you when you slowly open your eyes. Move your arms and legs slightly while you breathe in deeply once more. Do a gentle stretch on the exhale, and experience a feeling of alertness returning to your body and mind.

LETTING GO OF ANXIETY

Anxiety and panic can take many disguises in our lives, and they also show up in physical symptoms such as digestive problems or migraines. It is a natural part of the body's fight-or-flight response. Sometimes, however, anxiety occurs without a clear trigger, which can become problematic and even debilitating in severe cases.

Fortunately, meditation and sound can help. The script below deals with general anxiety. A couple of adaptations you can use to target specific places in your body where anxiety manifests are added at the end. Simply substitute more custom-targeted guidance for the general anxiety words below if you need to.

If you feel like combining this meditation with solfeggio frequencies, listen to the universal 528 Hz frequency for rewiring the neural pathways in the brain to release anxiety or 396 Hz, which promotes the cleansing of fear and feelings of guilt. The former frequency is associated with the solar plexus chakra and the latter with the root chakra.

- Find a comfortable spot to sit or lie down. Keep your arms by your sides when lying down or comfortably relaxed in your lap when sitting. Keep your legs and ankles uncrossed to help improve blood flow.
- Close your eyes if you feel comfortable doing so. If it makes you feel more anxious, fix your unfocused gaze somewhere ahead.
- You are safe and protected in this moment, and you can relax.
- Breathe in deeply from your abdomen. Keep your shoulders down and relaxed, do not pull them up to breathe.
- If anxiety makes it difficult to pull air in deeply because you feel constricted, do not fight it. Just take a breath as deeply as you can in the moment and savor the sensation.
- Breathe in again... and out.
- And in... and out.
- Fill your lungs as deeply as you can with air, allowing the breath to expand the feeling of restriction inside your body and mind.
- Breathe in... and out.
- And in... and out.
- Let go of any tightness and trembling. Allow the breath to push it out and away.
- There is nowhere else you need to be right now... Nowhere you have to rush to... No demands on your time. You are in a safe, restful place where you are welcome and loved.
- You have nothing to feel guilty about because you are in the right place and time for you. You deserve this time to relax and to fill your mind and soul with new energy to function at your best.
- You are doing the right thing. You are looking after your health.
- Breathe in again... and out.

- And in... and out.
- While you keep breathing calmly and deeply, become aware of the sensations in your body. Do not judge and do not evaluate. There is nothing wrong. Things are as they are. Observe them.
- Where do you feel physical sensations? Are there aches? Are there discomforts? Where are they? Don't try to change them; just note them.
- Breathe in again... and out.
- And in... and out.
- Start at the top of your head. Do you have a headache? Does your head feel tight, like there's a band around it?
- Does your neck hurt and feel tight?
- How about your face and jaw? Are you frowning? Are you clenching your teeth? Do any teeth hurt?
- Move down to your shoulders. Are they aching or tired? Are they bunched up?
- Do your chest and rib cage feel tight and constricted? Does it hurt to breathe deeply?
- Observe the middle of your body. Does it feel hollowed out and uncomfortable? Does it feel tight? Does it hurt in any way?
- Is there any discomfort in your abdomen? Do you feel nauseous? Do you feel hungry, but you can't put a name to what you're looking for? Do you feel bloated and heavy?
- Move your awareness to your hips. Is there any tension or pain?
- Breathe in again... and out.
- And in... and out.
- Observe your legs and feet. Are they relaxed? Are your toes turned up or are they relaxed?
- Now that you know where the tight spots are, go back to them one by one. Hold one place of tension in your mind while breathing in. As you breathe out, send the breath into the tightness. Visualize the muscles gradually letting go of tension as the breath fills them and opens them up.

- Feel the pleasant warmth of relaxation spreading across your body.
- Imagine you are breathing in pure calmness and relaxation and breathing out tension, tightness, and heaviness.
- Breathe in calmness... and tension out.
- And calmness in... and tension out.
- Keep replacing tightness and discomfort with open, relaxing calmness. Feel all the trembling inside you stop, leaving behind a blissful silence in which you float, feeling light and relaxed.
- Breathe in calmness... and tension out.
- And calmness in... and tension out.
- Now go back to the places in your body where you previously felt tightness. Do they feel different now?
- Take as long as you need to do this.
- [Pause]
- If there are places that have not released tension yet, keep sending calmness with your inhalations and letting tightness out with your exhalations.
- Breathe in calmness... and tension out.
- And calmness in... and tension out.
- Savor the feeling of softness and warmth that is flowing over your whole body. Snuggle into it. You deserve it.
- Feel the hardness that was packed into your core melting, becoming soft and warm.
- Rest in the soft warmth, enjoying it, savoring it.
- [Pause]
- Now become aware of your thoughts. Did they change when the sensations in your body changed? Are they calmer, slower, or fewer?
- Allow your mind to drift in any direction it wants. Don't focus on anything; just let your thoughts wander. See what they bring you without responding in any way.
- Breathe in quietness... and noise out.
- And quietness in... and noise out.

- Take as long as you want to enjoy this state of quiet relaxation. Keep breathing deeply and calmly.
- [Pause]
- Anchor the memory of this feeling in your mind and the fibers of your being. Whenever you feel anxiety coming on, remember the feeling and allow it to flood you with calmness and comforting warmth.
- Start returning to the awareness of your surroundings. Slowly allow the sounds and sensations of your physical world to penetrate your consciousness again.
- Move your limbs slightly. Keep breathing deeply and calmly.
- Open your eyes when you are ready.

ANXIETY IN THE STOMACH

- Direct your loving, calm attention to your stomach. Become aware of how it feels. Does it feel knotted up and tight? Do you feel empty and hollow? Do you have any pain? Do you feel nauseous or otherwise uncomfortable? Do you feel hungry without wanting food and not knowing what it is you really are looking for?
- Describe your stomach sensations in your mind. Give them words and pictures. Allow them to be and accept them. Think of them as messengers who came to show you where you need healing.
- Now that you have your mind pictures, you can let them float away.
- Return your attention to your breathing. Breathe in as deep as you can without forcing or pulling your shoulders up—try this for a count of four.
- 1... 2... 3... 4...
- Hold your breath for a count of two.
- 1... 2...
- Let it out through your mouth for a count of four.
- 1... 2... 3... 4.
- And breathe in.

- I... 2... 3... 4...
- Hold your breath for a count of two.
- I... 2...
- Let it out through your mouth for a count of four.
- I... 2... 3... 4.
- Feel your breath moving on the sounds of the music around you and allow the sound to penetrate the tight ball in your stomach. Allow the sound to gently work its way through the turmoil and discomfort you feel, leaving calm silence in its wake.
- Let the sound pick you up and float you on a cushion of relaxed peace. Feel the music move into every part of your body, leaving behind the same gentle, restful, light sensation.
- And breathe in.
- I... 2... 3... 4...
- Hold your breath for a count of two.
- I... 2...
- Let it out through your mouth for a count of four.
- I... 2... 3... 4.
- Return your attention to your stomach. Does it feel soft and open now? Does it feel calm and ready to accept life and its experiences again?

ANXIETY MANIFESTING IN FIDGETING HANDS

- Now return your attention to your hands. Did they stay still up to now, or did they move? If they want to fidget, allow them to do so now. Fidget all you want for 20 seconds.
- [Pause]
- Now stretch your hands and fingers as wide as is comfortable for you. Open them slowly and calmly... stretch them... stretch your arms out too. Hold the stretch for a moment or two... and release.
- Now ball your hands into tight fists, as tight as you can squeeze them... hold... and release.

- Open your hands again and stretch them, spreading your fingers wide and stretching your arms... hold them... and release and let your hands and arms go limp.
- Feel the warm, relaxed sensation in your hands now that they have had a good stretch. They might even tingle a bit.
- Let your arms and hands lie loose at your sides or in your lap. Savor the stillness that has come into your hands. Become fully aware of the calm, relaxed sensation and heaviness in them.
- Each time you want to move your hands, feel how they are too heavy to move. They are just... too... relaxed.
- Your hands and your arms are getting heavier... and more relaxed... They are growing to hold more heaviness.
- The heavy feeling is pleasant and reassuring. You are calm, restful, and happy.
- Breathe in deeply... and exhale.
- And breathe in... and exhale.
- Now fill your mind with a picture of the color blue. It doesn't need a form; it's just blue. See the blue in the most relaxing shade you can imagine.
- Visualize the relaxing blue moving into your hands and arms...representing the still, calm heaviness.
- When you feel the need to fidget coming on, imagine the color blue and experience the sensation of serene stillness and relaxation.
- Breathe in deeply... and exhale.
- And breathe in... and exhale.
- Immerse yourself totally in the color blue for a few moments... Take as long as you want.
- [Pause]
- Just breathe. Don't think about anything; just feel your calm, deep breathing. When you want to fidget, imagine the color blue and instantly experience the stillness returning to your hands and arms.
- Whenever you feel like fidgeting in the future, know you can picture the color blue and feel your hands relax.

- Breathe in deeply... and exhale.
- And breathe in... and exhale.

ANXIETY MANIFESTING IN JAW-CLENCHING

Many people complain of waking up with a toothache or headache because they grind their teeth and clench their jaws while they sleep. Clenching can also become subconscious behavior while concentrating on a stressful task, increasing the stress already being experienced.

- Zoom in on your mouth and jaw now and become aware of all the sensations there.
- Are you clenching your teeth now? Are your teeth, jaw, or gums hurting? Do you feel any tightness in the muscles around your jaw and the area of your throat? Does it feel difficult to swallow? Do you have any earaches?
- Don't measure or judge; just observe.
- Breathe in deeply now, and when you exhale, send the breath into your jaw.
- And breathe in... and exhale.
- Take the waves of the music you are listening to and the sound of your voice reading this script with your breath into your jaw, and feel how they lift and replace the tension there.
- Feel a coolness spreading in your mouth, and the tight, achy feeling disappear.
- Now empty your mind for a few moments and just... breathe.
- Breathe in deeply... and exhale.
- And breathe in... and exhale.
- Next, tense your jaw and hold your teeth together lightly. Not enough to cause discomfort, just lightly, and hold for a few moments.
- Notice the sensations in your face and jaw. Notice where muscles are tense now and if any aches have returned.
- Then let go slowly, savoring the loosening sensation.

- Breathe in deeply... and exhale.
- And breathe in... and exhale.
- Tense your jaw again and hold your teeth together a bit firmer. Not so it's painful, but just a little tighter. Notice the changes in your muscles and become aware of the sensations it brings. Hold the clench for a few moments.
- Let go of the tension all at once.
- Breathe in deeply... and exhale.
- And breathe in... and exhale.
- Let your lower jaw drop and hang slightly. Feel the free, relaxed feeling.
- Now, open your mouth widely, as widely as you can. Feel as if you're going to yawn and pull the muscles in your cheeks up, too.
- Relax everything, let your mouth close, and your muscles become loose once again.
- Hold your jaw in a comfortable position and memorize the feeling.
- Know that, from now on, when your jaw feels tight, this is a feeling you can come back to time and time again. It can train your brain to gradually release the tight grip.
- Take a deep breath, exhale, and lean into this loose, relaxed feeling for as long as you want.
- [Pause]

LOVING AND FORGIVING YOURSELF

Loving yourself, forgiving, and letting go of things you think you did wrong can be a huge issue for some people. It can stand in the way of emotional healing and balance.

Combine this meditation with the solfeggio frequency that relates to the heart chakra, which is 639 Hz. It promotes healing through love and brings about a profound connection to the self and others.

An alternative frequency to use is 741 Hz, which relates to the throat chakra. It heals and balances the ability to speak one's truth with love and peace and increases self-confidence.

- Find a comfortable position, whether it is lying down or sitting.
- If you are sitting, fold your hands loosely in your lap. Keep your feet next to each other on the floor.
- If you prefer lying down, stretch your legs out straight and do not cross your ankles. Let your arms lie on the bed or fold your hands over your middle.
- Place a pillow under your knees if that is more comfortable for you—your aim is loving yourself and allowing yourself space to be the glorious being you are.
- Become aware of the surfaces touching you. Are they warm, soft, smooth, or coarse? Notice the support it is giving you and where your body feels the support the most.
- Breathe in deeply and let the air fill your abdomen and your chest. Feel the air moving into your lungs and expanding your chest.
- Become aware of all the sensations in your chest. Do you feel any constriction? Do you feel open and receptive? Do you feel the need to close and protect?
- Let the openness spread to your throat, connecting your throat with your chest cavity.
- Breathe in... and out.
- And in... and out.
- And again, breathe in... and out.
- And in... and out.
- Feel the vastness inside you and know that is the true essence of the self you often hurt and judge. Know you have no beginning and no end, and you are truly wonderful and worthy of love.
- Know that you deserve to be loved and cared for, and accepted. You are precious and unique.
- Breathe in... and out.
- And in... and out.
- And again, breathe in... and out.
- And in... and out.

- Hold a warm feeling of acceptance and caring for yourself inside, and allow it to expand and fill you with warmth as far as it will go. Do not force anything; just let it move.
- [Pause]
- Form an intention in your mind to forgive yourself for all the times you did not love yourself. To forgive yourself for all the things you think you did wrong or neglected to do.
- Hold the loving, forgiving intention in your mind and give it a color and a form. Turn it around and look at it from all sides. Is it soft or hard? Is it round or square? Is it long or short? Is it a heart or any other recognizable shape?
- Is it pulsating? Is it emitting light? Is it sparkling?
- What is the color? Is it perhaps a warm pink or a deep, restful green? Or is it a calm blue? Perhaps an intense purple?
- Breathe in... and out.
- And in... and out.
- And again, breathe in... and out.
- And in... and out.
- See the loving intention in the full form and color you imagine it, filling you with its love. Imagine it pushing out any unkindness and hate and filling every corner of your being with love and appreciation, and forgiveness for yourself.
- Become aware of how peaceful this makes you feel. Feel the wonderful stillness that has descended over you like a soft blanket. Now the war inside is gone.
- Savor the peace, warmth, and quiet.
- Breathe in... and out.
- And in... and out.
- And again, breathe in... and out.
- And in... and out.
- [Pause]
- When you are ready, say the following affirmations in your mind:

- I forgive and love myself unconditionally and without boundaries.
- I accept myself unconditionally and without reservations.
- I care for myself, my health, and my inner peace because I know I deserve it.
- I care for myself with joy and ease; it is not a burden.
- I release any feelings of guilt and unworthiness because they no longer serve me.
- Breathe in... and out.
- And in... and out.
- And again, breathe in... and out.
- And in... and out.
- Repeat your affirmations again, as many times as you want.
- I forgive and love myself unconditionally and without boundaries.
- I accept myself unconditionally and without reservations.
- I care for myself, my health, and my inner peace because I know I deserve it.
- I care for myself with joy and ease; it is not a burden.
- I release any feelings of guilt and unworthiness because they no longer serve me.
- Breathe in... and out.
- And in... and out.
- And again, breathe in... and out.
- And in... and out.
- I forgive and love myself unconditionally and without boundaries.
- I accept myself unconditionally and without reservations.
- I care for myself, my health, and my inner peace because I know I deserve it.
- I care for myself with joy and ease; it is not a burden.
- I release any feelings of guilt and unworthiness because they no longer serve me.
- Breathe in... and out.
- And in... and out.
- And again, breathe in... and out.

- And in... and out.
- Move your awareness back to your chest and throat. Has anything changed? Do you breathe easier? Do you feel calmer and more relaxed?

Know that whenever in the future you find you're being unkind to yourself, you can come back to the loving intention you held earlier and let it spread its magic of warmth and love and forgiveness and acceptance again to fill your being.

RELEASING TRAUMA

Trauma can get embedded deep within our minds and bodies, causing disease and mental problems. It can be buried so deep we might forget that the traumatic event ever happened, but putting the instance to the back of our psyche will not heal the consequences of the trauma on our well-being.

Release conscious and subconsciously stored trauma with this guided meditation. Choose any nature sounds to play in the background while listening to your voice speaking the script. These sounds can consist of anything that calms and soothes you, such as a light breeze ruffling the leaves or water flowing happily over pebbles.

It is not recommended to choose upbeat sounds, such as a crackling campfire, even if you are particularly fond of the image. The flames are not restful, and such images can heighten sensations of anxiety that might be brought forward when working with traumatic memories.

- Find a comfortable chair to sit on, lie down on a bed, or choose a couch that is long enough for you to stretch your legs out fully. Keep your arms by your sides and your hands flat when lying down, or comfortably fold your hands over your midriff. If you choose a sitting position, hold your hands relaxed and loose in your lap. Keep your legs and ankles uncrossed to help improve blood flow.

- Close your eyes if you feel comfortable doing so. If it makes you feel anxious, fix your unfocused, soft gaze somewhere ahead or on the floor.
- Know that you are safe and protected in this moment, and you can relax.
- Breathe this assurance in deeply from your abdomen. Keep your shoulders down and relaxed; refrain from pulling them up to breathe. Feel a warm, safe feeling spreading through your abdomen, chest, and throat, enveloping your heart in soft restfulness.
- Exhale fully and visualize taking any tightness or discomfort out on the breath.
- Breathe the assurance of safety in again, and exhale stress and fear.
- Breathe in... and out.
- And in... and out.
- Take a moment to repeat to yourself, "I am safe. I am free."
- And again..."I am safe. I am free."
- Breathe in... and out.
- And in... and out.
- Feel any tight bands around your body loosening while you savor your affirmation as many times as you would like.
- "I am safe. I am free."
- And again..."I am safe. I am free."
- Breathe in... and out.
- And in... and out.
- [Pause]
- Now allow yourself to recall the memory of the trauma or as much of it as you can remember. Just let the picture flood your mind. Don't think rational thoughts about them; don't try to tell yourself what you should have done—just let the movie play in your mind.
- Turn your awareness back to your body. Do you feel new sensations anywhere that were not there before your mind movie?

- Acknowledge any feeling and physical sensation without trying to change them.
- Repeat your affirmations and breathe.
- "I am safe. I am free."
- And again..."I am safe. I am free."
- Breathe in... and out.
- And in... and out.
- "I am safe. I am free."
- And again..."I am safe. I am free."
- Breathe in... and out.
- And in... and out.
- [Pause]
- Now check your body for any specific location where you feel the tension stronger than anywhere else. It could be an ache or a vague sense of discomfort. It could be a feeling of constriction or nausea.
- Continue breathing deeply and calmly, and visualize sending the breath like a golden light to the affected part of your body. Imagine the golden light flooding and bathing that part, loosening tightness and soothing pain.
- If you feel emotions rising, let them rise, and acknowledge them as voices from your higher self that have come to cleanse and free you. Let them wash over you while you breathe deeply and calmly.
- Is there one emotion that stands out stronger than the others? Where do you feel this emotion?
- Send the golden light of your breath to the muscles and organs where you experience the strong emotion.
- Ask the muscles to become soft. Don't try to force anything; just ask them by repeating calmly, "Soft... soft... soft."
- You are not trying to make the emotions or the hurt go away by asking them to soften; you are simply asking them to soften around the discomfort.
- "Soft... soft... soft."
- Breathe in... and out.

- And in... and out.
- [Pause]
- Savor the softness that has come, and thank your muscles and organs for allowing the softness in.
- Acknowledge that the hurt and the tension are still there but that it is softer around the affected areas.
- Find peace in knowing that every time you ask them to soften a bit more, they will do so until they no longer hold on to the hurting, traumatic memories. The memories will simply float away, exhaled on the golden light of your breath.
- You are becoming whole once again, and all is well.
- "I am safe. I am free."
- And again..."I am safe. I am free."
- Breathe in... and out.
- And in... and out.
- Return your awareness to your surroundings when you feel ready. Stir your arms and legs slightly and open your eyes.

A HUMMING MEDITATION

Whether it is humming your favorite tune or sounding like a bumblebee without a melody, humming is a powerful enhancer of intentions and images.

You can either practice a humming meditation in the traditional way, keeping your hands relaxed, or you can put your thumbs in your ears with your fingers draped over your forehead. Closing your ears in this way will amplify the humming sound, making the vibrations even stronger.

The beauty in humming lies in the fact that regular daily activities don't need to be stopped if a quick vibrational reset is needed. You can hum softly under your breath while walking, driving, or doing anything where the sound won't disturb someone else.

For the following script, it is assumed that you are meditating only and keeping your hands relaxed. Adapt it in any way you would like.

- Sit or lie down comfortably. Keep your legs straight, your feet together, and your ankles uncrossed.
- Breathe in deeply from your abdomen, keeping your shoulders still.
- Exhale fully.
- Notice if you have any discomfort or pain anywhere in your body that you would like to send humming vibrations to.
- Reflect on whether you're holding any intention for something you want to achieve or a sensation or perception you want to change. Formulate your intention in words to yourself as clearly as you can.
- Breathe in again... and out.
- Breathe in... And let your breath out on a gentle hum. Don't force your voice, and keep it soft. You can keep your lips closed or open them slightly, whatever feels natural and comfortable to you.
- Breathe in... and out on mmm...
- And breathe in... and out on mmm.
- Breathe in... and out on mmm...
- And breathe in... and out on mmm.
- Become aware of where in your body you feel the vibrations of the humming. Are they in your head, your heart, your throat, or your stomach? Are the vibrations awakening any other sensations in your body?
- Keep humming softly for as long as you want, noticing the vibrations move through you.
- Breathe in... and out on mmm...
- And breathe in... and out on mmm.
- Breathe in... and out on mmm...
- And breathe in... and out on mmm.
- [Pause]
- Now, direct the vibrations to the body part that you want to heal or relax. Picture the vibrations as a golden spiral that gently turns, rubbing, and brushing that body part with calmness, softness, and health.
- Breathe in... And breathe the golden spiral out on mmm...

- And breathe in... and out on mmm.
- Breathe in... And breathe the golden spiral out on mmm...
- And breathe in... and out on mmm.
- Turn your mind back to the intention you formulated earlier. Visualize the words of the intention tangling with the golden spiral, becoming one with it. Imagine the intention being carried with the spiral to every fiber of your being.
- Keep doing it for as long as you want.
- Breathe in... And breathe the golden spiral out on mmm...
- And breathe in... and out on mmm.
- Breathe in... And breathe the golden spiral out on mmm...
- And breathe in... and out on mmm.
- [Pause]
- When you feel ready, stop exhaling the golden spiral and the hum. Breathe normally but deeply for as long as it takes to return your awareness to your surroundings.
- Breathe in again... and out.
- [Pause]
- Gently open your eyes.

CONCLUSION

I sincerely wish that the journey through sound healing you took with me in this book has changed your life for the better in profound ways.

Take what you have learned with you on the road to becoming the best version of yourself you can be, as you were intended to become from the beginning of time.

You are now equipped with an understanding of how important and fundamental all sound is for life. You understand how sound shapes us and continues to mold us—it is up to us to use it wisely.

You have also learned how to adapt sound to make your life easier, calmer, and hopefully, less painful.

You have, indeed, accomplished an act of creation. Well done!

May you travel forward with love, light, and courage.

REFERENCES

Abhang, P. A., Gawali, B. W., & Mehrotra, S. C. (2016). *Introduction to EEG- and speech-based emotion recognition*. Amsterdam Elsevier. https://www.elsevier.com/books/introduction-to-eeg-and-speech-based-emotion-recognition/abhang/978-0-12-804490-2

Aller, M., Giani, A., Conrad, V., Watanabe, M., & Noppeney, U. (2015). A spatially collocated sound thrusts a flash into awareness. *Frontiers in Integrative Neuroscience*, 9. https://doi.org/10.3389/fnint.2015.00016

Ankrom, S. (2019). *How to breathe properly for relieving your anxiety*. Verywell Mind. https://www.verywellmind.com/abdominal-breathing-2584115

Atkins, S. (2015, August 21). *A beginner's guide to essential Sanskrit mantras*. Sonima. https://www.sonima.com/yoga/sanskrit-mantras/

Bakken Center for Spirituality and Healing. (2015, October 19). *Deep listening*. Center for Spirituality and Healing - University of Minnesota. https://www.csh.umn.edu/education/focus-areas/whole-systems-

healing/leadership/deep-listening#:~:text=Deep%2olisten-
ing%2ois%2oa%2oprocess

Balezin, M., Baryshnikova, K. V., Kapitanova, P., & Evlyukhin, A. B. (2018). Electromagnetic properties of the Great Pyramid: First multipole resonances and energy concentration. *Journal of Applied Physics*, *124*(3), 034903. https://doi.org/10.1063/1.5026556

Balsamo, G., & Dagnese, L. F. (2012). *The Book of Breathing*. Robin. Basner, M., Clark, C., Hansell, A., Hileman, J. I., Janssen, S., Shepherd, K., & Sparrow, V. (2017). Aviation noise impacts: State of the science. *Noise & Health*, *19*(87), 41–50. https://doi.org/10.4103/nah.NAH_104_16

Berkovich-Ohana, A., Wilf, M., Kahana, R., Arieli, A., & Malach, R. (2015). Repetitive speech elicits widespread deactivation in the human cortex: The "mantra" effect?. *Brain and Behavior*, *5*(7). https://doi.org/10.1002/brb3.346

Bhaumik, G. (2019, December 27). *Sound healing explained - how it works and health benefits*. Destination Deluxe. https://destinationdelux-e.com/sound-healing-health-benefits/

Biblioteka Records. (2015, October). *The solfeggio frequencies*. BIBLIOTEKA RECORDS. https://www.biblioteka.world/our-blog/2020/9/27/the-solfeggio-frequencies#:~:text=The%2oSolfeg-gio%2oFrequencies%3A%2oWhere%2oDid%2oThey%2o-Come%2oFrom%3F&text=In%2othe%2o11th%2ocentury%2C%2oa

Boccia, M., Piccardi, L., & Guariglia, P. (2015). The meditative mind: A comprehensive meta-analysis of MRI studies. *BioMed Research International*, *2015*, 1–11. https://doi.org/10.1155/2015/419808

Booth, S. (2018, June 10). *Brain health with binaural beats*. Healthline. https://www.healthline.com/health-news/your-brain-on-binaural-beats#The-illusion-of-binaural-beats

Buddha Groove. (n.d.). *Traditional Tibetan tingsha cymbals / Meaning and origins*. Www.buddhagroove.com. https://www.buddhagroove.-com/buddhist-ritual-tool-tingsha/

Chaieb, L., Wilpert, E. C., Reber, T. P., & Fell, J. (2015). Auditory beat stimulation and its effects on cognition and mood states. *Frontiers in Psychiatry*, 6. https://doi.org/10.3389/fpsyt.2015.00070

Chepesiuk, R. (2005). Decibel hell: The effects of living in a noisy world. *Environmental Health Perspectives*, *113*(1). https://doi.org/10.1289/ehp.113-a434

Clason, D. (2019, September 16). *Tinnitus sound therapy - how it works*. Healthy Hearing. https://www.healthyhearing.com/report/52999-Tinnitus-sound-therapy-retraining-the-way-the-brain-perceives-sound

Cooper, B. B. (2013, August 21). *What is meditation & how does it affect our brains?* Buffer Resources. https://buffer.com/resources/how-meditation-affects-your-brain/

Cymascope. (n.d.). *Home of the cymatics*. Cymascope. Retrieved 2021, from https://www.cymascope.com/cyma_research/egyptology.html

Dargie, D. (1991). Umngqokolo: Xhosa overtone singing and the song Nondel'ekhaya. *African Music: Journal of the International Library of African Music*, *7*(1), 33–47. https://doi.org/10.21504/amj.v7i1.1928

Davisi, J. (2021, March 2). *10-Minute meditation for depression*. Www.youtube.com. https://www.youtube.com/watch?v=xRxT9cOKiM8

Deva, C. (2018, June 19). *Emotional and mental causes of illness. The list by Louise Hay*. Heartland Healing Arts. https://www.heartlandhealingarts.-com/blog/2018/6/19/emotional-and-mental-causes-of-illness-the-list-by-louise-hay

Encyclopedia.com. (2014). *Sound therapy*. Encyclopedia.com. https://www.encyclopedia.com/medicine/encyclopedias-almanacs-transcripts-and-maps/sound-therapy

Erkkilä, J., Punkanen, M., Fachner, J., Ala-Ruona, E., Pöntiö, I., Tervaniemi, M., Vanhala, M., & Gold, C. (2011). Individual music therapy for depression: Randomised controlled trial. *British Journal of Psychiatry*, *199*(2), 132–139. https://doi.org/10.1192/bjp.bp.110.085431

Estrada, J. (2020, March 25). *3 ways to bring your body vibrational balance using sound healing therapy*. Well+Good. https://www.wellandgood.com/sound-healing/

European Environment Agency. (n.d.). *Noise*. European Environment Agency. https://www.eea.europa.eu/themes/human/noise

Fellows, E. (n.d.). *Traveling the energetic highway: What are meridians?* Www.centerpointhealing.com. https://www.centerpointhealing.com/hyattsville/traveling-the-energetic-highway-what-are-meridians/#:~:text=The%20simplest%20definition%20is%20that

Feuerstein, G. (2011). *The deeper dimension of yoga: Theory and practice*. Shambhala.

Finne, P., & Petersen, T. H. (n.d.). *Traffic noise is dangerous to our health – but what do we do about it?* Forcetechnology.com. https://forcetechnology.com/en/articles/traffic-noise-dangerous-health-what-to-do-about-it

Flood, L. (2016, September 16). *Qi gong's healing sounds practice*. Chopra. https://chopra.com/articles/qi-gongs-healing-sounds-practice

Gabriel, R. (2015, January 15). *How to Use Sound to Heal Yourself*. Chopra. https://chopra.com/articles/how-to-use-sound-to-heal-yourself

Gadberry, A. L. (2011). Steady beat and state anxiety. *Journal of Music Therapy*, *48*(3), 346–356. https://doi.org/10.1093/jmt/48.3.346

Gingras, B., Pohler, G., & Fitch, W. T. (2014). Exploring shamanic journeying: Repetitive drumming with shamanic instructions induces specific subjective experiences but no larger cortisol decrease than instrumental meditation music. *PLoS ONE, 9*(7), e102103. https://doi.org/10.1371/journal.pone.0102103

Goldman, J. (1996). *Healing sounds: The power of harmonics*. Element Books.

Goldman, J. (2009a). The basic principle of sound healing. *Jonathan Goldman's Healing Sounds*. https://www.healingsounds.com/the-basic-principle-of-sound-healing/#:-:text=A%20concept%20of%20using%20sound,of%20using%20sound%20to%20heal.

Goldman, J. (2009b, March 25). *Everything is in a state of vibration*. Www.youtube.com. https://www.youtube.com/watch?v=gHb3ZyiQgyQ

Hanlon, B. (n.d.). *9 solfeggio frequencies*. Bríd Hanlon. https://www.brid-hanlon.com/healy-therapist-programs/nine-solfeggio-frequencies

Hatton, J. (2018). What are the dangers or side effects of binaural beats? [YouTube Video]. In *YouTube*. https://www.youtube.com/watch?v=aXi_hIdovpU

Hunt, J. (2020, May 28). *What is primordial sound meditation? The four soul questions | Personal mantra | Four intentions*. Www.youtube.com. https://www.youtube.com/watch?v=URwQoFvk9Qo

Inner Health Studio. (2012). *Relaxation for pain management: Free relaxation script*. Www.innerhealthstudio.com. https://www.innerhealth-studio.com/pain-management.html

Inner Health Studio. (2020). *Generalized anxiety relaxation: Free relaxation script*. Www.innerhealthstudio.com. https://www.innerhealth-studio.com/generalized-anxiety-relaxation.html

Isahak, D. A. F. (2005, March 27). *Five-elements qigong*. The Star. https://www.thestar.com.my/lifestyle/health/2005/03/27/fiveelements-qigong#:~:text=Today%20I%20will%20share%20with

Kaku, Dr. M. (2011). The universe is a symphony of vibrating strings [YouTube Video]. In *YouTube*. https://www.youtube.com/watch?v=fW6JFKgbAF4

Kappert, M. B., Wuttke-Linnemann, A., Schlotz, W., & Nater, U. M. (2019). The aim justifies the means—differences among musical and nonmusical means of relaxation or activation induction in daily life. *Frontiers in Human Neuroscience, 13*. https://doi.org/10.3389/fnhum.2019.00036

Kučera, O., & Havelka, D. (2012). Mechano-electrical vibrations of microtubules--link to subcellular morphology. *BioSystems, 109*(3), 346–355. https://doi.org/10.1016/j.biosystems.2012.04.009

Lazzerini, E. (2019, June 15). *How to cleanse crystals with a singing bowl*. Ethan Lazzerini. https://www.ethanlazzerini.com/cleanse-crystals-with-a-singing-bowl/

Lin, K. (n.d.). *Arthur Sullivan – The lost chord*. Genius.com. https://genius.com/Arthur-sullivan-the-lost-chord-lyrics

Lochte, B. C., Guillory, S. A., Richard, C. A. H., & Kelley, W. M. (2018). An fMRI investigation of the neural correlates underlying the autonomous sensory meridian response (ASMR). *BioImpacts, 8*(4), 295–304. https://doi.org/10.15171/bi.2018.32

MacMillan, A. (2017, April 5). *Why nature sounds help you relax, according to science*. Health.com. https://www.health.com/condition/stress/why-nature-sounds-are-relaxing

Marsab Music Management. (n.d.). *Cuncordu e tenore de Orosei*. Marsab. http://www.marsab.net/tenores-2/

Mauli. (n.d.). *What are the 5 elements in Ayurveda?* Mauli Rituals. https://www.maulirituals.com/blogs/news/what-are-the-5-elements-in-ayurveda

McCraty, R., Atkinson, M., Tiller, W. A., Rein, G., & Watkins, A. D. (1995). The effects of emotions on short-term power spectrum analysis of heart rate variability. *The American Journal of Cardiology*, *76*(14), 1089–1093. https://doi.org/10.1016/s0002-9149(99)80309-9

Mehta, R., Zhu, R. (Juliet), & Cheema, A. (2012). Is noise always bad? Exploring the effects of ambient noise on creative cognition. *Journal of Consumer Research*, *39*(4), 784–799. https://doi.org/10.1086/665048

Mind Tools Content Team. (2012). *Physical relaxation techniques: Deep breathing, PMR, and centering.* Mindtools.com. https://www.mindtools.com/pages/article/newTCS_05.htm

Miranda, Dr. R. A. (2020, February 22). *Do binaural beats work?* Www.youtube.com. https://www.youtube.com/watch?v=Om3zB35xxTo

Mogg, K., Bradley, B. P., Williams, R., & Mathews, A. (1993). Subliminal processing of emotional information in anxiety and depression. *Journal of Abnormal Psychology*, *102*(2), 304–311. https://doi.org/10.1037/0021-843x.102.2.304

Molesworth, BrettR. C., Burgess, M., & Gunnell, B. (2013). Using the effect of alcohol as a comparison to illustrate the detrimental effects of noise on performance. *Noise and Health*, *15*(66), 367. https://doi.org/10.4103/1463-1741.116565

Moss, A. S., Wintering, N., Roggenkamp, H., Khalsa, D. S., Waldman, M. R., Monti, D., & Newberg, A. B. (2012). Effects of an 8-week meditation program on mood and anxiety in patients with memory loss. *The Journal of Alternative and Complementary Medicine*, *18*(1), 48–53. https://doi.org/10.1089/acm.2011.0051

National Center for Environmental Health. (2019, October 7). *What noises cause hearing loss?* Centers for Disease Control and Prevention. https://www.cdc.gov/nceh/hearing_loss/what_noises_cause_hearing_loss.html

National Geographic Society. (2019, July 16). *Noise Pollution.* National Geographic Society. https://www.nationalgeographic.org/encyclopedia/noise-pollution/

National Institute on Deafness and Other Communication Disorders, Maryland. (2015, August 18). *How do we hear?* NIDCD. https://www.nidcd.nih.gov/health/how-do-we-hear#:~:text=Sound%20waves%20enter%20the%20outer

O'Brien, T. (2019, December 8). *Six healing sounds (simple) for anxiety depression.* Www.youtube.com. https://www.youtube.com/watch?v=i8UovBIlM10

Omnivos Therapeutics. (n.d.). *Education.* Www.omnivos.com. https://www.omnivos.com/education

Prestwood, K. M. (2003). Energy medicine: What is it, how does it work, and what place does it have in orthopedics? *Techniques in Orthopaedics, 18*(1), 46–53. https://doi.org/10.1097/00013611-200303000-00009

Price, S. (2021, April 13). *Cymatics for healthcare: Applying the science of sound in cancer surgery.* Health Europa. https://www.healtheuropa.eu/cymatics-for-healthcare-applying-the-science-of-sound-in-cancer-surgery/107471/

Pujol, S., Berthillier, M., Defrance, J., Lardies, J., Levain, J.-P. ., Petit, R., Houot, H., & Mauny, F. (2014). Indoor noise exposure at home: A field study in the family of urban schoolchildren. *Indoor Air, 24*(5), 511–520. https://doi.org/10.1111/ina.12094

Rivera-Dugenio, J. (2019). The language of our DNA-scalar energy. In *International Journal of Advanced Research and Publications*. http://www.i-jarp.org/published-research-papers/mar2019/The-Language-Of-Our-Dna-Scalar-Energy.pdf

Rodrigues, S. (2020, May). *Conscious listening and sound perception.* Explore Life. https://www.explore-life.com/en/articles/conscious-listening-and-sound-perception

Root-Bernstein, M., & Root-Bernstein, R. (2010). *Einstein On creative thinking: Music and the intuitive art of scientific imagination.* Psychology Today. https://www.psychologytoday.com/us/blog/imagine/201003/einstein-creative-thinking-music-and-the-intuitive-art-scientific-imagination

Rubik, B., Muehsam, D., Hammerschlag, R., & Jain, S. (2015). Biofield science and healing: History, terminology, and concepts. *Global Advances in Health and Medicine*, 4(1_suppl), gahmj.2015.038. https://doi.org/10.7453/gahmj.2015.038.suppl

Russo, M. A., Santarelli, D. M., & O'Rourke, D. (2017). The physiological effects of slow breathing in the healthy human. *Breathe*, 13(4), 298–309. https://doi.org/10.1183/20734735.009817

Santos-Longhurst, A. (2020, January 27). *Music as therapy: The uses and benefits of sound healing.* Healthline; Healthline Media. https://www.healthline.com/health/sound-healing#types

Satchwell, J. (2019, October 15). *3 ways to reduce pain with tuning forks.* Www.academyofsoundhealing.com. https://www.academyofsoundhealing.com/blog/3-ways-tuning-forks-can-reduce-pain

Scialla, J. (2019). *History of crystals and healing.* Crystalage.com. https://www.crystalage.com/crystal_information/crystal_history/

Scott, E. (2020a, June 29). *How noise pollution might be increasing your stress levels*. Verywell Mind. https://www.verywellmind.com/stress-and-noise-pollution-how-you-may-be-at-risk-3145041

Scott, E. (2020b, November 30). *Why noise is truly stressful and what to do about it*. Verywell Mind. https://www.verywellmind.com/how-to-reduce-noise-pollutions-negative-effects-3144733

Scott, E. (2021, January 5). *What You Need to Know About the Stress Hormone*. Verywell Mind. https://www.verywellmind.com/cortisol-and-stress-how-to-stay-healthy-3145080

Shanti Bowl. (n.d.). *How singing bowls work: The science of singing bowls*. Shanti Bowl. https://www.shantibowl.com/blogs/blog/how-singing-bowls-work-the-science-behind-singing-bowls

Shanti Bowl. (2021). *How to choose a singing bowl: Complete guide (Updated 2021)*. Shanti Bowl. https://www.shantibowl.com/blogs/blog/how-to-choose-a-singing-bowl

Smithsonian. (n.d.). *Smithsonian - tuning forks*. Americanhistory.si.edu. https://americanhistory.si.edu/science/tuningfork.htm

Snow, S. (2011). *Healing through sound: An exploration of a vocal sound healing method in Great Britain* [Thesis]. https://spectrum.library.concordia.ca/7351/1/Snow_PhD_S2011.pdf

Socratic. (2016, February 21). *What is the difference between an overtone and a harmonic?* Socratic.org. https://socratic.org/questions/what-is-the-difference-between-an-overtone-and-a-harmonic

Sørensen, M., Andersen, Z. J., Nordsborg, R. B., Becker, T., Tjønneland, A., Overvad, K., & Raaschou-Nielsen, O. (2013). Long-term exposure to road traffic noise and incident diabetes: A cohort study. *Environmental Health Perspectives, 121*(2), 217–222. https://doi.org/10.1289/ehp.1205503

Sound Coherence. (n.d.). *Tom Hunt*. Www.soundcoherence.com. http://www.soundcoherence.com/about

Stelter, G. (2016, December 18). *A beginner's guide to the 7 chakras and their meanings*. Healthline; Healthline Media. https://www.healthline.-com/health/fitness-exercise/7-chakras

Tenpenny, K. (2016, April 12). *Vocal toning- vowel sounds of each chakra and soul*. Www.youtube.com. https://www.youtube.com/watch?v=e5vbOpl6zS4

The Light of Happiness. (2021a, July 9). *9 best Tibetan singing bowls, plus 1 to avoid (2021 buyers guide) | The Light Of Happiness*. The Light of Happiness. https://www.thelightofhappiness.com/best-singing-bowls/

The Light of Happiness. (2021b, July 9). *9 best tuning forks for healing, plus 1 to avoid (2021 buyers guide)*. The Light of Happiness. https://www.the-lightofhappiness.com/best-tuning-forks-for-healing/

The Meditation Trust. (n.d.). *How is transcendental meditation different?* The Meditation Trust. https://www.meditationtrust.com/how-is-transcendental-meditation-different/

Thorp, T. (2021, January 14). *The Chopra Center*. The Chopra Center. https://chopra.com/articles/what-is-a-mantra

TMHome. (n.d.). *Origins - Where does transcendental meditation come from?* Transcendental Meditation: LATEST NEWS & OPINIONS. https://tmhome.com/why-should-i-take-up-transcendental-meditation/origins/

Tools for Wellness. (n.d.). *Fibonacci tuning fork set*. Tools for Wellness. https://www.toolsforwellness.com/product/fibonacci-tuning-fork-set/

Traditional Chinese Medicine World Foundation. (2019). *Meridian connection*. TCM World; https://www.tcmworld.org/what-is-tcm/meridian-connection/

Treasure, J. (2013). *Conscious listening*. Www.imdrt.org. http://www.imdrt.org/mentoring

Treasure, J. (2017). *How to be heard: Secrets for powerful speaking and listening*. Coral Gables, Fl Mango Publishing Group.

Treasure, J. (2020, September 18). *Transform your relationships with three types of listening*. Www.juliantreasure.com. https://www.juliantreasure.-com/blog/types-listening-relationships#:~:text=Outer%20listening%20is%20the%20process

Trice, E. (2020, August 15). *Buying my own singing bowl transformed my meditation practice*. Shape. https://www.shape.com/lifestyle/mind-and-body/tibetan-singing-bowl-meditation

University Of Maryland Medical Center. (2005, March 16). *Laughter helps blood vessels function better*. ScienceDaily. https://www.sciencedaily.-com/releases/2005/03/050310100458.htm

University of Toronto Computer Science. (2004). *What Is Sound?* http://www.cs.toronto.edu/~gpenn/csc401/soundASR.pdf

Voigt, J. (2012). *The six healing sounds: Chinese mantras for purifying the body, mind, and soul*. Www.qi-Journal.com. https://www.qi-journal.com/qigong-meditation/qigong-ch-i-kung/2809-six-healing-sounds

Voigt, J. (2013). *The man who invented "qigong."* Www.qigonginstitute.org. https://www.qigonginstitute.org

Wakeling, N. (2007, January 3). *Chakra toning*. Sound Intentions. https://www.soundintentions.com/sound-healing/exercises/chakra-toning/

Walsh, K. M., Saab, B. J., & Farb, N. A. (2019). Effects of a mindfulness meditation app on subjective well-being: Active randomized controlled trial and experience sampling study. *JMIR Mental Health*, *6*(1), e10844. https://doi.org/10.2196/10844

Wang, H., Tang, D., Wu, Y., Zhou, L., & Sun, S. (2020). The state of the art of sound therapy for subjective tinnitus in adults. *Therapeutic Advances in Chronic Disease*, *11*, 204062232095642. https://doi.org/10.1177/2040622320956426

Weller, L. (2020, September 3). *How the chakra system relates to the solfeggio scale*. Binaural Beats Freak. https://www.binauralbeatsfreak.com/sound-therapy/solfeggio-frequencies-chakra-system

WHO. (2021, April 13). *Noncommunicable diseases*. Who.int; World Health Organization: WHO. https://www.who.int/news-room/fact-sheets/detail/noncommunicable-diseases

Wired. (2019). A neuroscientist explains ASMR's effects on the brain & the body. In *YouTube*. https://www.youtube.com/watch?v=IiuUfX2cbhU

Yogapedia. (2017, January 8). *Yoga dictionary*. Www.yogapedia.com. https://www.yogapedia.com/definition

Yugay, I. (2019, January 10). *Everything you need to know about sound healing*. Mindvalley Blog. https://blog.mindvalley.com/sound-healing/?epik=djoyJnU9eFhxMTdqTFR2c2dSRUVCQXQ4QihNLTRJQkdLbi9HeWkmcDowJm49NiiISotrVWUxOUxzc3QyWDFGbGVDdy-ZoPUFBQUFBRoVINmxr

Zevitas, C. D., Spengler, J. D., Jones, B., McNeely, E., Coull, B., Cao, X., Loo, S. M., Hard, A.-K., & Allen, J. G. (2018). Assessment of noise in the airplane cabin environment. *Journal of Exposure Science & Environmental Epidemiology*, *28*(6), 568–578. https://doi.org/10.1038/s41370-018-0027-z

Images

3centista. (2020). A traditional djembe. In *Pixabay*. https://pixabay.-com/photos/djemba-africa-instrument-music-4931869/

Altmann, G. (2012). The right frequency is life. In *Pixabay*. https://pixabay.com/illustrations/heart-curve-health-pulse-frequency-66888/

AniaPM. (2021a). A rainstick. In *Pixabay*. https://pixabay.com/photos/rain-stick-music-instrument-6117677/

AniaPM. (2021b). Kalimbas range from fairly sophisticated to very basic. In *Pixabay*. https://pixabay.com/photos/music-kalimba-instrument-6117640/

Auntmasako. (2016). A set of tuning forks. In *Pixabay*. https://pixabay.-com/photos/tuning-fork-healing-brain-tuner-1902632/

Bartfai, L. (2018). Crystal singing bowls. In *Pixabay*. https://pixabay.-com/photos/sound-sound-health-meditation-3521140/

Braxmeier, H. (2011). A set of gongs, with singing bowls in the foreground. In *Pixabay*. https://pixabay.com/photos/gong-mark-up-idiot-self-tönendes-11484/

Ebrahimnia, F. (2021). Hanghang can vary from small to large. In *Pixabay*. https://pixabay.com/photos/hang-drum-music-musician-5684668/

Firmbee. (2015). Solfeggio and earphones. In *Pixabay*. https://pixabay.-com/photos/mobile-phone-iphone-music-616012/

Free-Photos. (2015). City noise does not even stop at night. In *Pixabay*. https://pixabay.com/photos/city-people-street-traffic-night-690158/

Lindl, C. (2019). Several monochords sharing a single sound box to demonstrate harmonic intervals. In *Pixabay*. https://pixabay.com/photos/body-monochord-monochord-haselholz-4352645/

Lolé, O. (2019). A hammered dulcimer. In *Pixabay*. https://pixabay.com/photos/hammered-dulcimer-instrument-strings-4481476/

Perry, J. R. (2014). A modern street musician playing a large didgeridoo. In *Pixabay*. https://pixabay.com/photos/didgeridoo-street-music-man-people-446132/

Photos. (2013). A traditional musician holding a native American flute. In *Pixabay*. https://pixabay.com/photos/native-american-courting-flute-176096/

Rickhuss, S. (2018). Gemstones used in natural healing. In *Pixabay*. https://pixabay.com/photos/natural-healing-gemstones-blue-bag-3371814/

Segado, J. F. (2015). Traditional Buddhist tingshas. In *Pixabay*. https://pixabay.com/photos/tingshas-buddhism-meditation-peace-1041584/

Sundermeier, A. (2019). Earplugs are not always the best solution. In *Pixabay*. https://pixabay.com/photos/ear-plug-noise-protection-4085688/

Time Traveler Al. (2020). Quartz rock crystal. In *Pixabay*. https://pixabay.com/photos/crystal-quartz-rock-crystal-5025318/

Wolter, T. (2019). Hearing is automatic but listening is not. In *Pixabay*. https://pixabay.com/photos/ear-mouth-nose-face-head-voices-3971050/

Zimmer, M. A. (2013). Singing bowls. In *Pixabay*. https://pixabay.com/photos/singing-bowl-singing-bowls-235266/

Barnes, S., Brown, K., Krusemark, E., Campbell, W & Rogge, R. (2007, October 11). *The Role of Mindfulness in Romantic Relationship Satisfaction and Responses to Relationship Stress.* Journal of Family and Marital Therapy. https://doi.org/10.1111/j.1752-0606.2007.00033.x

Baxter, S. (2019, October 20). *Vagus Nerve Reset to Release Trauma Stored in the Body (Polyvagal Exercises).* Vagus Nerve Reset To Release Trauma Stored In The Body (Polyvagal Exercises) - YouTube

Baxter, S. (2020, November 9). *Vagus Nerve Exercises to Rewire Your Brain from Anxiety.* Vagus Nerve Exercises To Rewire Your Brain From Anxiety - YouTube

Bell, A. (2017, July 21). *Somatic Psychotherapy.* Good Therapy. Somatic Psychotherapy (goodtherapy.org)

Bell, A. (2018, June 19). *Somatic Mindfulness: What Is My Body Telling Me? (And Should I Listen?).* Good Therapy. https://www.goodthera-py.org/blog/somatic-mindfulness-what-is-my-body-telling-me-and-should-i-listen-0619185

Brom, D., Stokar, Y., Lawi, C., Nuriel-Porat, V., Ziv, Y., Lerner, K. & Ross, G. (2017, June 6). *Somatic Experiencing for Posttraumatic Stress Disorder: A Randomized Controlled Outcome Study.* Wiley Online Library. https://dx.doi.org/10.1002%2Fjts.22189

Butler, A., Chapman, J., Forman, E & Beck, A. (2006, January). *The Empirical Status of Cognitive-Behavioral Therapy: A Review of Meta-Analyses.* Clinical Psychology Review. https://psycnet.a-pa.org/doi/10.1016/j.cpr.2005.07.003

Carbonelli, D. & Parteleno-Barehmi, C. (2016, May 11). *Psychodrama Groups for Girls Coping With Trauma.* Taylor & Francis Online. https://doi.org/10.1080/00207284.1999.11732607

Chambers, R., Chuen Yee Lo, B. & Allen, N. (2007, February 23). *The*

Impact of Intensive Mindfulness and Training on Attention Control, Cognitive Style, and Affect. Springer Link. http://dx.doi.org/10.1007/s10608-007-9119-0

Chen, Y., Hung, K., Tsai, J., Chu, H., Chung, M., Chen, S., Liao, Y., Ou, K., Chang, Y. & Chou, K. (2014, August 7). *Efficacy of Eye-Movement Desensitization and Reprocessing for Patients with Posttraumatic-Stress Disorder: A Meta-Analysis of Randomized Controlled Trials.* PLOS ONE. https://dx.doi.org/10.1371%2Fjournal.pone.0103676

Cino, R. (2017, November 24). *How to Decrease Anxiety Using Somatic Experiencing.* myTherapyNYC. https://mytherapynyc.com/how-to-decrease-anxiety-using-somatic-experiencing/#comments

Clarke, J. (2021, July 31). *What Is Gestalt Therapy?* Verywell Mind. https://www.verywellmind.com/what-is-gestalt-therapy-4584583

ConciousnessNOWTV. (2020, September 19). *How to use Pendulation to Decrease Stress and Increase Well-Being.* How to use Pendulation to Decrease Stress and Increase Well-Being - YouTube

Counselling and Meditation Exercises. (n.d.) Sligo Gestalt Counselling. https://sligogestaltcounselling.ie/try-these-counselling-exercises.html

Cutler, N. (n.d.) *Learning How to Unlock Tissue Memory.* Integrated Physical Therapy and Wellness. https://www.iptmiami.com/news/Learning_How_to_Unlock_Tissue_Memory

Depressive Disorders. (n.d.) Psychology Today. https://www.psychologytoday.com/us/conditions/depressive-disorders

Diaphragmatic Breathing Exercises. (n.d.). Physiopedia. https://www.physio-pedia.com/Diaphragmatic_Breathing_Exercises

Diaphragmatic Breathing: Everything You Need to Know. (n.d.). Evolve

Chiropractic. https://myevolvechiropractor.com/diaphragmatic-breathing/

Eckelkamp, S. (2019, October 9). *Can Trauma Really be 'Stored' in the Body?* mbg Health. https://www.mindbodygreen.com/articles/can-trauma-be-stored-in-body

Energy Psychology (2017, October 26). Good Psychology. https://www.-goodtherapy.org/learn-about-therapy/types/energy-psychology

Erdelyi, K. (2019, October 28). *What is Somatic Therapy?* Psycom. https://www.psycom.net/what-is-somatic-therapy/
Essential Somatics. (2019, February 1). *The Best Psoas Release.* (2) The Best Psoas Release - YouTube

Fallis, J. (2021, March 24). *How to Stimulate Your Vagus Nerve for Better Mental Health*. Optimal Living Dynamics. https://www.optimallivingdy-namics.com/blog/how-to-stimulate-your-vagus-nerve-for-better-mental-health-brain-vns-ways-treatment-activate-natural-foods-depression-anxiety-stress-heart-rate-variability-yoga-massage-vagal-tone-dysfunction

Feinstein, D. (2012, December 1). *Acupoint Stimulation in Treating Psychological Disorders: Evidence of Efficacy*. Sage Journals. https://doi.org/10.1037%2Fa0028602

Field, T. & Diego, M. (2008, March 4). *Vagal Activity, Early Growth and Emotional Development*. PubMed Central. https://dx.doi.org/10.1016%2Fj.infbeh.2007.12.008

Forgiveness: Your Health Depends On It. (n.d.) John Hopkins Medicine. https://www.hopkinsmedicine.org/health/wellness-and-prevention/forgiveness-your-health-depends-on-it

Friedman, L. (2019, November 15). *Using Somatic Experiencing to Cope with Anger.* Trauma & Beyond. Using Somatic Experiencing to Cope with Anger | Trauma Therapy (traumaandbeyondcenter.com)

Gaba, S. (2020, August 22). *Understanding Fight, Flight, Freeze and the Fawn Response.* Psychology Today. https://www.psychologytoday.com/gb/blog/addiction-and-recovery/202008/understanding-fight-flight-freeze-and-the-fawn-response

Giacomucci, S. & Marquit, J. (2020, May 19). *The Effectiveness of Trauma-Focused Psychodrama in the Treatment of PTSD in Inpatient Substance Abuse Treatment.* Frontiers in Psychology. https://doi.org/10.3389/fpsyg.2020.00896

Goodlet, N. (2020, November 30). *Vagus Nerve Stimulation Breathing Meditation Practice.* https://www.youtube.com/watch?v=kiQMaJJWcyQ

Hadley, H. (2017, July 19). *The Benefits of Somatic Breathing.* Total Somatics. https://totalsomatics.com/the-benefits-of-somatic-breathing/

Heidari, S., Shahbakhsh, B. & Jangjoo, M. (2017). *The Effectiveness of Gestalt Therapy on Depressed Women in Comparison with Drug Therapy.* Journal of Applied Psychology and Behavioral Science. https://japbs.com/fulltext/paper-02012017134122.pdf

Hoffman, S., Sawyer, A., Witt. A & Oh, D. (2010, April 1). *The Effect of Mindfulness-Based Therapy on Anxiety and Depression: A Meta-Analytic Review.* PMC. https://www.ncbi.nlm.nih.gov/pmc/articles/PMC2848393/

Holmes, J. & McGauran, J. (Executive Producers). (1988–present). *Home and Away* [TV series]. Seven Studios; Seven Network Operations Limited; Red Heart Entertainment; Keeper Media.

Hopper, S., Murray, S., Ferrara, L. & Singleton, J. (2019, September). *Effectiveness of Diaphragmatic Breathing for Reducing Physiological and*

Psychological Stress in Adults: A Quantitative Systematic Review. JBI Evidence Synthesis. https://doi.org/10.11124/jbisrir-2017-003848

IABET - Consciousness Through Art. (2020, April 2). *Art Therapy Exercise - Exploring Emotional Needs.* Art Therapy Exercise - Exploring Emotional Needs - YouTube

Jackson, K. (2019, February 4). *Pandiculations 101 with Think Somatics. (2)* Pandiculations 101 with Think Somatics - YouTube

Jackson, T. (2017, August 24). *Grounding: What to Do When You Feel Unstable.* Toni Jackson Counselling. https://tonijacksoncounselling.-com/2017/08/24/grounding-what-to-do-when-you-feel-unstable/

Jahnke, R., Larkey, L., Rogers, C., Etnier, J. & Lin, F. (2010, July 1). *A Comprehensive Review of Health Benefits of Qigong and Tai Chi.* Sage Journals. https://journals.sagepub.com/doi/10.4278/ajhp.081013-LIT-248?url_ver=Z39.88-2003&rfr_id=ori%3Arid%3Acrossre-f.org&rfr_dat=cr_pub%3Dpubmed&

Janet, S. & Gowri, P. (2017). *Effectiveness of Deep Breathing Exercise on Blood Pressure Among Patients with Hypertension.* International Journal of Pharma and Bio Science. http://dx.doi.org/10.22376/ijpbs.2017.8.1.b256-260

Jerath, R., Beveridge, C. & Barnes, V. (2019, January 29). *Self-Regulation Breathing of Breathing as an Adjunctive Treatment of Insomnia.* Frontiers. https://doi.org/10.3389/fpsyt.2018.00780

Johnson, J. (2020. May 27). *What to Know About Diaphragmatic Breathing.* Medical News Today. What is diaphragmatic breathing? Benefits and how-to (medicalnewstoday.com)

Jordan, S. (2016, February 7). *An Introduction to Focusing.* British Focusing Association. https://www.focusing.org.uk/an-introduction-to-focusing

Kelloway, R. (2019, March 29). *5 Somatic Experiencing Exercises to Keep Grounded During Coronavirus Uncertainty.* Life Care Wellness. https://life-care-wellness.com/somatic-experiencing-exercises-to-keep-you-grounded/

KoK, B., Coffey, K. & Cohn, M. (2013, May 6). *How Positive Emotions Build Physical Health: Perceived Positive Social Connections Account for the Upward Spiral Between Positive Emotions and Vagal Tone.* Sage Journals. https://doi.org/10.1177%2F0956797612470827

Langmuir, J., Kirsch, S. & Classen, C. (2012). *A Pilot Study of Body-Orientated Group Psychotherapy for the Group Treatment of Trauma.* APA PsycNet. https://psycnet.apa.org/doi/10.1037/a0025588

Leung, G & Khor, S. (2017, April 25). *Gestalt Intervention Groups for Anxious Parents in Hong Kong: A Quasi-Experimental Design.* Taylor & Francis Online. https://doi.org/10.1080/23761407.2017.1311814

Lindberg, S. (2019, January 9). *Psychopath.* Healthline. https://www.healthline.com/health/psychopath
Lynch, D., Laws, K & McKenna, P. (2009, May 29). *Cognitive Behavioral Therapy for Major Psychiatric Disorder: Does It Really Work? A Meta-Analytical Review of Well-Controlled Trials.* Cambridge University Press. https://doi.org/10.1017/s003329170900590x

Lyon, B. (2017, August 1). *Shame and Trauma.* Center for Healing Shame. https://healingshame.com/articles/2017/8/21/shame-and-trauma

Ma, X., Yue, Z., Gong, Z., Zhang, H., Duan, N., Shi, Y., Wei. G. & Li, Y. (2017, June 6). *The Effect of Diaphragmatic Breathing on Attention, Negative Affect and Stress in Healthy Adults.* PubMed Central. https://dx.doi.org/10.3389%2Ffpsyg.2017.00874

MacCarthy, M. (2019, December 17). *Somatic Low Back & Psoas Release.* (2) Somatic Low Back & Psoas Release - YouTube

Mertz, C. (2013). *The Effectiveness of Psychodrama for Adolescents who have Experienced Trauma.* Smith ScholarWorks. https://scholarworks.smith.edu/cgi/viewcontent.cgi?article=2024&context=theses

Meyer, A. (2020, June 20). *Subconscious Mind & Inner Child Explained: The Key to Wellbeing.* Medium. https://medium.com/invisible-illness/the-subconscious-mind-inner-child-explained-511b1ef93c7f

Miller, B., Littlefield, W., Morano, R., Wilson, D., Sears, F., Chaiken, I., Moss, E., Barker, M., Tuchman, E., Chang, Y., Hockin, S., Weber, J., Siracusa, F., & Fortenberry, D. (Executive Producers). (2017–present). *The Handmaid's Tale* [TV series]. Daniel Wilson Productions Inc.; The Littlefield Company; White Oak Pictures; MGM Studios.

Millman, R. (2019, March 24). *Healing the Inner Child | Tapping with Renee.* Healing The Inner Child | Tapping with Renee - YouTube

Millman, R. (2020, February 16). *Tapping to Heal the Inner Child and Letting Go of Shame | Tapping with Renee.* Tapping To Heal The Inner Child and Letting Go Of Shame | Tapping With Renee - YouTube

Moore, A. & Malinowski, P. (2009, March 18). *Meditation, Mindfulness and Cognitive Flexibility.* PubMed. https://pubmed.ncbi.nlm.nih.gov/19181542/

Morrisey, S. & Marr, J. (1984). Still Ill (Song) on *The Smiths.* Rough Trade.

Ortner, C., Kilner, S. & Zelazo, P. (2007, November 20). *Mindfulness Meditation and Reduced Emotional Interference on a Cognitive Task.* Springer Link. https://link.springer.com/article/10.1007/s11031-007-9076-7

Osadchey, S. (2028, August 8). *Somatic Experiencing (SE).* Good Therapy. https://www.goodtherapy.org/learn-about-therapy/types/somatic-experiencing

Pandiculation - The Safe Alternative to Stretching. (2010, September 30). Essential Somatics. https://essentialsomatics.com/clinical-somatics-articles-case-studies/pandiculation-safe-alternative-stretching

Psychodrama. (2016, May 16). Good Therapy. https://www.goodthera-py.org/learn-about-therapy/types/psychodrama

Richmond, C. (2018, November 29). *Emotional Trauma and the Mind-Body Connection.* WebMD. https://www.webmd.com/mental-health/features/emotional-trauma-mind-body-connection

Saadati, H. & Lashani, L. (2013, July 9). *Effectiveness of Gestalt Therapy on Self-Efficacy of Divorced Women.* Science Direct. https://doi.org/10.1016/j.sbspro.2013.06.721

Sensorimotor Psychotherapy. (2015, August 24). Good Therapy. Sensorimotor Psychotherapy (goodtherapy.org)
Shapiro, F. (2014). *The Role of Eye Movement Desensitization and Reprocessing (EMDR) Therapy in Medicine: Addressing the Psychological and Physical Symptoms Stemming from Adverse Life Experience.* The Permanente Journal. https://dx.doi.org/10.7812%2FTPP%2F13-098

Shella. T. (2017, May 26). *Art Therapy Improves Mood, and Reduces Pain and Anxiety When Offered at Bedside During Acute Hospital Treatment.* Science Direct. https://www.sciencedirect.com/science/article/abs/pii/S0197455617301053

Somatic Experiencing International. (2019, August 15). *What is Pendulation in Somatic Experiencing with Peter A Levine, PhD.* https://www.youtube.com/watch?v=LiXOMLoDm68&t=1s

Tomasulo, D. (2021, June 18). *Do You Need a Mama Psychodrama?* LinkedIn. https://www.linkedin.com/pulse/do-you-need-mama-psychodrama-dan-tomasulo

Transformations Treatment Center. (2018, October 1). *EMDR: Self-Soothing at Home. (2) EMDR: Self-soothing at home - YouTube*

Tune Up Fitness (2020, March 10). *Hum to Activate the Vagus Nerve.* Hum to Activate the Vagus Nerve - YouTube
Tune Up Fitness. (2020, March 10). *Vagus Nerve: Breathing for Relaxation.* Vagus Nerve: Breathing for Relaxation - YouTube

Valiente-Gomez, A., Moreno-Alcazar, A., Treen, D., Cedron, C., Colom, F., Perez, V. & Amann, B. (2017, September 26). *EMDR Beyond PTSD: A Systematic Literature Review.* Frontiers in Psychology. https://doi.org/10.3389/fpsyg.2017.01668

Van Korff, M., Crane, P., Lane, M., Miglioretti, D., Simon, G., Saunders, K., Stang, P., Brandenburg, N. & Kessler, R. (2005, February). *Chronic Spinal Pain and Physical-Mental Comorobidiy in the United States: Results From the National Comorbidity Survey Replication.* PAIN 10.1016/j.pain.2004.11.010

Virant, K. (2019, May 12). *Chronic Illness and Trauma Disorders.* Psychology Today. https://www.psychologytoday.com/gb/blog/chronically-me/201905/chronic-illness-and-trauma-disorders

Wagner, D. (2016, June 27). *Polyvagal Theory in Practice.* Counseling Today. Polyvagal theory in practice - Counseling Today

Warren, S. (2019, April 21). *What is Pandiculation?* Somatic Movement Center. https://somaticmovementcenter.com/pandiculation-what-is-pandiculation/

Winn, A. (2019, August 15). *Energy Psychology Demonstration - Correct Demo of Cooks Hook Up. (3)* Energy psychology demonstration - Correct demo of Cooks Hookup - YouTube

Yates, B. (2013, September 28). *Self-Love in About Five Minutes - Tapping with Brad Yates.* https://www.youtube.com/watch?v=tLWTzQWa2hg

Yates, B. (2014, February 28). *Self-Compassion - Tapping with Brad Yates.* https://www.youtube.com/watch?v=KHydpkmWydI

Yates, B. (2020, August 31). *Narcissists (Getting Free from Past or Present Pain) - Tapping with Brad Yates.* Narcissists (getting free from past or present pain) - Tapping with Brad Yates - YouTube

Zhang, M., Zhang, Y. & Kong, Y. (2020, May 18). *Interaction Between Social Pain and Physical Pain.* SAGE Journals. https://doi.org/10.26599%2FBSA.2019.9050023

Zwerican, A & Joseph, S. (2018, October 1). *Focusing Manner and Posttraumatic Growth.* Core. https://www.focusing.org.uk/an-introduction-to-focusing

Ascending Vibrations

YOUR FEEDBACK IS VALUED

We would like to be so bold as to ask for an act of kindness from you. If you read and enjoyed our book/s, would you please consider leaving an honest review on Amazon or audible? As an independent publishing group, your feedback means the absolute world to us. We read every single review we receive and would love to hear your thoughts, as each piece of feedback helps us serve you better. Your feedback may also impact others across the globe, helping them discover powerful knowledge they can implement in their lives to give them hope and self-empowerment. Wishing you empowerment, courage, and wisdom on your journey.

If you have read or listened to any of our books and would be so kind as to review them, you can do so by clicking the 'learn more' tab under the book's picture on our website:

https://ascendingvibrations.net/books

YOUR FEEDBACK IS VALUED

Why not join our Facebook community and discuss your spiritual path with like-minded seekers?

We would love to hear from you!

Go here to join the 'Ascending Vibrations' community:
   bit.ly/ascendingvibrations

CLAIM YOUR BONUS AUDIOBOOK

Download the 5+ Hour Audiobook *'Sound Healing For Beginners: Sonic Medicine Tor The Body, Chakra Rituals, & What They Didn't Tell You About Vibrational Energy'* Instantly for **FREE!**

If you love listening to audio books on-the-go, we have great news for you. You can download the audio book version of *'Sound Healing For Beginners'* for **FREE** just by signing up for a **FREE** 30-day audible trial. See below for more details!

Audible trial benefits

As an audible customer, you'll receive the below benefits with your 30-day free trial:

- Free audible copy of this book
- After the trial, you will get 1 credit each month to use on any audiobook
- Your credits automatically roll over to the next month if you don't use them
- Choose from over 400,000 titles
- Listen anywhere with the audible app across multiple devices
- Make easy, no hassle exchanges of any audiobook you don't love
- Keep your audiobooks forever, even if you cancel your membership
- And much more

Click the links below to get started:

Go here for AUDIBLE US: adbl.co/3wkoAhe

Go here for AUDIBLE UK: adbl.co/3stsPsV

www.ingramcontent.com/pod-product-compliance
Lightning Source LLC
Chambersburg PA
CBHW021701120626
46545CB00004B/1346